THE *NEW YORK* [barcode] P9-AGI-061
HER FANS HA

ANN-MARGRET
MY STORY

From her performances in films like *Bye Bye Birdie, Carnal Knowledge,* and *Tommy*, to television dramas including *The Two Mrs. Grenvilles*, to her dazzling stage shows, Ann-Margret is a woman adored, not just for her beauty and talent, but for herself. Until now we have known only Ann-Margret the star. At last, we hear from Ann-Margret the woman.

Ann-Margret: My Story is an exclusive invitation into a very private life, a revealing look at her relationships, triumphs and trials in and out of the spotlight. *Ann-Margret: My Story* gives us the real Ann-Margret—making her own way, seeking independence, and finding her voice both as a legendary performer and as a woman of guts, humor, energy, and inspiration.

"By one of America's sexiest and most celebrated entertainers . . . a riveting story that chronicles the seemingly charmed (but in reality strife-ridden) life and career of one of pop culture's female pioneers."
—*Publishers Weekly*

"Superstar legend Ann-Margret tells all . . . She remains one of the greatest entertainers of all time."
—*Live with Regis and Kathie Lee*

"An honest, heartfelt portrait of a real survivor."
—*Time Out* (UK)

"This kitten keeps landing on her feet, and in her new book, Ann-Margret talks all about it."
—*Entertainment Tonight*

"A fascinating autobiography."—New York *Newsday*

A Choice of the Literary Guild® and Doubleday Book Club
As seen in *Good Housekeeping*

Ann-Margret

MY STORY

BY ANN-MARGRET

WITH TODD GOLD

B

BERKLEY BOOKS, NEW YORK

The authors gratefully acknowledge permission to reprint lyrics from "Once Before I Go," by Peter Allen and Dean Pitchford, © 1982 Warner-Tamerlane Publishing Corp., Woolnough Music, My Macaroon Tunes, Jemava Music Corp. All rights reserved. Used by permission.

ANN-MARGRET: MY STORY

A Berkley Book / published by arrangement with
Ann-Margret Productions

PRINTING HISTORY
G. P. Putnam's Sons edition / February 1994
Published simultaneously in Canada
Berkley edition / April 1995

All rights reserved.
Copyright © 1994 by Ann-Margret Productions.
Front and back jacket photographs Copyright © 1994
by Harry Langdon.
This book may not be reproduced in whole or in part,
by mimeograph or any other means, without permission.
For information address: The Berkley Publishing Group,
200 Madison Avenue, New York, New York 10016.

ISBN: 0-425-14682-0

BERKLEY®
Berkley Books are published by The Berkley Publishing Group,
200 Madison Avenue, New York, New York 10016.
BERKLEY and the "B" design
are trademarks belonging to Berkley Publishing Corporation.

PRINTED IN THE UNITED STATES OF AMERICA

10 9 8 7 6 5 4 3 2 1

To my father, mother,
and Roger

AUTHOR'S NOTE

IN PREPARING FOR WRITING THIS BOOK, WHICH IS PERhaps the hardest thing I have ever done, I told myself I would conquer some fears and also wipe away some of the mist that had enveloped me for so long. I knew all about the Ann-Margret mystique. I was said to be a recluse, a fragile woman consumed by fear, a tragic heroine controlled by a strong husband. I was an enigma to many people, including those closest to me, and sometimes even to myself.

I felt it was time to change all that, to embrace candor and a willingness to try new things. For many years, I had harbored a fear of performing live in New York City. So, in the fall of 1991, I brought my act to Radio City Music Hall and faced the critics, the audience, my past, and all my inner demons. I figured I had better do it while I could still kick. Like all Swedes, I was raised to be intensely modest, but I must admit I was tickled by the reviews and the packed, enthusiastic audiences. Most importantly, I felt I had passed a test of strength, achieved a degree of courage.

I felt the same way about writing an autobiography and letting people hear the truth. I knew it wouldn't be easy to cast off my innate reserve and privacy, but I believed it was important that I write about the people and events that have shaped my life and career. Besides, if I waited too long, someone who didn't know me would do it, relying on press clippings and distortions.

As I see it, my tale is both unique and universal. I've had many successes, but also, like anyone else, my share of sadness. I'm a mom, a wife, and a crazy performer who likes to drive a motorcycle and kick up her heels. When certain music plays, I don't hear anything else. I'm very emotional, and if a song moves me, I try to include it in my act. It's almost a spiritual thing. I've just got to do it.

I'm sometimes mixed up, but I'm always me, Ann-Margret Olsson Smith, though I dropped the Olsson years ago because I didn't want my parents to feel any embarrassment if there was negative publicity from my being in show business. I'm also quite proud.

Shortly after I arrived in America as a little girl, my Uncle Arvid, a carpenter, fashioned a small wooden toy box for me and painted it marmalade orange. As toys became less important to me, I used the box to store the keepsakes of my girlhood—letters, ribbons, cards, awards, and treasures that meant the world to me.

I recall the times I sat on my bed, the bedroom door shut and the house quiet, and sifted through the box's sundry contents. Occasionally, I invited one of my cousins or friends to sit down with me and go through the box. I pulled things out, particular things—certainly not everything—and told stories that made me laugh, cry, smile, and mostly just remember.

This book is a lot like that great old toy box of mine. It's full of the things I've saved, the people I've treasured, the experiences I've been lucky to have. Good times, heartaches, triumphs, tragedies, celebrations, losses, mistakes, and incredible good fortune . . . I hope and pray that they're all in here.

INTRODUCTION

AS SOMEONE WHO HAS BEEN PROTECTED, CARED FOR, and shielded for most of her adult life, I knew I was absurdly, pathetically ill-prepared for what lay ahead. I slid behind the wheel of our car, in itself a departure, adjusted dark glasses over my wet eyes, and headed for St. John's Hospital in Santa Monica. I looked at my husband Roger in the seat next to me, tired and lethargic, drifting in and out of a netherworld of exhaustion, and I knew then the roles were reversing.

I thought how he had cared for me after I fell nearly twenty-two feet from a platform onto a stage in Lake Tahoe, about how much he loved me and protected me, and how fate was now telling me it was my turn to take over. Although it seemed an impossible undertaking, I knew I must do it. For both of our sakes, I had to become the assertive, take-charge woman I had never pretended or cared to be.

I pulled into the hospital, where Roger was scheduled to see a specialist to diagnose the mysterious ailment that had come on so insidiously. My tall, strong husband was never sick, but for longer than we could pinpoint—a year, perhaps—he had felt a gnawing fatigue, an unexplained tiredness.

"It's nothing," I remember him saying. "Nothing to worry about."

At first, I had tried to put it out of my head. I was preoccupied with my own problems. Three times during this period I had been sure I was pregnant, then had been bitterly disappointed. Hence, it was easy for me to deny what was happening to Roger, to pretend everything was fine.

Yet, there were days when Roger simply couldn't get out of bed, and for a man who was as driven, as frenetic as my husband, something was woefully wrong. In our family, Roger not only took charge of all the household details, he ran every aspect of my career—negotiating contracts, screening scripts, handling my investments, and producing my nightclub acts. Whenever I was onstage, Roger was in the wings, watching and worrying; if he thought I was exhausted at the end of a show, he would sometimes even lift me in his arms and carry me back to my dressing room.

But now, increasingly, Roger had to will himself to get dressed in the morning. His muscles were betraying him, and we were both terrified. It would have been so easy for me to have succumbed again to drinking, the weakness that had plagued me for five years. But somehow, I managed to collect myself, took charge, and insisted that Roger see a doctor. And he had nodded, a compliance that sent a chill through me.

As I listened to the diagnosis we heard after the visit to St. John's, I was calm. We were told on that day twelve years ago that Roger had myasthenia gravis, a neuromuscular disease that was incurable. This was the same illness that had robbed Aristotle Onassis of his vitality, and now it was threatening Roger.

It would have been natural for me to fold then, and I truly think many people would have suspected it of me, given my dependence on Roger. But there comes a point in life when clothes, money, and a large home in the hills mean nothing, when awards aren't worth the paper they're printed on, when jewels and fancy cars are worthless, when everything just stops.

Time stopped, then it started again in a new way. Roger and I would beat this, we decided, and I would shield him from all the worries and cares he had once assumed. I picked up the phone and talked to the agents; I learned about the stocks, bonds, and real-estate matters Roger had handled. I also attended to the leaking roof, broken appliances, and hillsides sliding after the rains. For some time now, Roger's three children had been living with us and I tried to handle, as best I could, all their problems as well.

I trudged along, worrying that I was making mistakes, asking lots of questions to make sure I wasn't being taken advantage of, but slowly and surely gaining confidence. I never let Roger know the extent of my fear or exhaustion, but there were plenty of harrowing nights when I cried, sitting in my backyard in the Los Angeles hills.

I must have been doing something right, because God was on our side. After visits to UCLA Medical Center and the Mayo Clinic, after months of various medications and treatments, doctors and worries, Roger's health slowly improved, but his disease could reoccur at any time.

Roger was quietly grateful, prayerful, and calm. I began thinking about the day there will be a cure, and felt a surge of hope. Both of us are very different people today. Roger has slowly asserted much of his old role in the family, but I will never be that same submissive, fearful woman.

I have come a long way from my sheltered youth. The shy little girl is still there, but she has stepped aside, making way for a stronger, more confident woman. I'm a tough, stubborn Taurus. And I come from equally tough stock. I did exactly what no one expected me to do, including me!

SOMETIMES THERE IS A MOMENT IN YOUR EARLY years that haunts you and defines your past, your present, even your future. For me, it was auditioning for what would become my official performing debut, the Morris B. Sachs *Amateur Hour,* a Chicago talent show that struggled to rival Ted Mack's. I was thirteen, with brown hair, a shaky smile, and a shyness so intense that I had sat paralyzed in the studio, tortured by nerves and fears. My terror had been palpable, visible to all around me, but miraculously ephemeral. The minute my name had been called, the minute the music started, the minute the other Ann-Margret Olsson had emerged, a prancing, gyrating, uninhibited performer totally consumed by singing, dancing, and pleasing the audience.

As I returned to my seat and savored the applause, I withdrew again and huddled at my mother's side.

"I can't believe she's the same girl. Turns it off and on," I heard someone say.

"I can't believe it's the same girl."

I repeated those words to myself again and again. I knew I would hear that comment throughout my career, and I have.

I suppose, in a way, there are indeed two Ann-Margrets. I wish I could tell you that I fully know and understand both of them, but I would be lying. I *do* know what makes Ann-Margret "The Performer" emerge, and it's very literally the sound of music. I hear a beat, a tempo that moves me and it's as if I'm transfixed. And it's been that way right from the beginning, when I was just a little thing with ringlets, big eyes, and an adoring audience of Swedish relatives.

*　　*　　*

In Valsjobyn, Sweden, where I spent the first six years of my life, music was the major release. In this tiny (population: 150) town of lumberjacks and farmers high up near the Arctic Circle, there were no movie theaters and few radios. But there was always the sound of my mother singing cheerful folk tunes, and by the time I was three, she and I were harmonizing virtually every evening. My mother's brother, Uncle Calle, often added his accordion. At get-togethers, my other relatives joined in, too. Of course, even then I was a ham and loved to take center stage. I quickly learned that I had a pleasant singing voice and that people responded to it. But what mattered most to me was the happiness I saw in my mother's face when she heard me sing. At three, I certainly had no conception of what it meant to be an entertainer, but I wanted to please my mother, grandmother, and Uncle Calle, just as I would want to please big-time audiences in the years to come. I had this desperate need to be a good little girl, to do what was expected of me, and in my house that meant singing.

I'm sure that some of this passion for music stemmed from loneliness. It was just Mother, Grandmother, Uncle Calle, and me for those first six years, and I missed the father I could not remember and fantasized about him terribly. I know Mother missed him, too, but given her nature, and his, this long separation was something that had to be.

Mother had lived in Valsjobyn all her life, and had been baptized Anna Aronsson. At five, she and her two younger siblings watched their father, whom I later called Moofa, leave the small village for more lucrative work in a stone quarry in Canada. A back injury forced him to return home eight years later, but the strain of being incapacitated, as well as the lengthy separation, resulted in his and my grandmother Mooma's divorcing.

I'm sure this devastated Mooma, but she had a Swedish stoicism, a reserve inherited from a people who endured hardships through severe, dark winters, and didn't complain. Probably this was not the most emotionally healthy way to deal with pain, but it was what both Mooma and my mother had learned from their parents and their parents' parents. Life was hard in the northern part of the world, but you dealt with it. I, too, would learn to grit my teeth, to hide all the disappointments until a time in later years when it would catch up with me and cause real damage. It was the Swede in me. It was the way my family functioned.

Moofa moved into a home across the river that flowed through the center of Valsjobyn, leaving Mooma on her own. Strong and independent, she took a baking course, borrowed money and built a small, three-room home. Soon Mooma had turned the kitchen and dining room into the village's most popular bakery-café.

At seventeen, my mother went to work with Mooma, and over the years she developed into an exceptional baker, a talent that escaped the next generation. To this day, I'm an utter catastrophe in the kitchen. As I've always said, "I don't cook, and I don't care."

Soon, Mooma's café became a town gathering place, a haven where Valsjobyn's residents exchanged news about births, deaths, and marriages. There was no real scandal and little gossip in town, where frugal, love-filled wooden homes dotted the rustic hillsides. The church steeple in the neighboring town of Hotagen rose like a moral compass, higher than any other structure. My mom was baptized in that church, took communion, and was eventually married there—all by the same minister.

There were no strangers where I grew up. Everybody knew each other. Even today, that insular world, free of strife, is my idea of a paradise.

But I'm not sure I could have stayed there, and my daddy apparently felt the same way. The cloistered small-town existence was making him restless. Gustav Olsson had a vision of life that extended beyond Valsjobyn. A strong man and a very taciturn one, he was possessed by the same restless, roving soul of the Swedish navigators who'd set sail centuries before from Ornskoldsvik, the coastal city where he was born.

As the eldest of two boys, Daddy was expected to take over his father's profitable taxi business at some point. But such a reasonable, sensible, comfortable life wasn't for him. Daddy had a definite rebel streak, the same streak I would exhibit years later as I forged a career in show business.

At seventeen, consumed by a spirit of adventure, Daddy set out for Canada. A year later, he hid beneath a truck, and crossed into the United States. A gypsy at heart, Daddy had no problem giving up his share of the family business to his brother, Hasse, and settling in Chicago, where he found work with the Johnson Electric Company. He also met my Auntie Mina and her husband Charley, who had arrived there years before.

Eventually, Mina and Charley returned to Valsjobyn. A few years later, in 1937, Daddy also returned to Sweden in order to claim a small inheritance his uncle Gustav, a renowned Stockholm surgeon, had left him. One night, deciding to visit Mina and Charley, he pulled his big black Plymouth in front of a barn where he knew almost everyone in the village had gathered for a dance.

Uncle Charley saw my father and ushered his Swedish friend from Chicago into the barn. Daddy surveyed the crowd, then waved to Auntie Mina. The next dance was a Swedish hambo, a fast-paced affair that set the barn floor awhirl. Then Daddy noticed that my aunt was standing off to the side, talking to a pretty young girl.

"That's Anna," my uncle said. "Anna Aronsson."

Without waiting, Daddy stepped across the barn floor and asked my mother to dance. She was nineteen, shy and sheltered. He was eighteen years her senior and had traveled extensively and collected a number of experiences, including two broken engagements. Daddy had a bit of the rascal in him!

The two mismatched Swedes danced the rest of the evening, rarely taking their eyes off each other. At the end of the dance, Daddy strapped her bicycle on top of his car and drove her home. He asked if he could see her again, and Mother replied, "Well, that's up to you, isn't it?" Mother's response said it all. She was practical and matter-of-fact by nature. Yet, there was a winsome charm beneath her careful reserve and Daddy was smitten.

The one thing Daddy hadn't anticipated while back in

his native country was falling in love. He constantly mentioned his life in Chicago, and he tried persuading Mother to move there with him. But she wouldn't even consider such a far-fetched notion. So Daddy canceled his plans and stayed. For once in his life, he was driven by forces he could not control, and this both troubled and intrigued him.

Every few weeks, he drove to Valsjobyn. Rather than say he was visiting a new girlfriend, he told his mother that he was going fishing. But she wasn't fooled. One day, as he was about to leave home, his mother called out, "Next time you go fishing up there, bring the fish home with you. I'd like to meet that special fish."

On Mother's twentieth birthday, Daddy proposed. The next winter, they were married in a simple family ceremony in Hotagen's white church. Afterward, they moved to Stockholm, where Daddy found work doing odd electrical jobs. Stockholm was frightening to Mother, who had never traveled beyond the provincial villages around Valsjobyn. I'm sure she was lonely and sad, though she kept it to herself. Within a few months, she was pregnant.

They were excited by the idea of parenthood. If the baby was a boy, he'd be Bo Lennart. If the baby was a girl, she'd be called Ann-Margret—after a Swedish swimming star Mother admired.

Not long after I was born on April 28, 1941, Daddy began communicating with his old employer, the Johnson Electric Company in Chicago, requesting whatever papers were necessary for him to return to work in the U.S. Mother was steadfast in her opposition to such a move, and it created quite a strain between my parents. But things were different then. In the traditional Swedish household, the man made the major decisions and the wife was expected to comply. My mother, of course, understood this not-so-delicate balance, but she was not, despite her reserve, a compliant woman.

It was also a difficult time. The world was in the grips of World War II. Sweden remained neutral, but the war still cast a pall of fright and uneasiness that was inescapable no matter where you lived. Even so, when Daddy's work papers arrived, he made plans to leave for the U.S.—alone.

Mother couldn't imagine a place as far away as America. Nor could she imagine going there. Yet Daddy's mind was made up. America was going to be our home. He would go first, but the family must follow. Mother was furious. After all, she was newly married and a mother. Furthermore, the move to Stockholm had been traumatic enough; she did not want to go to this place called Chicago.

But Daddy was adamant. He'd send for us when passage was safe, he informed Mother. With the war raging, that was hard to predict.

"And what if I don't want to come?" Mother protested.

The answer was simple. That wasn't a choice.

As Daddy made his way to the U.S. aboard a freighter, Mother closed our apartment in Stockholm and returned us to the more familiar, secure surroundings of Valsjobyn.

We weren't the only arrivals, though. Even though Sweden was neutral, more than one thousand uniformed young Swedish men encamped within the boundaries of Valsjobyn. With German soldiers in Norway, a mere ten minutes away, the soldiers were there for our protection.

We moved in with Mooma and Uncle Calle, and Mother went to work at the bakery, as she had done before getting married. It was like old times, except that the soldiers packed the café's downstairs rooms so tightly that it was almost impossible to walk from one room to the next without tripping over someone's boots. And I must admit I loved the attention. They encouraged me to sing and dance, and I delightedly complied.

One day I heard some of the soldiers using words that Mother had spoken to me about. Swear words. I immediately poked my three-year-old head out the curtain separating the kitchen from the café and scolded the soldiers.

"Fula ord!" I said, shaking my finger. "Bad words."

I was definitely raised to be a good, ever-so-polite girl, to avoid conflict and unpleasantness, and to this day, I bristle at bad language and loud words.

If there was conflict between my parents, and there was, I was shielded from it. It wasn't until I was an adult that I learned Mother exchanged heated letters with Daddy. She wanted him to return, while he insisted that we'd follow him soon. His stubbornness infuriated Mother as much as it frightened her. Her biggest fear was that she'd give in and leave Valsjobyn.

In the end, of course, she would, because a Swedish woman deferred to her man and stood by him, no matter the cost. Over the years, I'm sure I absorbed this attitude and let it affect my own marriage. But at the time, all I knew was that something in our family wasn't right. I wanted a daddy and he wasn't there.

By age four, my curiosity about Daddy was insatiable. I pestered Mother constantly with questions about him. Why didn't he live with us? What'd he sound like? Was he strong? My relatives always told me I resembled Daddy. I had his nose, eyes, and smile. But I wanted to hear more. Even better, I wanted to see for myself.

"Someday," Mother said.

"Really?" I asked. "Soon?"

It was then that Mother usually turned me around and gave me three kicks in the seat. A Swedish custom for good luck. *Tre Sparkar*. Still, to this day, I get my three kicks before going on stage.

"Soon," she said. "You must be patient."

Mother could answer only so much. She actually knew rather little about my father's background, about his innermost thoughts and the forces that motivated him in his life. Theirs was a curious match: two shy, stalwart individuals who took pleasure in a quiet camaraderie.

My father's absence played a big part in my desire as an adult to find a strong man to look out for me. Like my father, I dealt with sadness and loneliness in the private silence that was so much like Daddy's own personality, as well as a characteristic of being Swedish. I pledged that once reunited, our family would remain intact forever.

With the end of World War II, Daddy pressed harder for us to join him in Chicago, but Mother still balked at leaving home. Eventually, I later learned, Daddy issued an ultimatum. Either Mother came to America or they'd divorce.

Mother was against ending the marriage. Period. She'd suffered when her own parents had divorced, and she didn't want to inflict that pain on me. So as much as it distressed her, she agreed. She deeply loved my father and she wanted to keep the family intact. And so, we prepared to leave Sweden and all the relatives. Mother tried to be brave and I was elated, then terrified of leaving home, a syndrome that would exert itself more and more in the years to come. I would become both reclusive and an extrovert, the roots of which I now understand.

MOTHER AND I SETTLED INTO TOURIST CLASS ON THE steamer *Gripsholm.* During the twelve-day journey we entertained other passengers by harmonizing, and I played with two little girls I met on board the ship. But according to Mother, I spent most of the time pleading with her to repeat every tidbit that she'd ever told me about Daddy. I wanted to hear every story, every description of him over and over again. I didn't go to sleep at night without first looking at his picture.

On November 29, 1946, we sailed into New York Harbor. I understood little about the new country I was moving to, but someone on the ship had told me about the Statue of Liberty and all it represented.

Beyond that was the imposing skyline of Manhattan. We stood on deck dressed to the hilt. Mother wore a stunning fur hat and silver-fox shawl that she had designed. I put on the same white jacket, hat, white mittens, light-brown woolen stockings, and white boots that I'd worn leaving Valsjobyn. We wanted to look spiffy for Daddy.

The *Gripsholm* docked at Pier 44, and right away Mother and I began searching the crowd for Daddy. We held hands, squeezing tightly, as if that might help contain our anticipation.

''There's your daddy!'' Mother cried.

The moment I had dreamed about for so long was finally here, and it was even better than I had imagined. He looked exactly as he did in his photographs, handsome and strong. I was thrilled that I was his daughter.

Mother and I stuck close to Daddy while he claimed our trunks and loaded them into his car, a black Hudson. Although he spoke English and moved with familiarity, everything was foreign to us. We might as well have stepped on the moon. Daddy played tour guide. He drove us around Manhattan, pointing out Central Park, the Empire State Building, the Chrysler Building, and Times Square, and finally our hotel.

But that was only the start of a great first night in this new country. Daddy took us out to dinner at a coffee shop, read the menu to us, then gave the waitress our order. We didn't understand a word he said. Nor did we really know what was served to us.

I sat silently through the meal, not wanting to interrupt my parents. Apparently I was too quiet, though. Daddy asked if something was wrong. I shook my head. In truth, I was overwhelmed by the day's events. But I wasn't going to complain. No way. I didn't want to say or do anything that might ruin this special, long-awaited moment. So I sat with my hands in my lap, the picture of a perfect little girl.

But Daddy wanted to get to know me. He told me that he had arranged a surprise.

"We're going to see a show," he explained, but I still had no idea what he meant.

Daddy then took us to Radio City Music Hall. I stared at the giant marquee above the theater, trying to make some sense of the words illuminated by the bright lights. We took our seats, and Mother and I admired the crushed red velvet. As the theater darkened, I reached out for her hand. Then the curtain rose.

"First, we see a movie," Daddy explained.

"A movie?" I asked. "What's that?"

"Just watch," he replied.

The feature that night was *The Jolson Story,* the classic biography of entertainer Al Jolson, starring Larry Parks. Though the movie was completely unfathomable to me, and the words and story sailed beyond my grasp, I was captivated by the new, quite amazing experience. I watched with intensity, trying to figure out what was going on.

The next presentation, the stage show for which Radio City has always been famous, was much easier to understand. The program, titled *All in a Day,* was a series of musical vignettes. The stage filled with dozens of dancers, singers, and of course the Rockettes. I was mesmerized, transported to some other place.

When the show ended, I was speechless. How do you explain an experience that is beyond the reference of anything in your imagination? If you're a child, as I was, you simply look up at your parents and smile. The grin on my face said everything there was to say about what I'd just seen.

Daddy carried me to bed. This time when Mother tucked me in, she had help. I knew then that I would always try very hard to please my parents, and especially at this time my father, to be his good little girl. I suppose that when your father is absent for so many years, you fear that if you misbehave, he'll leave you again. I felt those days were over, but I would take no chances.

Daddy touched me gently on the forehead and looked lovingly into my tired eyes. I thought about the three good luck kicks my mother had given me whenever I asked if I could meet my father. "Someday," she would tell me, and someday had finally arrived.

FOX LAKE WAS ABOUT FORTY-FIVE MINUTES OUTSIDE of Chicago, and in so many ways, Daddy's description of it was right. The woodsy fishing resort reminded me of Valsjobyn. It even boasted more than a dozen transplanted Swedes, including relatives like Auntie Mina and Uncle Charley, who had moved back again from Sweden, as well as aunties Gerda and Gunilla, their husbands and children.

There was just one difference between Fox Lake and Valsjobyn. It wasn't my home. I felt strange, uncomfortable, out of place. I missed Moofa and Mooma, Uncle Calle, and all my friends. And I sobbed every day for the first few weeks. At first I felt that the only good thing about moving there was being a family.

The one-bedroom home on Hickory Street and Lake Avenue we moved into had the feel of a dollhouse. Mother and Daddy took the bedroom, and I slept on a pullout cot in the living room. Daddy lived in Chicago during the week because the commute was too long and too expensive. We saw him only on the weekends, and I'm sure this was very hard on Mother. In fact, I had no idea of the extreme homesickness she felt. She was only twenty-seven, and battling depression, which made her sick and prone to fainting spells throughout most of the first year. Leaving Valsjobyn was like ripping her heart out.

I suppose Mother was a lot like I was later on when I became involved with Roger. Daddy was more worldly than Mother, more experienced and more mature, and Roger was certainly more worldly than I when I started dating him. Both Mother and I were looking for father figures, men who would take care of us—even if, in her case, that entailed a sacrifice.

It was two years before Mother felt somewhat settled. By then, we were able to move into a green-and-white two-bedroom home on Lake Avenue that seemed just perfect for us. It had a screened-in porch, a dining room, basement, kitchen, and a big backyard. I even had my own room. Plus, Mother and Daddy saved enough money to buy a piano, which we put in a little room off the entry.

Once again, music filled our house as it had in Valsjo-byn, and gradually, Fox Lake began to feel like home. Although I know it must have still been very tough for my mother, I never heard her complain. Not once. I was the same way. While I dreaded the fear and nervousness of starting a new school, I kept it to myself. The other children were very kind to me, fascinated because they had never met a kid from a foreign country who couldn't speak English. But I felt awful inside. I didn't understand a word of the language, and I felt lost. Still, I didn't protest or gripe. That just wasn't the way Swedish children behaved. Just as you're taught never to boast, you're taught to grit your teeth and trudge ahead in the cold, knowing warmer days will eventually come.

In my second year of school, I won my first spelling bee, a measure of how hard I pushed myself.

And Mother watched out for me. At this young age, I could have suffered emotional damage from being the outsider in a strange culture, had Mother not helped me make friends by signing me up for dance lessons at the Marjorie Young School of Dance. Although it was a financial stretch, she felt it was important.

Marjorie Young was a great teacher who managed her class by traditional dance rules of patience and strictness. From the first day, I loved class and took to it with a natural ability. If I couldn't understand exactly what she said, I simply mimicked every move and gesture she made.

After dance classes, I hobbled home in pain. Mother winced at the sight of my aching, sometimes bleeding feet, and asked if I wanted to quit. My answer never varied. For me, the payoff was too great. At my first dance recital, two boys carried a large basket on stage. Then I popped out in a bright yellow tutu and belted a saucy rendition of "It Takes a Long, Long Train with a Red Caboose, to Carry My Blues Away." The next year, I tap-danced and sang "Cuanto Le Gusta" while wearing a bright green-and-white satin skirt and a high, floral headpiece that transformed me into a seven-year-old Carmen Miranda.

It was the start of my glitzy outfits and elaborate stage act—thanks to Mother. For each recital, she stayed up half the night, sewing my costumes with exacting precision, attaching thousands of tiny beads or sequins until her eyes hurt, determined that I'd never have to be without, even though we couldn't afford it.

When I was ten years old, we returned for a visit to Sweden. Since we were staying for such a long time, my mother first got permission from my fourth-grade teacher for me to miss school. Her stipulation was that I keep a diary of the trip. Daddy remained behind to work, and Mother and I set out early in May.

Our trip began in Ornskoldsvik, Daddy's seaside hometown; then it was on to Valsjobyn, where I made diary notations about climbing mountains and running among cattle and goats, playing with cousins in haystacks, and taking day trips with my aunts and uncles into neighboring towns. The *pièce de résistance* came when my Uncle Calle invited me to ride on the back of his motorcycle. He had a BMW, a bike that seemed really large and powerful to a ten-year-old. The sound of the bike's motor throttling up and down the roads was thrilling. I couldn't imagine anything more exciting than climbing on the back and feeling the surge of the engine and the wind in my face. I begged him to take me for a ride.

When my uncle took the bait and suggested we go for a spin, my mother hesitated before giving permission. She wondered if it might be too dangerous for a ten-year-old girl. Yet she was something of a daredevil herself. Daddy had owned motorcycles, and they had sped along these very same roads.

Uncle Calle outfitted me with a cap and goggles, and then I climbed on the back of his motorcycle. We raced through the outskirts of Valsjobyn, then crossed over the border into Norway. Uncle Calle drove fast and the ride was tantalizing. In the back of my mind, I knew that I had to actually drive that motorcycle. As soon as we returned, I asked Mother if I could get a bike of my own. She laughed. It would be a long time before I bought one of my own. But I never forgot that first ride.

Years later, I would roar around the canyons of Los Angeles on my motorcycle, a blithe spirit. In fact, this love of speed and danger is a side of me I may never truly understand. I'm sure that on some level I am reacting to my repressed upbringing, to the good little girl side of me. I suspect I have a deep need to break free of that, and courting danger is how I express it.

The whole vacation was memorable. At the start of school the following September, I read my diary to my new fifth-grade classmates. Then to the fourth grade. Then to the sixth, seventh, and the eighth grades. I think I read it to everyone in school.

One night Mother received a call from the mother of one of my classmates. She pleaded, "Mrs. Olsson, please don't let Ann-Margret read her diary anymore. I don't know what to do. My boy's been crying all day."

"What's wrong?" Mother asked.

"He wants to go to Sweden," she said.

Mother laughed. We understood.

4

I WAS AT SCHOOL THE DAY IN 1952 WHEN DADDY'S boss, Mr. Leonard Johnson, called Mother in a concerned, shaky voice. Gus had been hurt, he told her, badly hurt, and she was to come right away.

Mother got the name of the hospital, and then she called all the relatives. The support system provided by such a close community sprang into action. Everybody helped. Auntie Gerda volunteered to go with Mother to the hospital. Auntie Mina assigned herself the task of dealing with me when I came home. But Mother wanted to tell me herself. Just then, I pushed open the door and noticed her tears immediately.

"It's Daddy," she said.

I didn't know what to say and started to cry myself.

"He's going to be okay," she said, reassuring herself as much as me.

Then she explained the plan. I pleaded to go with her to the hospital, but she insisted it was a time for adults.

"I'll call as soon as I know something," she promised.

At the hospital, she was met by Mr. Johnson, who told her Daddy was working on a building, and had slipped and fallen two stories onto the concrete pavement, landing directly on his back. In retrospect, his fall was an eerie foreshadowing of my nearly fatal tumble from a similar height twenty years later. Both Daddy and I were lucky to be alive.

My father shattered his pelvis in four places. He also suffered numerous bruises, contusions, and sprains. When Mother entered the room, he was unable to move or communicate. The doctors had him rigged to a flotation device, which took the weight and pressure off his body. Although he would remain in that condition for a week, Daddy received a good prognosis for recovery, though a slow one, and Mother phoned home with the news, sounding as positive as could be expected. But we were all greatly relieved. Feeling as if I could let my breath out after holding it all afternoon, I thanked God.

As Daddy recovered, I repeated Mother's words of wisdom: God never gives us more than we can handle. It was true, and has proved true over the years time and time again. And I knew that I could handle a lot.

Daddy's ordeal proved that *all* of us could. He spent several weeks in traction, and then several more in the hospital. Then he was laid up for another five months at home. Not only was he debilitated, he was also devastated at not being able to support his family. Though he received some disability money as well as a bonus, the financial strain was severe. To help, Mother got a job cleaning house for our neighbors Mr. and Mrs. Alten. It was good, honest work, and it left her time to care for Daddy and me. When Daddy's slow recovery made hard times even rougher, Mrs. Alten offered Mother a different, more lucrative job as receptionist and caretaker of the Alten-Nelson Funeral Home, which they co-owned in the nearby suburb of Wilmette.

In exchange for Mother's services, we could live there rent and utilities free. This, of course, meant moving from Fox Lake and all the relatives, but we had little choice. For so long, I had been taught to be resolute, to accept adversity, but this time I had trouble meeting the family standard.

The funeral home had a tiny apartmentlike space—a family room, kitchen, bathroom, and living room that doubled as a room for the mourners. I slept on a fold-out sofa in the room where families waited before and after the services. This little room was adjacent to the viewing room. Sometimes, I had to wait until one or two in the morning before I could go to bed.

Those nights were so long and sad. Mother, Daddy, and I would wait in the dinette area, watching TV with the volume extremely soft. When the last mourners finally left, I'd go into my room and fold out the sofa. There was always smoke from cigarettes, so Mother opened the windows, while I curled up under the blankets.

In the insecure, fragile world of childhood, the traumas of sleeping in too-close proximity to a casket were nothing compared with the devastation of starting yet another new school. The semester was almost over when I enrolled in the sixth grade. I didn't know a soul. It was as if I had come from Valsjobyn all over again, and once again, I was plagued by the same anxiety and fear as before, perhaps even more.

Wilmette, a wealthy suburb, wasn't at all what we were used to. The fathers were mostly professionals, and many of the mothers were ladies who stayed at home and looked as pressed and perfect as Donna Reed, in their pretty dresses and pearl necklaces.

At school, a lot of the girls wore matching cashmere sweaters and pencil skirts. They seemed to own every color cashmere sweater made. I'd never seen so many. I'd never even seen *one,* not even in big department stores. Mother knitted my sweaters, while the majority of my wardrobe consisted of things my cousins outgrew.

I bit my lip and listened to all my mother's remonstrances about the clothes not making the person and so forth. It helped some, but not as much as when my sixth-grade teacher, Mr. Hampton, discovered that I could sing. After class, he complimented my voice and asked if I'd join the Glee Club. Not only did the Glee Club help my confidence, it also became the first outlet for my dreams of being an entertainer.

Just as I felt life was stable at last, early one morning I lifted my head from my pillow and heard sobbing coming from my parents' room. I hurried in and found Mother on the bed, her face red and puffy, and she couldn't stop crying. Without asking what was wrong, I wrapped my arms around her. Daddy gave me the news.

"Mooma died," he said softly.

I looked at him for a disbelieving second, then began crying as hard as Mother. Mother departed for Valsjobyn immediately and spent five weeks there, leaving Daddy and me at home. It was a devastating, heartbreaking time for us, grieving Mooma's death from afar, wanting to be with the family back in Sweden, and coping without Mother. Mrs. Alten fixed me breakfast every morning, and Daddy left work early to be home when I got out of school.

One day I came home and Auntie Mina met me instead. She said that Daddy had fallen again, this time from a ladder outside a dairy where he was working. It turned out that he had accidentally breathed ammonia fumes leaking from a tank. Luckily, Daddy suffered only a minor concussion and came home later that evening.

Mother learned about this close call only after she came back home from Sweden, but by then, Daddy had nothing more than a persistent backache. She added to it by hugging him with all her might. We'd encountered some rough times since leaving Sweden, there was no question about that. But Mother somehow always insisted that there was a bright side. We were a family, she'd say. As long as we had each other, everything would be okay.

AFTER ALMOST FIVE MONTHS OF CONVALESCING, Daddy was his old self again. He returned to work full-time, enabling us to move from the funeral parlor into the upper half of a duplex in Northfield, a nearby suburb smaller than Wilmette. The difficult times faded in the background.

For all these years we had done without TV, but now we had a big black-and-white set and sat back each evening after dinner, watching our favorite shows. I discovered the Morris B. Sachs *Amateur Hour,* the local equivalent to the Ted Mack *Amateur Hour,* and loved watching the singers, dancers, ventriloquists, mimes, jugglers, baton twirlers, and comedians. I fantasized about going on the show myself, but didn't say a word about it to anybody. I didn't have the nerve, but luckily, someone else did.

Gus and Helen Randall were like godparents to me, and even contributed money for my dancing lessons. Daddy knew Gus from the Swedish clubs in Chicago. Helen was a pretty woman with white-blond hair and electric blue eyes. They had first seen me sing and dance some five years earlier at a birthday party for my Auntie Gunilla and decided from that impromptu performance that I had talent worth nurturing. One night after supper, as all of us watched the Morris B. Sachs *Amateur Hour*, Helen suggested that I try out for the show.

"She's a natural," Gus said excitedly.

There was just one problem.

"How do I get on?" I asked.

While Gus investigated how and when I could audition, I eagerly rehearsed. Several weeks later, I faced the show's producers in a downtown Chicago studio that was full of hopeful performers, their parents, and their prodders. This was my big moment.

I waited silently, trying to hide the fact I was a knot of nerves and fears.

"Ann-Margret Olsson?"

I nearly jumped out of my seat, before composing myself. I took a couple of deep breaths and regained control. Almost magically, mystically, I became that other person, that character who cast away her shyness and stepped in front of the producers, ready to perform.

"Whenever you like," a producer said.

I closed my eyes and focused. My heart pounded.

As soon as the music started, everything was fine. I sang and moved as if I were at home or at school with friends.

"Wonderful," the producer said when I finished. "Wonderful."

Somehow, I knew I would be given a place on the show, and I was. Viewers picked the show's winner by phoning in their vote for best performance, and Mother also made sure every Swede in the vicinity tuned into the show. I didn't give one thought to winning. I just wanted to do well, and make my parents proud.

On the big night, my dress was the one I wore as a bridesmaid at my cousin Greta's wedding several months earlier. I sang "Make Love to Me," a popular song that sounded risqué considering my age, though it seemed to go over well. Then Mr. Sachs announced that I'd won first place. I was deluged with prizes—a white orchid, a wrist watch, and a check for seventy-five dollars.

As the winner, I made another appearance on the talent contest the following week. This time, I lost. I took it without disappointment, knowing that I'd tried my hardest and done my best. It was, as my mother pointed out, part of realizing that everybody has their time in the sun.

NEW TRIER HIGH SCHOOL IN WINNETKA, ONE OF THE best schools in the state, was well-known for its great music and drama program. As a freshman, I was more than a little intimidated by this school where cheerleaders were admired, performers were celebrated, high grades were expected, and a good social life was very important. Prohibited by my parents from dating until I was sixteen, I turned my attention to fitting in as best I could. The biggest event of each year was Lagniappe, a talent show produced, directed, choreographed, and performed by students.

I showed up for tryouts, but was so uneasy about introducing myself to the panel of juniors and seniors conducting auditions that I practically backed into the room hoping nobody would notice. I studied the judges and noticed Annie Fraser, a junior I'd seen on campus who was full of energy and talent.

"I'd like to sing," I said. "And also dance."

Sing? Dance? Annie later told me that she shuddered. This girl has difficulty saying her name, never mind performing, she thought. She turned to the others. Someone else on the selection panel worried that I'd fall over from nerves. They whispered among themselves. But I closed my eyes, collected myself, and let the familiar strains of "Bill Bailey" bring out the performer in me. Annie and the others were surprised and relieved.

"Terrific," Annie said afterward. "You're in."

I wanted to continue fitting in. So, the summer of 1957, I went to a cheerleading camp in Indiana. Camp was supposed to last a week, but on the second day, a counselor pulled me out of practice and took me straight to the infirmary, where a doctor examined me and then quarantined me in a tiny cabin. I had the chicken pox.

My parents arrived the next day and took me home, and naturally, I was devastated. A week later, on the morning of my appearance on the Don McNeill *Breakfast Club,* a well-known talent show syndicated out of Chicago, my face was still covered by the red spots left over from the chicken pox.

"What am I going to do?" I cried to Mother as I dressed for the show.

"You aren't sick," she said. "So you will do your best."

I had wedged my foot in the door of the Don McNeill *Breakfast Club* because one of Mr. McNeill's producers, Mr. Peterson, had a son, Tom, who was a friend of mine in school, and he had put in a good word. Once at the studio, I learned that Mr. McNeill was on vacation. However, his replacement was Ted Mack, *the* Ted Mack of *Amateur Hour* fame.

The makeup and hair people delicately tried to cover the spots on my face and brush my hair so that it would hide some of the spots on my forehead. But once it was time for me to sing "Them There Eyes," I underwent the usual transformation, the Ann-Margret shift from reticent to unrestrained.

After my performance, Mr. Mack asked if I wanted to appear on his *own* show. Did I!

But then I realized that an appearance on the Ted Mack *Amateur Hour* meant traveling to New York. Given our tight financial situation, I figured that Mr. Mack's offer was a wonderful compliment, but not likely.

But I had the best stage parents in the world. Never pushy, always supportive and loving. With help from my godparents, they came up with enough money for the trip. Mother and I were so-o-o excited. It was a gilded moment, our first time back to Manhattan, the city where our journey in this country had begun eleven years earlier.

I agonized over what to wear on the show and settled on a burgundy velvet dress with a scooped neck, which I'd borrowed from my cousin Ann. Feeling that "Them There Eyes" was my lucky song, I selected it for the show. But

I lost to a man who played "Lady of Spain" on a big Mexican leaf, and once again, I listened to my inner warning to "take it in stride." My mother's teachings, my Swedish upbringing had stressed humility, and I did my best to not feel disappointed. But, all things considered, I felt like a winner, because I actually got through the song.

One of my mentors in my high school years was Dr. Peterman, who headed New Trier's music department and became one of the important figures in preparing me for the future. One of my girlfriends pushed me into his office, and asked Dr. Peterman if he wanted to hear someone sing.

"I mean, she can *really* sing," she said.

He shrugged. If he knew of my Ted Mack performance, he wasn't letting on.

"Okay," he said with resignation. "Sing."

"I wish someone could accompany me on the piano," I suggested, feeling nervous and on the spot.

"Forget the piano," Dr. Peterman said. "Just sing."

"Yes, sir."

Midway through "Bill Bailey," one of my staples, I could tell that Dr. Peterman was surprised. Afterward, though, he simply said he looked forward to working with me in some of the school's productions. Once I knew Dr. Peterman better, I understood that he was already preparing me for new challenges. He knew how difficult show business was, and he didn't want to inflate my expectations with praise.

Soon after, school was out for the summer and I got a job as a salesgirl in a department store. Every morning I put on makeup, a special uniform, and took the El downtown. I also made a determined effort to find an agent. I got out the Yellow Pages and spent my lunch hours going on umpteen disheartening interviews. My voice teacher Mildred Davis knew how badly I wanted to perform and gave me the name of Hal Munro, an agent who also had his own band on weekends, playing socials and clubs. Mr. Munro seemed to like me, but more than that he also happened to be in dire need of a singer. Suddenly, I had a job.

For the next couple of years, I would spend most weekend nights singing with Mr. Munro and his band, traveling around Chicago and throughout Illinois, Indiana, Wisconsin, and Michigan. But one day that summer, Mr. Munro phoned with an intriguing offer. He'd booked a female singer with the Danny Ferguson Band at the Muehlebach Hotel in Kansas City, but she had suddenly dropped out. Was I interested in the job?

"It pays ninety-eight dollars a week, not including room and board," he said as if that was a bigger factor than having to ask my parents, being away from home, preparing for the start of my junior year, tryouts for the cheerleading squad . . . all sorts of things.

My parents consented, knowing how very much I wanted a career in entertainment. I was told I had to start two days later, on a Sunday. Daddy woke me early Saturday morning and loaded the car with luggage. Mother was going to stay with me in Kansas City. When we got there, Daddy helped Mother and me settle into our hotel, then drank several cups of coffee, and turned around and drove the five hundred fifty miles home so he could be at work on Monday. That was my dad. He was always such a trooper.

Meanwhile, I memorized an hour or so of new material, rehearsed with Danny Ferguson, and then performed at the hotel Sunday night. Lacking any real stage presence then, I relied on enthusiasm and adrenaline as I stood in the center of the stage and clutched the microphone. But the engagement went better than anyone had anticipated, and we were held over two additional weeks, which meant that I missed the start of school. But Mother reasoned that I was still getting an education—just not a traditional one.

As Dr. Peterman promised, I progressed well in the theater department. I starred in both *Manhattan Towers* and *Plain and Fancy,* but the real performing highlight of my high school career occurred during the 1959 Lagniappe. For my rendition of "Heat Wave," which I choreographed, I slithered out from behind the grass door of a Tahitian set in a tight, chartreuse dress slit up my leg, slow-danced center stage, and belted out, "She started this heat wave, by letting her seat wave . . ." Almost as soon as I began to move there was a rustling in the audience by parents who thought my interpretation way too steamy. Several other parents walked out. There it was again—the "other" Ann-Margret, a sultry siren who really had no idea of how different she was on stage. I was hurt when I heard my friend's father had walked out.

"You've got to understand," my friend explained. "He really likes you. And he respects you. He just got a little—"

"A little what?" I asked.

"Nervous," he said. "You know, nervous."

I suppose I was a dangerous creature in those days, with no knowledge of her effect on people. But I just continued innocently on, fixated on performing.

After graduating, I planned on attending Northwestern, which had accepted me earlier in the year. But I was torn between school and singing. Before leaving New Trier, I sought advice from Dr. Peterman. I asked what he thought might happen to me as a performer in the world outside high school, and braved for the worst.

Dr. Peterman smiled. He looked almost surprised that he and I hadn't already had this conversation.

"Look, kiddo," he said in a serious tone, "with your talent as a singer, dancer, and actress, plus your face, you could realize big things in Hollywood."

I was stunned. This man who I respected had articulated my innermost dreams.

"I predict the movies for you," he added.

"You're kidding."

"I'm not," he said. "With hard work . . ."

"It's impossible," I interrupted.

"With the right breaks," he continued. "With a little luck. You can, as I said, do big things."

I gave Dr. Peterman a hug and left his office, grinning from ear to ear.

7

STILL BUOYED BY MY TALK WITH DR. PETERMAN, I plunged into Rush Week at Northwestern. I put on my best outfit, applied makeup, curled my hair, and tried to be as sophisticated as I could while running from sorority to sorority, attending luncheons, tea parties, dinners, and assorted get-togethers.

My first choice was Kappa Alpha Theta, the same sorority to which Annie Fraser, my friend from New Trier, belonged. I went through the initial day of partying and events. Then, at the end of that evening, I came down with a bad flu, and went straight to bed, thus missing the rest of the week of socializing. As a result, I assumed my chances of pledging a sorority, especially Kappa Alpha Theta, were ruined.

Yet apparently my name was the source of some high drama when the Theta's selection committee went into its final round of discussion. Somehow I remained in contention, but there were a few girls who wondered if I had the right stuff and asked if I had a recommendation from any Theta alums.

Annie exploded. She ripped off her sorority pin and threw it across the room in disgust. "If you don't pledge Ann-Margret, you don't have me either," she exclaimed. With that, she slammed out of the sorority, a true friend.

A few nights later, Mother came into my room, where I was still in bed with a temperature. The doorbell had rung a few moments earlier, though I hadn't heard it. Mother told me to get out of bed and look outside the window. And there stood the girls from the Theta house on the front lawn, each one holding a lighted candle. Bundled up in a warm robe, I opened the window and tried to say hello, and thanks, but all that came out were tears of joy. My new sorority sisters serenaded me with the Theta song and initiated me on the spot.

One day at the Theta house, Carol Thomas, a sorority sister, mentioned that a friend of hers, Scott Smith, was organizing a combo. Carol explained that an agent from Los Angeles had recently asked Scott about doing an act. He'd already lined up bassist Ring Warner and drummer David Zehring, both students like me. Now, he needed a girl singer.

Did I want to meet him?

Sure.

Scott and I met several weeks later at the Theta house. Tall and dark-haired, he had already graduated from Northwestern with a degree in speech, served in the army, considered entering the ministry, then reconsidered and set his sights on show business.

Scott sat down at the keyboard and I sang along. After a few numbers, I was hired and rehearsals began a few days later. Over lunch at the Hut, a campus hangout, we dubbed ourselves the Suttletones, figuring the spelling pun might get some attention. We all chipped in to have Maurice Seymour, a well-known Chicago photographer, snap our publicity photo. We were ready for business. Scott had met all kinds of people in the various clubs where he had performed, including a man named Frenchy Medlevine, who owned the Sands, and managed a number of similar clubs in the area. Through Frenchy, we landed a booking at the Sands. And we also signed to make Frenchy our manager.

We did three long sets a night, working on a small stage directly behind the bartender—so close I felt as if I could use my high heel to mix drinks.

As time passed, my time with the Suttletones overtook the hours I devoted to school. Ordinarily, I didn't get home until around two or three a.m., which made study somewhat difficult. I found myself racing through the day in anticipation of the time when I could step on stage at night on the weekends.

Somewhat predictably, perhaps, Scott and I started dating. Pretty soon, my whole life was music, and my priorities were clearly shifting away from the campus.

My friend Annie worried that maybe I was too one-dimensional. Between classes, shows, rehearsal, and Scott, I had hardly any time for socializing. I was a Theta in spirit only; my actual presence at the house was almost ghostlike.

"I'm worried you're short-changing yourself," Annie said one night as we caught up on each other's lives over dinner at the pancake house just off campus.

"You work every weekend. You also have school. Is this what you want?"

"I'm loving it," I said.

"So you're happy?"

"Deliriously," I replied.

And I was. Imagine dreaming about being an entertainer since you were a small girl, and then getting a chance to do just that. I was wrapped up in a glowing haze, a young woman with no fear of the future, eager to cast aside the hardships of the past. In truth, it was a magic time in my life.

In late May, as I wound up my freshman year, Scott received a call from an agent whose partner had caught several of our shows at the Sands. There was an opening at the Nevada Club, in Las Vegas. Did we want the job?

The engagement would last two weeks, commencing after school let out in June. The agents said there would be more work after that, and, naturally, we let ourselves dream of a big future. None of us could imagine a summer quite as good as this one promised to be.

Frenchy tried talking me out of it. "Why don't you just finish school, stay here, get married, and have babies?" he asked.

"No, not yet. I want to be an entertainer."

"Do you know how tough it is out there? I don't want you to get hurt."

"I've been warned. But I still want to try."

"There's just one problem," Scott said. "And maybe it's not so big."

"What's that?" I asked.

"Ann-Margret, you know how strict your parents are. Do you think they'll let you go?"

I gave him a reassuring smile, but privately, I was doubtful.

8

I HAD NEVER BEEN A CONSCIOUS MANIPULATOR OF my parents, but subconsciously, I knew how to win their approval. They doted on Ann-Margret the performer and anything that would enhance my career was sure to win their approval. Hence, I decided that my parents should see us on stage before I asked them about Las Vegas. Scott thought I was making a mistake, because the Mist, the nightclub we were playing outside Chicago, wasn't exactly a wholesome atmosphere. Opening around midnight, the Mist didn't close until after sunrise. We only worked weekends, but we worked both of its rooms, the bar in front and the rear showroom, until four or five a.m.—sometimes even eight.

In the showroom, we opened for Belle Barth, a comedienne and singer famous for her risqué jokes, and one of the objects of Scott's concern. I must say Belle was very sweet to all of us.

My parents were older than old-fashioned and simply didn't use the sort of language that made up most of Belle's act. In fact, I could still hear myself as a little girl in Valsjobyn, mimicking Mother as I told the soldiers in the bakery not to swear: "Fula ord! Fula ord!"

But I had faith. During our set, I watched the table where my parents sat with my aunts and uncles. They looked as proud as royalty. Afterward, I told Scott not to worry, because if the Suttletones were a hit with my relatives, Belle was an even bigger one. Perhaps, until that moment, I had misinterpreted propriety for prudishness. Not only did Daddy and my uncles Charley and Roy laugh, my uncles repeated some of the jokes they heard that night for the rest of their lives. One of my very favorite things that my Uncle Charley said when he thought something was funny—he'd say, with a big smile on his face and always with his hand slapping his knee, "Vall, dat vuss uh corker!"

We had the big discussion about Las Vegas the next night over dinner. I asked Scott to come for support, and he wound up explaining the agent's offer and doing more of the talking. When it came to business, I felt tongue-tied and preferred to let someone else explain things, a harbinger of my attitude toward Roger in later years.

My parents were impressed by what the Suttletones had achieved in such a short time. They were also impressed by Scott. Moreover, they believed in me. When it came to helping me do my best, they felt the same as they had when I was seven and Mother stitched thousands of little beads and sequins on the costumes I wore to recitals. They wanted me to have every chance in the world to succeed in whatever I wanted to do in life.

"Well, I'm glad all of you will be working together," Mother said.

I sprang out of my chair and hugged Mother. They'd said yes!

The night before we left, which was the day after school finished, Daddy came into my bedroom wanting to talk. Almost always, Daddy was a man of few words, quiet and introspective. But the eve of my departure for the summer was an emotional occasion. I stopped packing, which consisted mainly of throwing a bunch of sweaters and stretch pants into a suitcase. Daddy and I sat on the bed. He apologized for not having a lot of advice to give me about show business.

"But maybe," he said, "I've learned a few things that I can tell you about."

Looking into my eyes, he patted my knee and smiled. I fought back tears. Though Daddy rarely said anything about his past, he recounted some of the travels he'd made as a younger man and warned me to be on the lookout for characters who might try to take advantage of my inexperience in handling business matters. It had happened to him, he said. Then Daddy asked me a favor.

"Of course," I said.

"Ann-Margret, I want you to promise me you'll never take a drink of alcohol."

"You know I don't drink, Daddy." I had never had a drink. Nor had I puffed a cigarette.

"I promise," I said.

Now I know that Daddy struggled with alcoholism as a young man, and that he feared it was in the genes. As it turned out, he was right. But at the time, I was puzzled. I felt it wasn't my place to ask additional questions, so I nodded and quickly shifted my thoughts to the trip ahead.

Before we left, I made my decision to drop my last name and simply go by Ann-Margret. It wasn't an affectation. Nor was it an attempt to be different. I didn't know of any performers who went by one name. It was just my way of ensuring that my parents were not hurt, embarrassed, or bothered by anything that might happen as a result of my being in show business.

And so it was. Not Ann. Not Miss Margret. But Ann-Margret.

The four of us filled Ring Warner's station wagon and Scott's Austin Healy—the Healybird—with luggage and equipment and left early in the morning. Except for Scott's radiator blowing outside Salt Lake City, we arrived in Las Vegas without incident. Scott, who had vacationed with his family in Vegas, had briefed us on what to expect—a main street lit by neon signs, hotels rising up from the desert sand like concrete cacti, and packed casinos.

But we did an emotional turnaround when we got into town. We got lost and couldn't find the Nevada Club, where we were booked. We had to ask for directions, and then, finally, we pulled up in front of the club. Scott located the club's entertainment director, who seemed confused, then apologetic. The club, he explained, had extended the previous act, meaning we had no job. Scott got on the phone with the agent in L.A. who'd booked us into the Nevada Club. He said that he was very sorry, but as long as we've come this far, we should continue on to L.A. and see what happens there.

We issued a collective shrug. At nineteen years old, you

take such matters in stride. We'd driven to Las Vegas from
Chicago. How much farther was L.A.?

"Only three hundred miles," Ring said.

"That's less than half a day's drive," Dave Zehring
chimed in.

We needed no convincing, and so we climbed back in
our cars. None of us had been west of Colorado before. So,
we regarded this as a minor setback in our grand game plan,
and also an exciting adventure.

9

IT WAS DARK WHEN WE ARRIVED IN LOS ANGELES, EXhausted but with our idealism intact. We headed for Hollywood and checked into a one-bedroom unit at an inexpensive hotel on Sunset Boulevard. The three guys slept on the living-room sofa and floor. I accepted their offer to take the bedroom.

Monday morning we drove to the agency, where our agent greeted us warmly and introduced us around the office as a promising group from Chicago. We got directly to the point: Was there any work?

"Not at the moment," the agent said. "But something will come up. I'm sure of it."

"When?" we asked.

"Soon."

What could we say? Nothing. But we didn't hide our feelings of disappointment.

"Listen, kids," he said. "Jobs pop up every single day. Call here twice a day—at ten and four—and we'll tell you whether or not we have something."

We called. Every day. Like clockwork. But the answer stayed the same. Sorry kids, nothing yet.

In the meantime, we rented a Spanish-styled duplex in the Hollywood Hills, explored the city, and worked on ways to stretch our meager savings. A few weeks later, in early July, our funds had dropped to where we subsisted primarily on toast, hard-boiled eggs, and water. But none of us wanted to give up.

Without any job prospects, I finally proposed finding another agent, and I suggested the same method I'd used to get my first job—the Yellow Pages. Again, we had nothing to lose. So Scott and I made a list, and we auditioned for anyone who agreed to meet with us, a process we quickly learned wasn't much fun.

At one point in this adventure, a wonderfully kind agent named Harry Bloom listened to me and Scott do our routine, eyed my long brown hair, and sent me to audition for the role of Maria in the movie version of *West Side Story*. Sure, I knew that I'd never get the part, but I still pursued the lead.

He gave us the address of the Pierre Cossette Management Company. We arrived at the right office, but they weren't auditioning for that role. Bobby Roberts, a manager who worked with Pierre, met with us anyway. I told him about the Suttletones.

"There aren't many jobs," he said. "Maybe something will happen in the future."

One of our next peregrinations was to the office of Georgia Lund, an agent I'd found in the phone book. Georgia, a dynamite lady who was perhaps the only woman in Hollywood at the time who owned her own agency, specialized in booking small clubs and restaurants. She was *great* to us. She explained it was high season in the clubs, and most of the acts had been booked at the start of summer, but something could change. Indeed, several days later, she called—to say she had booked us for two weeks at the Villa Marina, a really lovely restaurant-supper club in Newport Beach. Down to our last pennies, we finally had a real honest-to-goodness job. Without wasting time, we drove to Newport, checked into a nearby hotel, and splurged at the grocery store for the first decent meal we'd had in weeks.

Newport Beach was in the peak of its summer social season, and a magnet for Hollywood's boating crowd. The Villa Marina was one of the most popular gathering places. Don Sharp from the *I Love Lucy* show came in, then he brought composer Henry Mancini and his wife, Ginny, and then they invited Mr. and Mrs. Edgar Bergen.

We performed three sets a night, and never to less than a sell-out crowd. With good word-of-mouth, the Villa Marina extended us another three weeks. We were ecstatic, and the desperation of the previous weeks evaporated. We lived near the beach, *and* got paid for doing what we loved to do. We were kids, we were rich by our standards, and we were deliriously happy.

As for my relationship with Scott, the difficult times we had been through had taken a toll. We agreed to remain good friends, and I was relieved. He'd wanted us to get married, but I felt too young to be seriously involved with one person.

Soon, I began dating actor Peter Brown, who starred on the popular Western series *Lawman*. Peter had seen several of our shows, then introduced himself one night. He was handsome, glamorous and fun, and we made a date. And we saw each other many times that summer. Peter even took me to several Hollywood parties and premieres. In fact, that was my first introduction to the glitter and hoopla of "Hollywood." He also found out that I had never been to Disneyland, so he took me, my parents, and our dear friend Karin Ottoson.

Peter handled everything so smoothly, including his fans, and he was always wonderful to them. That's something I've always remembered and admired about him.

At the end of our engagement at the Villa Marina, Georgia Lund phoned with another job: two weeks at the Commercial Hotel, in Elko, Nevada, a town of rugged, friendly cowboys, a town still imbued with a strong sense of the old West. Singer Vikki Carr, who was just beginning what would be a superb career, was the headliner, and she was great to us. The stage was situated above the bar and it overlooked several rows of slot machines. Between songs, we overheard gamblers swapping tips on which machines were hot. I didn't play, because the money was too dear to me. Also, I knew my parents would never approve of gambling and subconsciously, they were always on my mind.

Throughout the summer, I'd phoned my parents almost daily with descriptions of each performance. My enthusiasm was boundless, infectious, and by the time we reached Elko, my parents made plans to see us in person. They joked that because I always called collect, it would be cheaper to fly to Nevada than to pay the long-distance phone bill.

Their visit made me realize how homesick I was. We swam and caught up on family news and I bought Mother a gorgeous bracelet at a store I liked downtown. I pointed out the hot slot machines to Daddy. In a good-natured way, he wanted to know how I knew about such things. Mother supplied the answer.

"Gus, our little girl is growing up."

10

WHETHER IT WAS LUCK, TALENT OR A COMBINATION of the two, after the Elko engagement wound up, we managed to land two weeks at the Riverside Hotel in Reno. The Riverside was our best booking to date. The room was cozy, and the stage was large enough that I finally had some room to stray from the microphone. With room to move, I did what came naturally when I heard good music. I snapped my fingers, tossed my hair, did whatever it took to convey the feeling of the words and music to the audience. I suppose that was the genesis of the Ann-Margret frenetic feline moves that have punctuated my style and my career. Believe me, I don't orchestrate all that much of them—it's a natural response to the music.

People have always asked if I was influenced by anybody in television, movies, or music when I started in show business. My answer has never varied. No. When I said hello and good night, I was Ann-Margret Olsson. But in between, I was an actress who, instead of saying dialogue in a scene, sang the words to songs and let the music guide her movements.

One night at the Riverside Hotel, a man named Frank Taylor came backstage after the show to offer words of encouragement and congratulations. Frank was producing *The Misfits,* which was being shot outside of town. The movie starred Montgomery Clift, Clark Gable, Marilyn Monroe, and Eli Wallach, and was the talk of Reno.

Mr. Taylor was generous in his praise and warned that he'd be back. So, the next night, he returned, bringing Montgomery Clift. After the show, they came backstage and Montgomery Clift, sensing how scared I was, gave me a friendly hug and promised to see us again.

Sure enough, several nights later there was a small commotion in the back of the showroom. Frank Taylor and Montgomery Clift were back, joined by Eli Wallach.

The threesome came backstage after the performance and visited for a generous period of time, asking more about our backgrounds, and offering encouragement. Before leaving, they invited us to the set to watch them film.

It was the first time any of us had visited a movie set, and I was nervous as could be. Everybody looked busy, important, and I didn't want to interfere in any way. So I stood quietly, trying to be as inconspicuous as possible, while at the same time trying to absorb everything going on.

Then Eli Wallach recognized me. He waved, and came toward me, and by his side was Clark Gable.

"Clark Gable, Miss Ann-Margret Olsson."

He brought over his chair and sat down beside me.

"So I heard that you attend Northwestern?" he asked.

"Yes," I nodded.

"They have a fine theater department," he said. "Are you involved in that area of study?"

"Yes, I am," I nodded again. "Speech. Maybe theater later."

I didn't want to say too much, in part because I didn't want to say anything wrong. Later that night, as I'd done after each of these encounters, I phoned home and breathlessly recreated for my parents my brush with Hollywood's stars.

I also explained how, just before leaving, I had caught a glimpse of Marilyn Monroe. From the distance, Marilyn struck me as a beautiful woman with a porcelain delicacy. I had no idea of the marital difficulties she was going through at the time with Arthur Miller. I sensed only the special splendor and style that made her a star.

"It was just a brief moment," I told Mother. "I wished it had been longer."

Several years later, Marilyn's stand-in, Evelyn Moriarty, coincidentally became my stand-in on a film and has worked with me ever since. I told her that I'd visited the set of *The Misfits,* and she remembered it well. She recalled how Marilyn had asked, "Who's that pretty brunette sitting by the lake with Frank and Monty?"

I was shocked. I couldn't believe that she noticed a stranger sitting in the heat. But Evelyn insisted.

I would've loved to have known her. I would've understood her, I think. To me, she was a vulnerable woman, who only wanted to be accepted and loved, but somehow was mistreated, used, and often abused by Hollywood, the studio system, and by men. Just thinking about her makes me upset at how people take others for granted and often don't appreciate them until it's too late. Marilyn was one of those who wasn't helped soon enough.

Because the Riverside Hotel extended us another six weeks, we stayed in Reno long after the film company left. But at the end of August, the job ended and we finally had to contemplate the future.

And that was our dilemma. By this time, I had become intoxicated with show business. I glowed on stage, and thrived in that ambience. School, by contrast, was dull and unglamorous, a very poor second. In the back of my mind, I knew I should complete my education, but I knew what my heart told me to do. Scott also shared my sentiments. But Ring and David Zehring weren't quite as sure they should drop out of Northwestern for the slim chance of stardom.

We put off the heavy-duty talk until we got back to L.A. Once there, Ring and David opted to return to college and finish their degrees. It was a tough, agonizing decision, but the right one for them. Scott, who'd already received his diploma and was in graduate school, chose to stick with the Suttletones and see where it led. So did I. There wasn't even a question, just a proviso: I needed to get my parents' permission.

11

AS I HEADED BACK TO CHICAGO, I FELT THE FAMILIAR warmth of childhood and subtle parental pulls. It would be good to see Mother and Daddy again, but how would they react to my suggestion of becoming a college dropout? My parents knew my inclinations. We'd discussed it many times on the phone, so Mother was prepared when I brought the subject up yet again. This time, I asked with utmost seriousness, what she thought about my postponing school in favor of performing.

''You're so bound and determined to get into entertainment that I don't think you'd be doing yourself any good going back to Northwestern right now,'' she said. ''You have to do what you think is right.''

Daddy agreed. He reminded me that he'd also sought to fulfill his dreams as a teenager by hopping aboard a freighter bound for Canada and then sneaking across the border into the U.S. even though his friends and family thought him nuts. I loved hearing that story and loved that he cared enough about my hopes to give his approval.

''Don't worry,'' he said. ''We believe in you.'' As immigrant parents, I'm sure they harbored desires to see their only daughter get her college degree. But they never let on, and for this I will always thank them. They knew me so well, and were willing to subvert their goals for mine. I was on my way.

While I was in Chicago, Scott replaced Ring and David with a brand-new rhythm section. By the time I returned, we had another engagement—several weeks in the lounge at the

Dunes Hotel, in Las Vegas, the city of our first disappointment.

The Dunes was big time. I decided my wardrobe, which still consisted mostly of castoffs from my cousins, needed glamorizing. So I splurged and bought a pair of Spring-o-lators—clear plastic mules, with very high rhinestone-studded heels. My mother laughed when I told her about the purchase, but those shoes, the trendiest thing going in 1960, made me feel ready.

Tony Bennett headlined the main showroom at the Dunes. We shared the lounge with the greatly talented New Orleans trumpeter Al Hirt and his band, and he commanded all the good set times, of course, while we played off-peak hours. It was a tough gig. People stood in line for tickets to see Tony Bennett, but during our set times seats were available, and those who came into the lounge just wanted to talk, smoke, drink, gamble, rest. If they were entertained, so much the better.

Still, we created a small buzz. Tony Bennett listened several times, as did Al Hirt. Symbolically, the Dunes was a turning point for us. After that, we went back to L.A. believing that we were in show business and not merely college students working on a lark.

And with that came new, nettlesome problems that influenced the future of the group. One afternoon, Bobby Roberts asked me to come in and explained he wanted to sign me. Not the Suttletones. Not Scott *and* me. Just me. He talked about continuing in nightclubs, but also about my making records and movies.

"It's up to you," Bobby said.

I honestly hadn't thought about doing anything outside of the Suttletones, at that point, but it all sounded so intriguing. Bobby smiled. He'd baited the hook, and I'm sure he felt confident he could reel me in.

A few days later he called.

"Have you heard of George Burns?" he asked.

I might've been _____ rs. Then he settled _____ gs: "Bill Bailey," "Have a _____ Knife."

ater I learned that at the tim

reputation for discovering new talent was unsurpassed; in previous holiday shows, he'd introduced newcomers Bobby Darin and Bobby Rydell, and now they were rising up the charts. I knew I would have trouble resisting this, but I had one reservation.

"What about Scott?" I asked.

"If you get the job," he explained, "there's a spot for him to accompany you."

But Bobby also had a reservation. He asked about Scott's and our combo's old deal with Frenchy, our manager from Chicago. We'd signed a contract, which was long forgotten, yet Bobby knew that if we ever achieved some degree of fame and began to make money, we'd hear from Frenchy.

"So we've got to get you out of that deal," he said, and we agreed. I didn't know much about Bobby as a manager then, but he had managed to hook me up with George Burns and that was enough to convince me that he was the right man to handle my career.

In November 1960, Bobby drove Scott and me to General Service Studios, where George Burns maintained an office on the lot. I was totally disarmed by Mr. Burns.

"How ya doin,' kid?" he asked in that great, gravelly voice of his. He puffed intermittently on his cigar. His eyes sparkled with playfulness.

I'd worried about what to wear for the audition, as I only had three outfits, and settled on tight, black toreador pants, which were shiny and worn from lots of wear, a light-blue, long-sleeved, round-neck lamb's wool sweater that I'd also had for a while, and old black pumps with little high heels and pointed toes that had seen better days. I referred to that outfit as my uniform. Mr. Burns seemed to approve.

Since he didn't have a piano in his office, we walked to a nearby soundstage, where an upright was pushed into a corner. Scott took off an empty birdcage that was on top of an old dusty tarp covering the piano and dusted off the keys. Mr. Burns, sensing my nerves, relaxed me with flirtatious one-line _____ into a chair and nodded. I did three son_____ Time," and "Mack the _____

Many years _____

the lineup for Mr. Burns's show, which included the great
Ames Brothers making their final appearance together and
a juggler named Frances Brunn, was already set. He'd only
agreed to see me as a favor to Pierre Cossette, Bobby's
boss. But as soon as I finished the last song, Mr. Burns
stood up and walked toward me with a bright smile.

"How'd you like to go to Vegas and do the show with
me?" he asked.

I heard the words clearly, but didn't believe them. Or
rather I *couldn't* believe them.

"Are you joking?" I exclaimed.

"Not unless you're paying me," he cracked.

"Well, yes," I said excitedly. I mean, here was the big
break I'd dreamed of. "I'd love to. *We'd* love to. Wow,
that'd be great."

I couldn't have wished for a better mentor than George
Burns. He was professional, bright, funny, and, above all
else, kind, generous, helpful, and really sensitive to people's feelings. He truly respected women. In my segment
of the show, I had three songs. Then, at the finale, Mr.
Burns and I did a vaudeville bit in which he sprinkled sand
on the stage and we performed a little soft-shoe "sand
dance" on it.

We rehearsed endlessly at his home, which appealed to
me. He and I were both perfectionists, and somehow despite all the differences—age, experience—we were in sync
in a funny way. What really impressed me about Mr. Burns
was his relationship with his beautiful and gracious wife,
Gracie Allen. Whenever he wanted an honest opinion, he
called Gracie. Hers was indeed the final word. He trusted
her totally, and I took careful measure of the importance
of that ability to trust another human being so completely.
I'm absolutely sure that their relationship influenced my
willingness to trust Roger, as I would do years later.

As rehearsals intensified and the late December opening
night drew closer, Scott and I received a surprise. Frenchy,
our old manager, called. He happened to be in Beverly Hills
and just wanted to check in on our progress. He also knew
very well, as we did, that he still had us under contract.

We set up a meeting at the Hamburger Hamlet, a dimly

lit restaurant in Beverly Hills. Frenchy was extremely nice and cordial. Scott talked and got straight to the point: We wanted a release from our contract. Frenchy contemplated the situation with a face that refused to betray his feelings.

"I'll tell you kids what I can do," he finally said. "Since what we're talking about is business, I'm willing to let you buy yourselves out of our contract. If I'm hearing you correctly, you want to be free and clear."

"That's right," Scott agreed.

"Then what you need to know is—"

"How much—"

"That's right," Frenchy said. "How much. I'm thinking that what seems fair is—"

I held my breath and kept my eyes on Scott, who was cool under pressure.

"Six thousand dollars," Frenchy said.

Yikes. To us, six thousand dollars was practically all the money in the world. But we didn't flinch.

"Fine," Scott said. "We'll get it to you."

I've always had very fond memories of Frenchy. He was truly very kind to me. And I felt he deserved to be paid. Although the amount was prohibitive to both of us, I'd lived the past summer like a field mouse, saving almost every dollar I made, so when I checked my savings account, I found enough money to cover the debt. Frenchy got paid, and Scott and I got peace of mind, freedom, and a trip to Vegas.

12

AT THIS EARLY STAGE OF MY CAREER, I HAD ALREADY learned to distinguish the shadings of my performance anxiety. This time, as I faced the empty stage of the Congo Room, the Las Vegas Sahara Hotel's showroom, I felt stark terror. In a few hours, the room would be packed with people, people staring at *me*. My terror grew, then glancing at the empty tables, I heard a familiar voice.

"Annie!" called Mr. Burns.

Lots of people have called me Annie. But he's the only one who's ever done it in a way that doesn't bother me.

I returned his smile, but noticed his enthusiasm had quickly been replaced by a look of concern. He studied me carefully, slowly, puffing his cigar like a draftsman looking over completed blueprints for errors.

"Is that the outfit you're wearing tonight?" he asked.

I wore an orange-red velvet pants suit, brand-new and very chic, purchased at a Beverly Hills boutique right before I left L.A. The suit cost more than I'd spent on clothes in my entire life, but the show was an event and I wanted to look good. I'd actually told Mr. Burns about my new outfit the day before, and he'd said he got excited just thinking about it.

But now . . .

"It's velvet," I said as my self-assurance disappeared. "It's very stylish."

He didn't answer. Instead, there was a long pause.

"What happened to the sweater and pants that you wore to the audition?" he asked. "The *tight* sweater and the *tight* pants." Then he told me something I've never forgotten.

"Annie," he said, "people don't only wanna hear your

voice. They wanna see where it's comin' from.''

I turned around, hurried to my room, and changed into my black toreador pants and sweater. When I returned to the showroom, Mr. Burns grinned and gave me a gentle pat on the back as if to say ''good girl.''

That night the Conga Room overflowed with revelers as well as a slew of agents and talent scouts from L.A., though I was oblivious to their whereabouts. Sick to my stomach with anxiety, I watched the show from the wings until just before my cue. Offstage, Mr. Burns bussed my cheek for good luck, then introduced me as ''a girl straight out of her first year at Northwestern.'' All of a sudden, I forgot about my queasy stomach and lost myself in the music. I did the three songs I'd sung for my audition. It was as if I sang on automatic pilot. The minutes flew by.

A little later, I returned for the show's finale with Mr. Burns. Reaching into his jacket pocket, he took out a handful of sand and sprinkled it on stage. Then he gingerly took my hand in his, and together we soft-shoed over the sand. To look at my face, though, was to know that I was dancing on cloud nine.

That night Mr. Burns congratulated me on a good show and paid me one of the ultimate compliments.

''Annie, every time I do a show, I go out loving my audience,'' he said. ''Tonight I saw that same look in your eyes.''

''That's how I feel,'' I replied.

''Don't ever lose it,'' he said.

I've never placed much emphasis on reviews. I've always felt strange reading them, even the good ones. But the next morning someone eagerly read me *Variety*. In the ''New Acts'' column, there was a review of Mr. Burns's show that mentioned me prominently. ''George Burns has a gold mine in Ann-Margret,'' it began. ''She has animation in both face and body, blends a winning personality into her singing. More important, she has a definite style of her own, which can easily guide her to star status.''

Was I ecstatic? Who wouldn't be! I tried not to get too excited about the review. I knew that such things were as meaningful as weather reports—people's opinions changed all the time. But still, it was hard to control my feelings.

After the next night's show, everyone gathered in Mr. Burns's large dressing suite for a Christmas Eve celebration. I was subdued and homesick. Mr. Burns, noticing my mood, came over to me and asked if anything was wrong. I told him the truth. I missed my family. For the second year in a row, I wasn't able to spend the holidays with them.

"Come here," he said, guiding me into the room in his dressing suite where he actually dressed. "I've got a phone in here. Call your parents."

"Really?" I asked. "Are you sure?"

"Yes," he said. "They'd like to hear from you, and I know you want to speak to them."

Without hesitation, I had long conversations with both my parents. Before I hung up, even Mr. Burns took the receiver and said hello and told them what a good job they'd done as parents. Afterward, I hugged Mr. Burns, thanked him profusely, and told him how much the call had cheered me.

I don't remember exactly how it came out, but then I told him that my parents weren't at home in Wilmette. They were visiting relatives in Valsjobyn, Sweden. I felt badly about the long-distance charges, but he laughed and said not to worry.

I forgot about it, until the next night's show, when I heard Mr. Burns talking about it in his routine.

"She talked to them for half an hour and when she hung up Ann-Margret was crying," he said. "But when I found out they were in Sweden and I got the bill, I started to cry."

Several nights later Mr. Burns surprised me again. He called several hours before the show and asked if I had a dress that I could wear on stage. A dress? Given our discussion at dress rehearsal, I was puzzled.

"I do," I answered. "But why?"

As Mr. Burns explained, his wife, Gracie, had suggested that I might change outfits. Apparently, a couple of the waitresses in the showroom, each one of whom acted very motherly toward me, mentioned that the tight pants and sweater I wore could be giving a misleading impression. Touched by all the concern, I laughed and told Mr. Burns that I'd wear whatever he thought best.

"Better do what Gracie says," he replied.

13

SLOWLY, I DRIFTED BACK TO EARTH AFTER MY WORK-
ing with George Burns. In January 1961, I settled into my
L.A. apartment and tried to establish a bit of a routine. I
dated my old friend Peter Brown several times, and I
checked in with my manager and wondered what, if anything, would follow the Vegas engagement. But that conversation only underscored my naiveté.

It turned out he'd been busy fielding phone calls about
me. RCA wanted to sign me to make records; Twentieth
Century–Fox offered to give me a screen test. And *Life*
magazine had already assigned a writer and photographer
to profile me for a story on a young hopeful trying to get
that "big break" in Hollywood.

From then on, I felt as if I were in an animated movie.
In a period of five days, I met with the head of Twentieth
Century–Fox and scheduled a screen test. I signed with
RCA to make an album. And I met with *Life* magazine's
Los Angeles bureau chief Richard Stolley, who introduced
me to the people who would be following me around for
the next few weeks, reporter Shana Alexander and photog-
rapher Grey Villet.

It was soon clear that Hollywood was opening its doors
to me and not Scott, which, unfortunately, jeopardized our
partnership. I'd tried not to think about this situation, but
it was becoming unavoidable. Scott was immensely talented, very gifted, and there was a definite chemistry between us, yet clearly we would have to part.

Scott continued to work with me on different projects for
a month or so longer, and he also had options of his own.
RCA was speaking to him about making his own album

when the U.S. Army intervened. Scott was called up by the reserves, and sent to Fort Huachuca in the Arizona desert, where he finished his military obligation just as others were being drafted and sent to Vietnam.

Meanwhile, with the crew from *Life* in tow, I met with director Robert Parrish at his house. Mr. Parrish handed me the script, which was for a remake of *State Fair,* and explained that I'd test for the lead.

"I promise you," he said, "the test will be no worse than six or seven hours in the dentist's chair."

The only painful part of the screen test was a predawn wake-up call the next morning. By six-thirty, I'd passed through makeup and wardrobe. By late morning, I was in front of the camera, playing the Jeanne Crain, good girl part from *State Fair,* opposite a wonderful actor named David Hedison.

After lunch, I did the second-half of my screen test, what was called the "personality test." In addition to reading a scene, they wanted to see how I moved and sang. I changed into a red sweater and my black toreador pants and underwent a complete makeover. My hair was brushed wild, my eyebrows colored, and my lips painted a bright red. I burst out laughing when I finally saw myself in the mirror.

Back on the soundstage, where a handful of crew waited for us, I mentioned to Mr. Parrish that I felt a lot more comfortable performing to an audience—if that was possible. He opened the doors and some more people wandered inside. With Scott playing piano, I did several songs from the act we'd honed over the summer. I really got into it. With fingers snapping and hair flying, I moved across a wide swath of stage, showing my wild side. By now, I knew it was only a matter of minutes before my secret self emerged on stage, but the audience was surprised.

Afterward, the crew applauded and someone mentioned to me that these seasoned stagehands never did that. I was pleased, if slightly embarrassed. Nearby, Mr. Parrish leaned against a camera and talked to Shana Alexander.

"The kid's a real schizo," he mused.

But then came the really hard part: waiting for the studio to review my performance. In the interim, the *Life* magazine crew traveled back home with me to meet my family in Fox Lake. One of my relatives threw a brunch and Shana and Grey got to meet the family, including all my aunts, uncles, and cousins. My Uncle Roy threw me over his knee and pretended to spank me as he'd done when I was little. Daddy and I danced the "hambo" across the living room and into the kitchen where Shana was interviewing Mother.

"How is it having your only daughter in Hollywood?" she asked.

Mother thought for a moment, then replied, "Boy, has our phone bill been big!"

After a few days, Shana and Grey got their story and returned to L.A. I enjoyed this first encounter with the press, though in later years I would grow more wary. But right then, I couldn't wait to read the article.

On January 17, Peter Brown phoned. He was traveling to Green Bay, Wisconsin, to appear on a telethon, and had a brief stopover in Chicago. He wanted to know if I'd meet him for an early breakfast at O'Hare airport.

Early turned out to be five a.m. I arrived with my parents, and Peter, too, had someone with him, a friend who was also going to the telethon—actor Roger Smith. Since I didn't watch much TV, I had no idea Roger starred on the popular series *77 Sunset Strip*. Peter explained that as he introduced us. Then, Roger and I had a brief conversation.

"So you're trying to be an actress?" he asked.

"Yes," I nodded.

"How's it going?"

"I was just tested at Twentieth Century–Fox," I replied.

Roger expressed interest, but many years later, he confessed that he said to himself, "Poor thing. This sweet, innocent baby will be devoured by the wolves out there." He never let on, though. And after breakfast, I kissed Peter goodbye and told Roger that it had been very nice meeting him.

"Good luck," he said. "Maybe we'll see each other sometime in L.A."

"Sure," I smiled. I thought: "What a nice man." But that was it. Because I had never seen his show, I had no conception of what a big star he was. He was a friend of

Peter's, so I'd be nice and polite. Yes, I noticed how handsome he was, but sparks just didn't fly then. I can't explain it, but I do know they did later.

Not long after, Robert Parrish telegrammed with news that my screen test had been terrific. Then Fox called and said they wanted to sign me to a seven-year contract. Soon after, a very flattering article on me appeared in the Sunday supplement of the *Chicago Sun-Times*. And on January 27, *Life* magazine hit the stands with a fourteen-page spread that showed both sides of me—the performer going through her first screen test and the more traditional girl hanging out with her Old World family. I was *beyond* thrilled. I knew I should be calm. I knew how ephemeral this business was, but I couldn't help my feelings. I was teetering on delirious.

On February 5, 1961, my mother's birthday, I returned to L.A. and bought a car, mostly out of necessity. With Fox signing me for more money than I'd ever dreamed of making, I splurged on a sporty, red-and-white stick-shift Falcon that appeared as if it could keep pace with my frenzied schedule. Less than a week after being home, I recorded my first RCA single, "Lost Love," and the next day taped *The Jack Benny Show*.

For my TV debut, which had been arranged at the Sahara a month earlier when Jack Benny himself asked me to guest on his show, I dressed in a shirtwaist satin brocaded dress with three-quarter sleeves given to me by Helen and Gus Randall, sang two songs, and even tried my hand at comedy.

"I come from Wilmette, Illinois," I said to Mr. Benny. "And I was born in a trunk."

"Oh, your folks are in show business?" he asked.

"No," I replied. "Luggage."

That punch line drew a laugh from the audience. Mr. Benny gave me one of those looks of his. The audience laughed even harder.

"Aren't you ashamed of yourself?" he asked.

I nodded, trying not to laugh.

"That was a joke, right?" he asked.

I nodded again, but then lost control and let myself chuckle along with the audience.

"A pretty good one, too," Mr. Benny said. "Who gave it to you?"

"George Burns," I answered.

The breaks I got back then were incredible. Movies, music, television. Plus mentors like George Burns and Jack Benny!

How lucky could a girl get? I savored it all, feeling young and lucky and terribly happy.

14

I WAS STILL A NEOPHYTE IN HOLLYWOOD AND HAD no notion of how one studio loaned its contract players out to another. Yet it appeared that if things went well, my first movie wasn't going to be with Fox but instead with Paramount Studios, where I met with legendary director Frank Capra.

His list of credits included film classics like *It Happened One Night* and *It's a Wonderful Life*. I worried he might ask me a question I couldn't answer, which would've embarrassed me. The films I knew best, the only ones I could talk about with authority, were *Rebel Without a Cause* and *Battle Cry*.

Besides that, I wasn't sure whether I wanted to act or sing. I was still merely reacting to my success, not plotting my career, and things were happening too fast.

But my worry was for nothing. The interview was a brief one. Mr. Capra, as I always called him, was casting *Pocketful of Miracles,* which would turn out to be his last directorial effort.

Rather than have me read a scene, Mr. Capra asked me to sing a song. I didn't know how to interpret that. After all, was it possible to audition without actually auditioning? I didn't have enough experience to know that every audition is different. Some people want you to do several pages from a script, while others want to talk as if you were old friends. Mr. Capra didn't even show me a script. Instead, he listened to me sing, then we chatted, and then the meeting was over. Obviously, he knew what he was doing, but I didn't.

"Don't worry," I told myself on leaving. "You can sing.

You have a record contract to keep you busy.''

My first single, "Lost Love," which was written by Johnny Otis and H.B. Barnum, came out two weeks after my interview with Mr. Capra. One morning as I lay in bed, I heard the song through the walls of my apartment. One of my neighbors must've had their radio on. I leaped out of bed and turned my radio on.

"Oh my God!" I screamed. "That's me!"

I finished recording the album in Nashville, where I hooked up with some of the best musicians in the business. Floyd Cramer played piano, Chet Atkins was on guitar. I also worked with the Jordanaires, Elvis Presley's backup singers, and the Anita Kerr singers. In those days, we recorded music and vocals together as if it were a live performance.

The album was titled *And Here She Is: Ann-Margret* and was released in early March. It came with a nice endorsement from Mr. Burns. "If anybody besides me is going to sing 'Lovie Joe,' I'm glad it's Ann-Margret," he wrote on the liner notes. "Actually, she gives it several 'touches' I was never able to, not the least of which is femininity."

Then he added, "You can hardly beat that combination of talent and beauty. Of course, when I first started I was known for my talent and beauty, too, but Gracie retired."

The album offered something for every taste: big-band numbers, standards, and the bouncy pop single "I Just Don't Understand," which soared up the charts and inspired *Time* magazine to call me a record industry rarity— "a girl singer who can really make a pop song pop." I couldn't believe it; I'd been singing like that since I was a little girl.

As if this little bubble of excitement wasn't enough, in April, the Jack Benny special aired. In May, Mr. Capra requested another meeting with me. However, before we met, his office sent me the script for *Pocketful of Miracles*. I was confused.

"Does this mean I have the job?" I asked my manager.

"Keep your fingers crossed," he replied.

Little did I know, I had some help in the matter from a few influential friends. Marty Rackin, the president of Paramount, showed my screen test to Mr. Capra. Then Bud Yorkin and Norman Lear, a hot producing-directing team, took it upon themselves to call Mr. Capra on my behalf. They had auditioned me for their film adaptation of *Come Blow Your Horn,* and apparently felt terrible they couldn't use me.

All of this made my next meeting with Mr. Capra even shorter than the first one. After mentioning that he'd liked me on *The Jack Benny Show,* he said that he wanted to use me in the film. And that was it. Once outside, I screamed.

Then came the publicity, the part of the business with which I've always been uncomfortable. Nothing makes me more wary than answering questions about my personal life, which is why this book has been so many years in coming! The headline above my interview with Hedda Hopper announced me as, "Hollywood's Newest Garbo." Louella Parsons's story trumpeted, "Career Is Swinging Along." Another columnist announced, "Swedish Girl New Cinderella."

About that time, I started dating a businessman named Burt Sugarman. Burt knew Mr. Burns's son Ronnie and asked me out for coffee. A few years my senior, Burt was light-years ahead in terms of life experience. He'd been married, had a child, and had proven his sharp instincts in business.

Burt came into my life at just the right time. I was a young, inexperienced nineteen-year-old. With so much happening so quickly, I yearned for someone strong in my life, someone who could serve as a protector and anchor and yet still be fun. Burt was exactly that sort of guy.

But my schedule soon made dating difficult. In late May, I started work on *Pocketful of Miracles,* whose cast included Bette Davis. I loved the thrill of driving up to the studio gate that first day of work, then going to makeup, wardrobe, and finally, to the soundstage. But once there, I realized I'd entered a world in which I had no experience.

I didn't know the difference between a medium shot and a long shot. Basic stuff. More than anything, I didn't want my inexperience to put me in any situations I'd regret or that would draw unwanted attention to me.

"You'll do just fine," said Miss Davis, who played Apple Annie, the mother of my character, Louise. I was never on a first-name basis with her, but then again, I was a very formal, traditional person in that regard. "Mr." and "Miss," now "Ms.," were what I felt comfortable with and still do.

It was quite something to be getting my screen baptism playing opposite this movie legend. It would've been intimidating had she not been such a generous, patient teacher! I now know how difficult she was sometimes said to be, but to me, she was wonderful.

My first close-up was an interesting experience. We'd done the scene several times. Each time I grew more intense, wanting to be perfect and please Mr. Capra. But all of a sudden, Miss Davis halted the action.

"No, no, no," she interrupted, looking from me to Mr. Capra, clearly displeased by something. "We have to stop."

Mr. Capra could've gotten upset with her. He had every right because, after all, he was the director, and she'd usurped control of his set. But Mr. Capra was a gentle, soft-spoken, intelligent, understanding man. His eyes revealed the pleasure he found in his work. And he got on well with Miss Davis.

"Yes?" he asked. "What is it?"

"Where's Ann-Margret's hairdresser?" Miss Davis demanded. "And her makeup person? This just doesn't look right."

Everything stopped and everyone looked at me. I disliked being the focus of attention like that. It made me uncomfortable. But when Bette Davis asked a question or made a demand, people reacted. She had a strong, knowledgeable presence and commanded respect. And like any great actress, she knew how to use that to her advantage.

People came running. They fussed over my hair and face. When they finished, Miss Davis ushered me to a quiet corner, inspected the work, and then straightened my dress.

"Ann-Margret," she explained, "this is *your* close-up.

And you want to look the very best you possibly can. All right?''

"Yes, ma'am," I nodded.

She led me back to my mark and took another long, careful look at me from straight on. Then she turned to Mr. Capra.

"All right," she said. "*Now,* we can shoot it."

In September, I finally started work on *State Fair,* and though I had tested for the part of Margy, the chaste farm girl, I was recast as Emily, the bad girl, a switch based on my personality test. The studio bosses thought I looked too sensuous and seductive to play such an innocent. The "wild" Ann-Margret, the side that I couldn't control, had shaped my role.

Director José Ferrer decided that my long hair, which fell to the middle of my back, should be dyed orange, a color called "Titian," to be exact. They felt it matched my character and captured the attention of the movie's naive farm boy, played by Pat Boone. I gave Pat his first screen kiss in that movie, though there was no off-screen romance. Pat was married and I had a boyfriend.

In the picture's big production number, "Isn't It Kind of Fun," my character, Emily, changed mid-song from a gingham-clad milkmaid to a wild seductress in a skintight, sequinned top, a little tulle skirt, sheer black tights, and black stilettos. We rehearsed that number for three weeks and spent a week of twelve-hour days shooting it. It was grueling, tedious work, but I loved it all.

Meanwhile, Burt and I spent New Year's Eve in Las Vegas, where we attended a party at the Sands and danced through the night. In February, just as *State Fair* was finishing, Burt surprised me with a diamond ring and asked me to marry him. I was taken aback, and a little numb, but I did love him. But what did I know about marriage? I don't think I paused to really explore the commitment marriage entailed. I was young and very impressionable. Was Burt really the right man for me? I'm not sure I adequately probed my feelings, but I was very young and naive.

Meanwhile, I turned my attention to the upcoming Academy Awards. Without my knowing it, there was an intense, behind-the-scenes lobbying effort to get me on the Academy Awards telecast as a performer. Various people called the producers on my behalf, including George Burns, Jack Benny, Bud Yorkin, Norman Lear, Marty Rackin, Pierre Cossette, Dick Pierce from RCA, and Bobby Roberts, who later took all the credit, but it worked. Although practically unheard-of for someone as little known as me to appear on such a prestigious show, I was assigned to sing "Bachelor in Paradise," one of the Oscar-nominated songs.

My parents flew out to share in the excitement of the *State Fair* premiere, but they were decidedly unenthusiastic about my engagement. They adored Burt and they respected his intelligence. But they didn't want me to get married.

"You're too young," Daddy said as emphatically as I'd ever heard him.

"You are just twenty," Mother said. "You have a whole lifetime ahead of you."

My parents weren't the only ones who felt that way. In the weeks leading up to the Oscars, I began rehearsals for an appearance on the Andy Williams special. I sang "Moon River," accompanied by the song's composer Henry Mancini. One day during a photo shoot for *TV Guide,* Andy noticed the ring on my finger and asked if it was new.

"It looks like an engagement ring," he said with the tone of a question.

"Yes. I'm engaged."

"You're kind of young, aren't you?" he asked.

I wrestled with the dilemma day and night, but the bottom line was my parents. Years later, when I met Roger, I would cross them, but not now. Although certain of how I felt about Burt, my parents were the most important people in my life and I didn't want to do anything that would upset them. At the end of March I returned the ring to Burt. Talk about difficult. My heart sat in my throat. My stomach was a mess.

It was nothing against him, I explained. The timing was just wrong. I wanted to slow down. Be friends.

But like any twenty-year-old coming off a broken engagement, I was an emotional wreck. And there was just a

week or so before my appearance on the Academy Awards
show, the most watched television program in the world. I
didn't care about the show. I thought my life was over.

But something deep within me managed to surface. Yes,
I was heartbroken. But I was also a performer and this was
my moment. I would get on that stage and give it my all.

15

I STILL HAVE A VIVID IMAGE OF THE SUN SETTING over the ocean on April 9, 1962, as Mother, Daddy, and I got into my convertible Falcon—my Northwestern sticker in the back window—and drove to the Santa Monica Civic Auditorium, where the Academy Awards were being held. We avoided the throng of press and photographers by using the rear entrance—though of course nobody would've recognized me, since my first movie had only just been released.

My parents were escorted to their seats while I was whisked off to hair and makeup and began mentally preparing for the performance I'd rehearsed for weeks with the assistance of my friend, choreographer Maggie Banks. I was supposed to start after Vince Edwards and Shelley Winters finished presenting the award for Best Cinematography. They were unexpectedly interrupted when a man, later dubbed "the Imposter," snuck past guards, ran on stage, and handed them a homemade Oscar.

The delay only increased the tension I already felt standing center stage behind the red curtain. My heart pounded. I tried to put out of my mind the fact that forty million people around the world were watching. It didn't matter that most of them would, as one writer put it, momentarily ask, "Who's she?" My parents, relatives, and friends were watching, and I didn't want to let them down.

After Vince and Shelley finished the presentation, I received no introduction. The spotlight focused on the curtain. My hand slipped through the opening and I snapped my fingers. Very snazzy. A snare drum provided the beat, then the rest of the orchestra kicked in, and I danced out on stage. Bob Hope, the master of ceremonies, stepped out on the far end of the stage as the song wound to a close. I strolled over to him, stopped, gave him a long, provocative look, and disappeared offstage.

Bob Hope looked almost startled as he said, "Who was that? I never saw her before. I thought it was a dancing pony."

Backstage, I jumped up and down, relieved that the number was finally over. My parents, who were beaming with pride, met me backstage. We left and finished watching the show at the house of Bobby's boss, Pierre Cossette.

I had rehearsal with Andy Williams the next day and planned on resuming my schedule as if nothing extraordinary had happened. However, before I left the house, my manager called to read me the reviews from the show.

"Oh, you don't have to," I said.

"They're incredible," he exclaimed. "This is the stuff people dream of."

"That's so nice. But really—"

"Listen," he insisted.

He read me parts of Roland Barber's review in *Show* magazine, which described me as looking like "a girl in her first formal . . . who'd set out for the Junior Prom but through some horrible mistake had found herself on stage at the Academy Awards . . . Then she began to sing. As she sang, she danced, and a transformation took place: from Little Miss Lollipop to Sexpot-Banshee."

My manager boasted that his office was so inundated with calls that several temps were hired just to handle the phones. The offers included a film with David Merrick, nightclub dates, live concerts, and even performing at the opening of a cantaloupe festival. Bobby struck while the fire was hot. In retrospect, he should have been selective, but he signed me to half a dozen pictures spread across Columbia, MGM, and Twentieth Century–Fox.

Virtually overnight, I was booked for the next few years. It looked great on paper. In reality, it would've been impossible to make all those films in the stipulated timespan. But I didn't know about that. I was swept away by the excitement, while Bobby promised that was merely the

start. I had no approval of scripts, cast, directors. Nothing.
I was a commodity, someone to be stuck in whatever film
the studio decreed. But what did I know? I was no different
than lots of girls who come to Hollywood willing to trust
whoever is willing to help them.

Indeed, things would've been perfect if not for a disturbing phone call from my mother one afternoon. She
caught me at the apartment before I left for a meeting at
Columbia Studios, where I was about to begin shooting *Bye
Bye Birdie*.

"What's wrong?" I asked, reacting to the tinge of alarm
in my mother's voice.

She explained that earlier in the week, Daddy had come
home from work with a limp, complaining of exhaustion.
He'd insisted nothing was wrong, that he'd just stepped the
wrong way on a ladder. However, as the week progressed,
his limp had worsened and he continued to feel fatigued.
Finally, Mother had forced him to see the doctor, who had
diagnosed a mild stroke.

"The doctor told him to relax," Mother continued. "He
said to take a drink after work, come home, put his feet
up."

I wanted to jump through the phone and hug my father.

Suddenly, I made an impulsive, but totally from-the-heart
proposal. "This is silly," I said. "We're a family. There's
no reason we should be living this far apart. I want you
and Daddy to move out here."

For a family as closely knit as mine, it made sense. It
was the only thing that made sense. Money wasn't a factor.
I was receiving just under six figures for *Birdie,* such an
astronomical sum to us that it didn't seem real. Beyond that,
though, we missed each other. We wasted so much time
traveling between L.A. and Chicago and talking on the
phone.

It was decided that my parents would remain in Wilmette
until Daddy's strength returned. Then they'd drive out to
L.A. I would've preferred they fly out immediately, but
Daddy insisted on driving. It was his old wanderlust at
work. He wanted to see the country.

I began shooting *Bye Bye Birdie,* a film that was really

quite portentous for me. *Birdie* would captivate the hearts of audiences and make me an instant star. Such swift incandescence, I would learn, is not always the easiest way to build a career.

Birdie was a satire about all the frenzy that erupted in the late 1950s when Elvis was drafted into the U.S. Army. I portrayed Kim, an all-American teenager from Sweet Apple, Ohio, who, in the biggest publicity stunt ever, is selected to appear on the *Ed Sullivan Show* and kiss rock idol Conrad Birdie goodbye as he sings "One Last Kiss," a song written especially for the occasion.

Nothing like this had ever happened in Sweet Apple. The only one who does not appreciate the excitement is Kim's boyfriend, Hugo, who's played by Bobby Rydell. The rest of the cast included Jesse Pearson as Birdie, Paul Lynde and Mary La Roche as my parents, and Maureen Stapleton, Janet Leigh, and Dick Van Dyke, whom I'd recently met on the Andy Williams special.

Ironically, I'd never seen Elvis perform. I'd missed his big appearance on the *Ed Sullivan Show* in 1956.

But for whatever reason, director George Sidney decided that I was perfect for the part of Kim McAfee. He'd even selected me before we met, having spotted me dancing at the Sands in Las Vegas the previous New Year's Eve. A while later, he sent me a script for *Birdie,* then arranged a meeting in his office. He always reminded me that he'd had to keep from smiling at how I'd put on a pleated skirt and flats to try and look sixteen.

"I saw how you looked in Las Vegas," he confessed. "It wasn't sixteen."

In the midst of shooting, my parents arrived and moved into my one-bedroom apartment on Canon Drive in Beverly Hills. The landlords, Mr. and Mrs. Jorgensen, were Danish and provided company while I was away, but we were crowded. I gave my parents the bedroom and slept on the sofa, though I'm not sure how much rest I actually got.

"You must be concentrating so hard," my mom said one morning. "You were dancing in your sleep."

I started dating singer Eddie Fisher, who told me he'd wanted to meet me since the Academy Awards. As always, though, my parents came along on the first few dates. Eddie understood. He was very into family, too, and quickly grasped that my attitude was love me, love my parents. Once, he even arranged for all of us to see him perform at Lake Tahoe. And after we'd been going out a while, he gave me a cute Yorkshire terrier puppy that I named Scoobie, who lived for many years and became part of my family.

But I wasn't keen on entering another serious relationship, and so dated several others, too. I saw music producer Lou Adler, and talent agent Jack Gilardi. Jack represented Bobby Rydell and Onna White, and visited the *Birdie* set often. I eventually asked him why he didn't ever stop and say hi or ask me to go out and talk. So we set a lunch date.

Six months after we finished *Bye Bye Birdie,* the editing completed, the studio happy, Mr. Sidney decided he wanted to shoot more film for a new beginning and end, with just me.

The studio thought he was nuts. If I'd been in their shoes, I probably would've thought he was nuts, too. Who was I?

But Mr. Sidney felt so strongly about his instinct and vision that he put up sixty thousand dollars of his own money to shoot what became *Birdie*'s signature opening and closing—me on a treadmill, a wind machine blowing my hair, as I sang the title song, "Bye Bye Birdie." The studio later reimbursed him.

As we prepared for the movie's opening in New York, Mr. Sidney was absolutely convinced I had a date with destiny. So was my manager. I didn't know what to think.

But just in case, I brought along my parents.

16

FOR MOTHER, DADDY, AND ME, THE TRIP TO NEW York for *Birdie*'s world premiere on April 5, 1963, had the excitement and emotions of a homecoming. We checked into our hotel, spent a day sight-seeing, and pinched ourselves as the limousine took us to the premiere.

Sixteen years earlier, Daddy had met us at Pier 44 and taken us to the show at Radio City. This time, we got out of the limo and stared up at the ANN-MARGRET emblazoned with the names of all the other stars in the movie on the marquee. There were also large photograph cutouts and giant posters of me dancing.

Speaking in Swedish so nobody could understand, we asked each other, "Can you believe this?"

Sitting between my parents, I watched them smile more than I watched the movie. I've always had a hard time watching myself on screen without feeling unease and inhibition. I don't see myself. It's someone else and I don't know who that person is.

My parents weren't the only ones who loved the picture. From the opening, *Birdie* was a smash. The first week, it grossed more money than any film in Radio City's thirty-year history. Although I expected *Birdie* to do well, I wasn't prepared for all the attention I got. The *Daily News* called me a "knockout." *Life* magazine, which put me on the cover again, said my "torrid dancing almost replaces the central heating in the movie theater."

Was this what Dr. Peterman had meant when he said someday, if I got lucky, I could make it big? It was a lot to handle—exciting, demanding, fun, weird. I loved the work, but didn't like reading about myself, and I especially disliked talking about myself. Interviewers asked me what it was like to be a star. But I tried to explain, I wasn't a star.

"Bette Davis is a star." Me? "Someday. Maybe."

More questions. What did I hope to accomplish?

"Everything," I said. I gave the simple, pat answers stars gave in those days and the press expected it. I was supposed to be glowing and ingenuous and I tried to comply.

At a small supper party Mother and I arranged at our house for friends and family to celebrate *Birdie*'s success, Daddy and I danced on the patio, and he complained of feeling ill. Worried, I helped him in, put him to bed, and told Mother. But later that night, Daddy revealed the cause of his illness. He'd had too much to drink.

"Well, it's a party," Mother said. "You'll have to be careful next time."

It wasn't quite that simple. Daddy then explained that he'd had a drinking problem for years. Mother was shocked. He hadn't ever told her. Until then. Slowly, painfully, and sadly he continued. Years before they'd met, he'd had quite a problem and friends got him admitted to a hospital outside Chicago. After a month's stay, he left and had never taken another drink until the doctor in Wilmette advised him to have a little schnapps every afternoon.

So little was known then about substance abuse. But a shot of whiskey after dinner to relax turned into more than Daddy could handle. Although Mother and I were unaware of it, Daddy admitted his old problem had crept back into his life.

I looked into his eyes and felt the sadness and strength that kept this problem hidden from us. He was such a private man. I remembered the promise he had extracted from me years earlier. Another piece of the mystery solved.

Luckily, we were a strong family. Mother hugged Daddy. Both of us pledged to help. And Daddy resolved simply to stop drinking, yet again. With his extraordinary resolve, he was able to do so. I'm sure it caused him deep emotional and probably physical turmoil. But talking about such things was not his way.

* * *

With *Birdie* a box-office smash across the country, I reached what I now realize is a rare and enviable position for any performer. I was "hot."

My manager once again decided to capitalize on this frenzy of interest in me, though clearly he would have been prudent to go more slowly, to consider the long-term effects on my career. Before the start of summer, he'd signed me to even more pictures—five with Columbia, two with Fox, two with MGM, and two with Frank Sinatra's production company, Essex Films. At the time, I was swept up in the excitement, too, and had no inkling that I was quickly growing overextended and overexposed.

To give you a sense of how much in demand I was in those days, and I say this with bemusement, not immodesty, President Kennedy issued a request for me to sing at his private birthday party in Manhattan at the Waldorf-Astoria. So, at the end of May I flew to New York. The previous year Marilyn Monroe had sung "Happy Birthday." My performance wouldn't be quite as personal, but still I wanted to live up to the honor of being asked.

As proof of how trusting I was, I'd received two extra party invitations but Bobby had told me they were for him, and I believed him. Later, I found out they were for my parents. I was devastated and still get furious when I think about how my parents would've loved to have met the President of the United States.

In any event, the party was already underway as I walked into the banquet room, arriving precisely at the time that had been arranged for me to sing. I stared through the lights and found the President's handsome face. Looking directly at him, I delivered a sultry rendition of "Baby, Won't You Please Come Home," which seemed to go over quite well, judging by his smile.

Afterward, I accepted an invitation to a private party at an ambassador's elegant East Side brownstone. When I got there, President Kennedy greeted me warmly and asked me to sit beside him. I recognized Pierre Salinger, but noticed that I was the only entertainer present. There I was, an electrician's daughter from Sweden, in the midst of Camelot. I thought I'd die of nerves. By now, even I have heard all the stories about how much President Kennedy liked to have women around. But I can tell you he was nothing but correct to me. And very charming!

"This is a long way from Valsjobyn," President Kennedy smiled.

The President, who had a small pillow tucked behind his back, revealed a surprising knowledge of my background. Clearly, he'd been briefed; he knew about my Swedish roots, my parents' names, the important role George Burns had played in my career, as well as the reviews given *Bye Bye Birdie*. I was amazed.

In the midst of our conversation, I spotted his brother Robert across the room. He motioned Robert over, and we shook hands. Then the President asked if I'd sing another song.

"How about 'Bye Bye Blackbird'?" I asked.

"Good," he replied.

"But only if everybody sings along," I said, flashing a sneaky smile.

I would never have had enough nerve to do it otherwise.

"If you put it that way," the President laughed. "We'll try to do our best."

Soon after, I excused myself from the festivities, which were still going strong. Although I was terribly upset about leaving a party where the President of the United States was the honored guest, I had an early plane back to L.A., and I didn't want to miss it. I was the same good girl inside: I had a job to do in L.A. and nothing would deter me.

17

EXCEPT FOR A PIANO, THE MGM SOUNDSTAGE WHERE
Elvis and I met was empty. In the background, a few of
his guys hung around observing their boss, a ritual I would
soon come to expect. Under the watchful gaze of director
George Sidney, a studio photographer snapped shots of
what the film company executives figured would be a his-
toric moment.

"Elvis Presley, I'd like you to meet a wonderful young
lady, Ann-Margret," said George Sidney. "Ann-Margret,
this is Elvis Presley."

The significance was lost on Elvis and me. I reached out
my hand and he shook it gently.

"I've heard a lot about you," we said at the same time,
which made us laugh and broke the ice.

It also allowed me to catch a glimpse of Elvis's famous
smile, set off to the left, slightly crooked, very warm and
nice.

In a few months, the posters advertising *Viva Las Vegas*
would tout us as "that Go-Go guy and that Bye-Bye gal,"
but that day we looked rather straitlaced. Elvis wore a conservative suit and a tie, and I must say, he looked great. I
was in a white knit double-breasted jacket and a white knit
A-line skirt. We were both very conservative, very correct.
Little did we know we both shared a devil within.

Elvis told me he'd enjoyed *Bye Bye Birdie* and again
offered that sweet smile. I thanked him. I wished that I'd
seen him perform so that I could return the compliment.
Alas, I didn't have much to say and just smiled back.

That was the extent of the meeting. For all the hysterics
that surrounded Elvis, without question the world's most

celebrated entertainer, and the headlines I generated because of *Birdie*, neither one of us outwardly professed any particular excitement at meeting the other. I'm not really sure why I was so calm about meeting "the King." After all, this was *Elvis*, a man who had captured the heart of almost every woman in America. Little did I know he would soon capture mine.

We left with a good sense of each other. I realized Elvis was as shy and ill-at-ease meeting new people as I was. If nothing else, at least we had that much in common. Later, he told me that he, too, thought that he detected a kindred soul in me—a smile, a glance. He sensed something was there, some kind of chemistry. But neither of us was the type who would've risked our sensitive egos with any remark that showed inner feelings.

We were quiet, polite, and careful. But I knew what was going to happen once we got to know each other. Elvis did, too. We both felt a current, an electricity that went straight through us. It would become a force we couldn't control.

Over the years many people have written about what they think happened next between Elvis and me, but until now I've never addressed those special, treasured, intimate moments.

But there's just no getting around it. Our relationship was too big a part of my life to ignore. He had touched something deep within my psyche.

Somehow, Elvis has been distorted into the sort of figure that he feared—more myth than man. But the Elvis Aron Presley I knew was very much a young man at the peak of his creative powers and enjoying life to the fullest. He was happy and fun. He was also loving and good. The thing that caused him his biggest problems was the enormous fame that engulfed him, because at heart Elvis was no saint or king but rather a kid.

When work on the film started in Las Vegas, he was in a great mood. In the picture, Elvis played Lucky, a guitar-strumming race-car driver whose life is turned upside down by a chance encounter with me, Rusty, a swimming teacher with show-biz aspirations. We get together, but only to find ourselves competing in a hotel talent contest.

I'm sure the producers knew that the fast-paced, boy-meets-girl musical would certainly be improved if the chemistry between Lucky and Rusty were right. Initially, Elvis and I might've admitted that the only heat between us came from the hot desert sun. But others saw sparks from the start.

A reporter from *McCall's* magazine, on the set the first day of shooting, watched Mr. Sidney putting us through a ten a.m. rehearsal and wrote, "Elvis makes a face and shakes his head. It is a flirty, cute expression that isn't in the script, but it delights Ann-Margret. She laughs and flirts right back. . . . Whenever the dialogue brings Ann-Margret and Presley together, their roles suddenly become more than play-acting. An electricity from the two charges the crew with alertness."

The reporter asked if Elvis and I planned to date. I recoiled from the personal question.

"I really couldn't say," I replied.

But only because I didn't want to. From day one, when we gathered around the piano to run through the film's songs, Elvis and I knew that it was going to be serious.

That day, we discovered two things about each other. Once the music started, neither of us could stand still. Also, we experienced music in the same visceral way. Music ignited a fiery pent-up passion inside Elvis and inside me. It was an odd, embarrassing, funny, inspiring, and wonderful sensation. We looked at each other move and saw virtual mirror images. When Elvis thrust his pelvis, mine slammed forward too. When his shoulder dropped, I was down there with him. When he whirled, I was already on my heel.

"It's uncanny," I said.

He grinned.

Whatever it was, Elvis liked it and so did I. Both of us were very shy and we hardly said anything, but every time we began singing, we couldn't help but notice the similarities in the way we performed. It was like discovering a long-lost relative, a soul mate.

Not long after shooting began Elvis asked me out. First, I'm told, he spent some time investigating me, doing a little intelligence work to make sure I wasn't attached to anybody.

When word got back that I was single, he acted. "Rusty," he said, calling me by my character's name, "how about going out with me and the guys to see a show?"

I couldn't wait. We slipped out late at night, a whole group of us. It was an innocent, friendly date. How could it have been anything else? We weren't alone for one second. In time that would change. I was used to having my parents accompany me on dates, so Elvis's entourage wasn't a problem. His guys always treated me wonderfully. A couple of days later, we went out to see Don Rickles. Although we snuck in late, Don spotted us in a booth and we quickly became comic chop suey, grist for his quick mind.

As time went on, Elvis grew more and more comfortable around me, and most trusting, which was very rare with him. Usually, Elvis was surrounded by his guys. They were a combination support system and buffer to keep outsiders at bay. But I sometimes noticed that soon after I came over, everyone would suddenly leave, just disappear, and we'd be alone.

"Where'd everyone go?" I asked.

"They were busy," Elvis said, with a smile.

Many years later Joe Esposito, one of Elvis's closest pals and right-hand man, told me that he'd secretly pass the word that everybody had to clear out. It was always so sudden, but I never noticed. I guess I had on blinders.

The more time Elvis and I spent together, the more we learned how eerily similar we were. Some things were obvious, such as a love of motorcycles, music, and performing. We'd both also experienced meteoric rises in show business; we liked our privacy; we loved our families; we had a strong belief in God.

We both found solace in the quiet of the night. While the rest of the world slept, we talked until three or four in the morning, alone and not bothered by the pressures and demands of our occupations. Our talks were wide-ranging and earnest, spanning everything from work to the latest songs on the radio, from the news to sports.

At first we didn't do much talking about *us*. We let ourselves come together naturally, without analyzing the attraction or worrying about it. It was fun, joy, admiration, and love in its purest form. Our feet barely touched the ground. Early in the relationship, Elvis asked Esposito what it was about me that he couldn't get out of his head.

"She's the female you!" Joe exclaimed.

On the set, Elvis and I always had ideas and we worked with a sixth sense. One day we were in my dressing room with choreographer David Winters, who wanted to talk to us about working out moves to the song "Cheek to Cheek." He put on the tape. We listened to it once, watching each other from across the room, staring into each other's eyes and thinking. We didn't say a word. We didn't have to.

"Put it on again, okay?" Elvis asked.

The moment the music started, Elvis and I just started to move. Nothing had been rehearsed, but to watch you wouldn't have known that. We covered the entire room, bumping into the furniture, shoving it aside, circling each other like a couple of caged animals. In that spontaneous burst of creativity, we choreographed almost all the moves. Afterward, we looked at David.

"Great," he said. "Just do that."

We weren't much tamer off the set. We loved harmonizing to Jimmy Reed blues tunes. One night at Elvis's house, we'd finished dinner and were watching TV with the guys and some of their girlfriends, an average, lazy night at home, when Elvis and I grew a bit restless and silly and put on an impromptu show.

No rehearsal was necessary—only the excuse to do what came naturally. We snuck out of the living room. Then, without warning, he pushed open the big double glass · doors. Everyone turned and looked. We were both on the ground, stretched out like cats, and in a husky growl he sang, "You got me running." I answered in a similar voice, "You got me hidin'." As we traded lyrics, we crawled across the carpeted room in time with the music while everyone clapped and laughed.

By the time the production returned to L.A., our relationship was the "best kept" secret in town. The columnists loved us. In August, Hedda Hopper interviewed me—supposedly about *Bye Bye Birdie*'s royal premiere in London that November. We did indeed discuss that. She actually instructed me how to curtsy to royalty, having been taught herself by Noel Coward.

"You put one foot behind you and give a little dip, keeping your back straight," she said. "And there you have it."

But after a quick lesson, Hedda switched subjects, to what she described in her L.A. *Times* column as "the love business."

"Have you had dinner at Elvis's house?"

"Yes."

"Were all his boys there?"

"I don't care to comment."

"Oh, so you're going to be coy?"

"No, but you always put me on the spot, and I never know what to say."

"You're doing fine—just say nothing."

Which was what I did. My parents were the only ones to whom I opened up and confessed Elvis's and my closeness.

As soon as *Viva Las Vegas* began shooting in L.A., Elvis became a regular visitor to our apartment on Wanda Drive. I remember one night when he and some of the guys dropped by unexpectedly. He'd just bought a brand-new Rolls-Royce limousine, and he wanted to show it off. We were finishing dinner when we heard a ruckus outside and went to check it out. And there were Elvis and the guys, each trying unsuccessfully to maneuver the huge car up the steep, narrow driveway. After I bought my parents a house in Beverly Hills, Elvis came there, too.

I remember once after a long day of shooting, Elvis gave me a ride home on his Harley Davidson. We roared across the MGM lot, outside the gate, and got as far as Venice and Overland—about three blocks away—when his bike ran out of gas. It sputtered, stopped, and died. Luckily, there was a gas station at the corner. Elvis went to pay, then came back looking a bit chagrined.

"I don't have any money," he said. "Do you have a couple of dollars?"

I checked my purse and pockets. I too looked embarrassed.

"Nothing," I said.

A second later, both of us were laughing. It was truly funny. Elvis Presley and Ann-Margret, stuck on a corner, out of gas, with no money. But of course the young attendant recognized Elvis, asked for an autograph, and then filled the tank. All of us thought it pretty funny. Then Elvis and I zoomed to my parents' house. The next day Joe Esposito went to the station and paid for the gas.

At first Elvis didn't believe I really rode motorcycles, but once he saw me maneuver my bike, he was impressed. On the picture, I did most of my own stunts and he usually watched from the background. We rode all over L.A. unrecognized. It was a terrific release. Both of us shared the same passion for Harleys—the sound, the speed, the thrill of pushing one hundred on a straightaway and feeling the immense power. Whatever it was that made me so uninhibited, so defiant of danger, Elvis shared it. We were indeed soul mates, shy on the outside, but unbridled within. We both lived on the edge and we both were self-destructive in our own ways. Years later, I would struggle to save myself. I only wish I could have saved Elvis.

But at that moment, we thought nothing could go wrong.

I remember one time Elvis suggested we go for a ride. For some reason I sensed he was up to something. He loved playing practical jokes. I got dressed for one of our long motorcycle rides, but once I got outside, I saw that we weren't going to ride our regular bikes. For a change, Elvis had bought a tandem bicycle. But that was fun, too. We pedaled all over the hills of Bel Air. People honked, we waved.

One of the things Elvis loved to do most was take long rides in his car late at night. We used to drive all over the city, listening to music, to tapes Elvis made of music we both liked, and talking. Always talking. I knew I'd crossed into a certain uncharted territory when Elvis asked to be alone with me, but later the frequency with which that happened made me happy. It meant Elvis truly trusted me.

Oh, he trusted his father, Colonel Parker, and a couple

of others, but no one else. He had an instinctive feeling
about people. I remember once he told me he'd secretly
used a small tape recorder to bug a business meeting and
afterward found out a guy who claimed to be one of his
friends had disparaged him by belittling his talent. Rather
than fire the man, Elvis did worse—he never acknowledged
him again.

But he opened up to me. Like everyone else, Elvis had
dreams and desires, hopes and hurts, wants and weaknesses.
He didn't reveal this vulnerable side until everyone had
disappeared, until those private moments when we were
alone, after darkness had blanketed the city and we'd
parked somewhere up in the hills and could look down
upon the sprawl of L.A. or up at the stars.

People think of Elvis as having everything, but that
wasn't at all true. He had a great capacity to love, and he
wanted to be loved in return, but he knew the world he
existed in, the life he led, as well as all the people who
surrounded him, who hurt him, who wanted something
from him—everyone but a few—made it virtually impossible for him to ever feel that affection; and if he did, he
didn't know whether or not to trust it.

There was a void in Elvis's heart. He talked of how he
missed his mother Gladys, who'd died some five months
after he'd been inducted into the army. He'd describe her
in the most heartfelt manner and talk about what a plain,
simple woman Gladys had been. He explained how she'd
never been interested in the luxuries his money could buy.
She didn't care. She only wanted to be able to love him
and see him truly happy.

Elvis realized how similar we were in regard to the closeness we shared with our families. In many ways, both of
us, despite fame and whatever else we'd achieved so
quickly, had remained very childlike, and emotionally dependent. We wanted to find that same nonjudgmental, un-
qualified love that our parents gave us.

His wish was that we could stay together. But of course
we both knew that was impossible, and that's what was so
very difficult about our relationship. Elvis and I knew he

had commitments, promises to keep, and he vowed to keep his word.

Both of us knew that no matter how much we loved each other, no matter how strong our bond, we weren't going to last. We tried not to think about it.

Sometimes that was impossible. We talked about marriage. We were so alike, so compatible. Elvis didn't like strong, aggressive women and I posed no threat there. He, on the other hand, was strong, gentle, exciting, and protective. Just the qualities I liked. In terms of our careers, there was no conflict, only respect.

Perhaps the rest of the world had no problem imagining us married, but that vision was helped along by the fantasy our movie created. *Viva Las Vegas* concludes with Lucky and Rusty marrying in a lavish ceremony, which was shot at the Little Church of the West, a real wedding chapel in Las Vegas. After that scene—while the movie was still in production—MGM released publicity photos taken there. Within hours, it seemed that every Hollywood gossip had us engaged.

The wave of speculation followed me to London for the premiere of *Bye Bye Birdie* in November. Queen Elizabeth's pregnancy prevented her from attending the royal festivities, but Prince Philip received me and Bobby Rydell, who also attended the special screening.

Afterward, at a press conference, I was bombarded by questions concerning Elvis. Nobody cared about the movie. They wanted to know about my relationship with the King of Rock and Roll. I tried to be straightforward.

"We're seeing each other," I said. "That's all."

Yet a few days later, stories appeared in rather disreputable publications that Elvis and I were going to wed. I was dumbfounded. Friends and relatives called. I asked where they'd heard such lies, and they told me that they'd read I'd held a press conference to announce the big day. I was crushed, then badly hurt, by the deception. But I was also concerned about Elvis. I didn't want him to be hurt, too, or to think that I would ever try to take advantage of him. Then I got *really* angry.

My parents, who'd accompanied me to London for the

publicity tour, urged me to call Elvis and explain the headlines myself before they were blown out of proportion.
When I did, Elvis said he'd expected as much from the
aggressive London press and wasn't upset. He asked if I'd
been hurt, and I told him I was terribly hurt by the lies.

After London, my parents and I attended the *Birdie* premiere in Stockholm, where the newspapers all carried front-
page stories about my ascent in Hollywood. Then we took
a side trip back home to Valsjobyn, where the entire town
met us and chauffeured us by sled to our old house, where
Uncle Calle lived, and still does. Friends and relatives lined
the entire path. I was so overwhelmed I could hardly speak.

"Ann-Margret, you got bigger," Uncle Calle said. "But
you're still the same little girl."

I hadn't been back since I was ten years old, but I was
happy to see that my idea of paradise remained intact.
Nothing had changed.

18

SOON AFTER I GOT HOME TO LOS ANGELES, EVERY-thing about the world was suddenly, horrifyingly different. On November 22, I drove into Beverly Hills to shop. I parked my car, but before I got out, I sensed something eerie outside. Then I noticed the people on the sidewalk all had the same stunned expression. They walked around looking dazed, almost in shock. People in cars pulled over. It was as if everything around me was slowing down, stopping.

I turned on the radio and heard the horrible news: President Kennedy had been shot in Dallas. All of a sudden, I was as numb and confused as everybody else. Time stopped for me as it did for everyone in the nation. I could not do anything but sit in the car and listen, hanging on every word the announcer spoke.

I started to cry. Only six months earlier I had sung at the President's birthday party. I had coaxed him into a sing-along. I had looked into his eyes and been dazzled by his smile. I had fallen under the magic Kennedy spell.

I drove to Elvis's house and found him glued to the TV. I sat down next to him. We stayed like that for what seemed an eternity—watching, waiting, and crying over the President's death.

It didn't matter that Elvis and I were in show business. In that horrible time, we were Americans, ordinary, concerned citizens, who, like everyone else, were devastated by the tragic loss of our country's president and our generation's finest leader. Elvis and I clung to each other, tried futilely to make sense of what had happened, and prayed for the future.

By late February, Elvis began to work on the next in the series of movies he would grow to detest for their predictability and shallowness. In later years, we'd sometimes commiserate, because from the time we made *Viva* I'd always told him what a fine dramatic actor he could be. Elvis just looked down. He thought so, too, but realized that forces he couldn't control kept him from growing.

By that time, our relationship had, by necessity rather than choice, shifted gears. There were other factors in Elvis's life that forced him apart from me, and I understood them. Elvis had always been honest with me, but still it was a confusing situation. We continued to see each other periodically, until we had dated for almost a year. Then everything halted. We knew the relationship had to end, that Elvis had to fulfill his commitment.

From the set of my next movie, *Kitten with a Whip,* I started to speak of Elvis in the past tense. "Elvis and I *were* seeing each other," I admitted to columnist Sheila Graham in a rare moment of unguarded frankness. When she asked about our rumored engagement, I quickly added, "We were never engaged."

That was the truth.

I now began putting all my energies into my career. I was offered *Cat Ballou,* the western spoof that won Lee Marvin an Oscar, but my manager apparently declined the job without informing me. I suppose he felt it was in my best interests.

It was only years later that I learned about the offer. Would things have been different had I known? I wonder. At the time, I still trusted Bobby's judgment implicitly. I didn't know right from wrong when it came to business. He had signed me to umpteen pictures at various studios, which meant that to a certain extent I was forced to accept whatever film the studio dictated. In this case, it turned out to be *Kitten with a Whip,* an interesting, ambitious attempt at *film noir* that was doomed by its exploitative-sounding title.

Discarding the wholesome image I earned in *Birdie* and *Viva Las Vegas,* I played a renegade, schizophrenic, re-form-school escapee, a girl billed in the ad campaign for the picture as "frightening and unpredictable."

It was a big change, but also a challenge as an actress. In preparation for my first dramatic role, the film's director and writer, Douglas Heyes, worked with me for three weeks before shooting began. We went through every scene, discussing character, dialogue, and motivation. He was very strict with me, and I learned a lot, perhaps too much.

My performance in *Kitten* was so gritty and intense that people were confused. They preferred me as the innocent sweetheart in *Birdie*. And journalists questioned my judgment in playing this part.

Kitten did well at the box office despite some atrocious reviews. It also sorely tarnished my reputation with fans. (The same problem frustrated Elvis. People didn't want us to change.)

Still, there was a payoff. Vincent Canby, the *New York Times* movie critic, praised my acting in *Kitten,* and director Mike Nichols saw the movie and years later, remembering that he'd liked me, cast me in *Carnal Knowledge.*

My next picture, *Bus Riley's Back in Town,* written by William Inge, was exactly what a script should be—challenging, dramatic, a good story. Inge, a sweet, sensitive man who'd written one of my all-time favorite movies, *Splendor in the Grass,* had adapted his novel about a wealthy man's bored wife whose high school boyfriend reenters her life and rekindles her passion.

But the high hopes I had for that movie were dashed when the film was delayed by studio executives who thought *Bus Riley's* suggestive content too daring for the image of me they hoped to market. That resulted in endless editing, and then finally an order to reshoot half a dozen key scenes. Inge took his name off the picture. I protested, but to no avail.

Meanwhile, I moved directly into another picture more in line with my earlier films. *The Pleasure Seekers,* a remake of *Three Coins in a Fountain,* was a musical about three girls who travel to Spain seeking love and adventure. But ultimately *The Pleasure Seekers* caused the same problem as *Kitten:* Audiences simply did not want to envision me as a sophisticated woman of the world.

In August, I appeared on the Sunset Strip in four giant billboards. In one, I leered toward the street. In another, I perched astride a motorcycle. All of them said one thing—"Ann-Margret." These billboards, which cost a lot of money, were supposed to exploit me as a "property" and would be followed up by more PR, my manager boasted.

I'd already spent one hundred thousand on publicity over the past three years, he explained, and had budgeted up to ten percent of my earnings on promotion in the future. This was news to me. "Is this right?" I asked.

"Yeah," I was told. "No one's ever done anything like this."

But there was a reason no one had done anything as brazenly self-promotional. The billboards created great resentment toward me throughout Hollywood. Why did I need to promote myself so aggressively when I was already signed to so many pictures? Was I that ambitious?

I wasn't particularly aware of the reaction that started to build within Hollywood, partly because I went straight into another picture, *Once a Thief,* which kept me both distracted and out of town, in San Francisco. As the filming wound up, I decided to see a movie with a couple of friends from high school who lived in San Francisco. We arranged to meet in my hotel lobby, and I still remember that moment with vivid clarity. I wore boots and an olive-green three-quarter coat, very glamorous, with a fluffy collar.

As I stood there, two young men came over to say hello. I had briefly met Allan Carr before in Hollywood. And I had also been introduced to the other guy, Roger Smith, that early morning at O'Hare airport in Chicago when I was dating Peter Brown. Nice guy, no sparks. But, as they say, that was then.

Roger, it turned out, had first spotted me in the hotel lobby but didn't think I'd remember him now that I was a star. He would've passed by without saying anything if Allan hadn't prodded him to walk over and say hi. I remembered him immediately. Roger explained he was in town doing a nightclub act at the Hungry i. We talked till my friends came.

"How about coming by tonight?" Roger asked. "I'll arrange for a table."

"That's so nice," I replied. "Thank you. But I can't. I'm already going to a movie."

"How about after the movie?" he asked. "I don't go on until pretty late."

"I wish I could," I apologized. "But I've got to go to bed. I'm working tomorrow. Early call. It's the last day, then everybody goes home."

"Congratulations," Roger said. "But if you have a change of heart—"

Just as we'd done four years earlier, Roger and I said goodbye and didn't expect to see each other again, except, perhaps, in passing at some event. This time, something clicked for me at that meeting. I loved Roger's smile, his dimples, and the way he looked at me. I was truly sorry I had to work and couldn't see him.

In order to complete the last sequence of shots, we needed the weather to be foggy—traditional Bay Area pea soup. But the weatherman didn't cooperate. We awoke to sunshine, and hence filming was postponed. The same thing happened day after day. After a time, we became weary of waiting and de-energized by the skies everyone else adored.

Then one morning my phone rang.

"You're still here?" the caller asked.

"Roger!" I said, recognizing his voice immediately. "Isn't it amazing?" Secretly, I had hoped this would happen and was thrilled to hear his voice.

"I read in Herb Caen's column that you were still in town," he said. "You need fog?"

"Yes, and there is none," I said, pretending to be sad. "Next they'll run out of sourdough."

"Well, why don't you come down and see my show?" Roger didn't even try to conceal his delight. "As long as you're here."

"I will," I said. "If—"

"If?"

"If the weather doesn't get worse."

It didn't, but I still waited several days before I let Roger know that I'd see him at the Hungry i. As usual, I took along a couple of chaperones—the assistant director and sound man—and the three of us entered the club a few minutes after Roger had started. The bill included comedians Don Adams and Bill Cosby.

Roger played his guitar, sang, and told some jokes. At six-two, he was very good-looking, with hazel eyes. He was also funny, quick with a line, and extremely charming. I also sensed a deep inner strength and confidence as I watched him perform.

"Interested in having some coffee?" he asked after getting off stage.

"I'd love to," I answered.

Moving into another room, we got a table for five—plenty of room for my entourage, Roger, and Allan. Roger and I clearly wanted to get to know each other, but we were like two heads of state surrounded by advisors. Still, we managed a few moments of hushed talk, during which Roger asked me to dinner.

"Maybe tomorrow?" he suggested. "You and me."

I pondered the question. Roger must've gotten a bit nervous, because he quickly added, "And Allan. Allan and I would love to take you to dinner."

I realized Roger understood me. Or was starting to.

"Okay," I said. "Tomorrow night."

We went to an Italian place decorated with lots of red and had a private booth. Allan and I sat in the booth and Roger faced us, in a chair. And it was fun and enticing and unnerving in that I knew I was captivated by this handsome new man in my life. The more I talked to Roger, the more I wanted to know about him. I was also fascinated by Allan. While Roger was a thoughtful, serious man of few words, someone who pondered each question, Allan was the life of the party. He knew so much about show business and could hardly contain all he knew. They complemented each other perfectly.

Who knows what they thought of me? At one point, Allan began to tell a story about several actors I'd met, and I stopped him right in the middle of what most people would consider a delicious bit of gossip. It's all right if the subject is there to defend himself—that could even make for interesting conversation. But if he's not present, I don't want to hear about it.

"Stop," I told Allan.

He and Roger looked at me as if something was wrong.

"I don't think it's right," I said.

"What?" Allan asked.

"I know several of the people you just mentioned. I don't like gossip."

"We aren't saying they're mean," Roger explained.

"I know," I said. "I know what you're saying. And I don't think it's nice to speak about them when they aren't here." I suppose I was a real Goody Two-shoes, but I had been raised that way and had so far managed to both view and eschew Hollywood values. I just wasn't going to gossip.

Allan is a wonderful raconteur and saves up his stories for when he goes out. I'm sure my attitude deflated him, but Roger later told me he himself was impressed. He said he had never known anyone with that kind of honesty, that moral streak. He had seen it in movies, but never in real life.

I asked Roger to tell me about himself and learned that he was born in Los Angeles in 1932. He was around five when his mother, Leone, noticed him mimicking people and enrolled him in a class for child actors. He also started singing and tap-dancing lessons. Soon, he was appearing in shows that raised money for war bonds. It was Roger's mother who scrimped and saved to be able to give Roger lessons, as she really believed in his talent. To this day, Roger always gives her the credit for his being in show business.

At twelve, Roger's father, Dallas, a clothing manufacturer, moved his business to Nogales, Arizona, a small town on the Mexican border. Roger appeared in every theater production at Nogales High and was president of the school's acting club. He was also a star linebacker on the football team and won a scholarship to the University of Arizona. There he fell in with another guy, Travis Edmonson, who taught him how to play guitar, and they became famous for serenading the girls' dormitories with Spanish love songs. They also won the school's talent show, whose grand prize was an appearance on the Ted Mack *Amateur Hour.*

My face brightening, I interjected, "I was on that show, too. How did you do?"

"We were terrible," Roger laughed. "We did a song, goofed it all up, and didn't even wait around. We left, went down to a coffee shop, and sat around complaining and moping, until somebody came in and told us that we'd won."

"You won?" I don't think I revealed at that moment that I had lost.

"Yeah. We couldn't believe it. Shows how much confidence we had."

Anyway, with the Korean War escalating, Roger decided to get his service commitment out of the way by enlisting in the Navy Reserves. Stationed in Honolulu, he spent his free time on the beach, playing guitar and attracting crowds, which included the wives of William Powell and Jack Lemmon, as well as Jimmy Cagney. All three actors were on the Big Island for the filming of the movie *Mister Roberts.* Cagney suggested Roger try his luck in Hollywood, and even told him to look him up when he got there.

"But of course, we'd been drinking and he never gave me his phone number," Roger said.

Still, it was the message Roger wanted to hear. The minute his naval duty was over, he packed up and headed for Los Angeles, where he gave himself two months to succeed or else return to Nogales and his dad's business. His efforts to find Cagney ended where they usually began—with the guard at the front gate of each studio telling him to scram. Finally, he just wrote Cagney in care of each studio and hoped one letter would reach him.

Meanwhile, Roger's time limit ran out. He told his landlady he was leaving the next morning, then performed his final set at a local coffeehouse where he'd been playing for free. Just as he got into his car to leave, a man who turned out to be a talent scout from Warner Brothers knocked on his window. He had seen Roger at the coffeehouse, and asked if he wanted to come in and read. That was a Friday. On Monday he went to the studio and was put in a drama class.

Not long after, Roger began dating a girl in the class, who had a reading scheduled at Columbia. She asked him to do the scene with her, and the studio ended up signing Roger. Then he heard from Cagney, who was on location, but received his letter and sent instructions on how to contact him when he returned.

Not until we knew each other much better did Roger add that he also married Victoria Shaw, an actress who starred in the *Eddy Duchin Story,* and became a father.

But that was fine. What I didn't know certainly didn't interfere with the story, which I marveled at. Roger had clearly traveled an interesting road, and I saw why he was so sure of himself, much more able to take control of his career than I was of mine.

Dumped by Columbia, Roger interviewed at Universal, where Cagney was making a picture, and he was immediately put under contract. He made two movies with Cagney—*Man of a Thousand Faces,* and *Never Steal Anything Small.* Roger also played Patrick Dennis in *Auntie Mame,* one of the great classics.

Next came his big break. He signed a contract with Warner Brothers' TV department and was cast as Jeff Spencer, a hip detective in the new series *77 Sunset Strip.* Between 1958 and 1964, every teen in America and plenty of adults, too, snapped their fingers to the show's great opening theme and sat riveted. Now that I've seen the reruns, I can see why every woman in America was infatuated with this interesting man who was entering my life.

Roger went on to tell me that he'd met Allan early in the summer of 1964 in Milwaukee, where he was touring in the play *Sunday in New York.* Allan, a boy genius who loved the theater and started in it at a very young age, had traveled from his Chicago home to see Roger's play. Confessing his dream of doing something in show business, Allan complimented Roger on his acting and they talked through the night.

They met again at the end of summer when Allan read that Roger was breaking in a nightclub act at the same Milwaukee hotel. Afterward, Allan repeated how impressed he'd been with Roger's act and was amazed to learn that Roger had improvised the whole thing, just made it up as he went along. "Imagine," Allan said, "how good it could be if you wrote the act."

Roger suggested they work on it right then, and Allan accepted the offer. So they stayed up all night writing, laughing, and singing, and the new, improved show was held over another week. During that time, Allan suggested that he start managing Roger's career, and Roger accepted. Many years later, all of us laughed at such blind trust, but Roger has great instincts. He sensed how smart Allan was, and how capable. He'd met a lot of people in Hollywood, but none like Allan Carr.

Allan said they needed to go someplace where Roger could get attention from critics, like the Hungry i. Roger wanted to call first. Allan insisted that they only had to show up and audition and all would work out. Within the week they were in San Francisco and on stage.

Which brought us back to the table, where Roger attempted to ask me some personal questions, without much luck. But he complimented me on my work, particularly the performance I'd given on the Academy Awards. He admitted it had amazed him.

"Having met you, this quiet girl, I never would've guessed," he said.

"I've heard that before," I laughed.

The rest of the evening went fine. Roger noted with happiness that the weatherman was predicting clear, sunny skies for an indeterminate length of time. I mentioned that I planned on renting a car the next day and driving to Monterey, and Roger insisted that I take his rental car.

I let myself be convinced, and the next day I gave him a bear hug and took off down the coast.

Meanwhile, he and Allan spent the entire day talking about me. Roger admitted he was smitten. Allan wanted to talk about the mistakes I was making in my career.

"You have to talk to her, Roger," Allan urged. "Tell

her she's making some big mistakes in her career.''

"You're crazy," he answered. "I'm not going to get into all that. I just met her."

"I can't believe it," Allan continued.

"It's none of my business," Roger said. "I just want to ask her out on a date. By ourselves."

Little did Allan know that as they talked, Roger sweated over a love note he'd written to me on the map in the glove compartment. It was short, sweet, and poetic. "Here's a map of the Monterey area. Hope you have a good time. I love you. Roger."

He regretted leaving it there as soon as I had driven off, and worried that he'd gone and said too much too soon. Why hadn't he just signed it, "Love, Roger"? he agonized. When I returned his car, I gave him a thank-you hug and didn't mention a word.

"Did you find your way all right?" he asked.

"Just fine," I said. "It was a great drive. Spectacular view of the ocean all the way."

"Did you find the map in the glove compartment?" he asked.

"I didn't have to," I said. "I just followed the signs on the road. Found my way perfectly."

Whew! Roger breathed a sigh of relief.

Roger phoned later that evening, sounding gleeful as he told me the next day's weather report. Sunny and mild. Then he mustered up his courage and asked me out—with just him.

I said that I couldn't wait.

We drove to San Jose and parked at the small airport, which piqued my curiosity. Then we walked onto the tarmac where the planes were parked. It was as beautiful and sunny out as the weatherman had promised. Figuring we were going to take a flight somewhere, I followed Roger and looked for our pilot.

As we stepped up to a white plane, Roger opened the door and motioned for me to get in. I put one foot up, then hesitated.

"Who's going to fly this thing?" I asked.

"I am," he said.

Maybe that was it. Maybe that was the moment I fell in love. I don't know. But I looked at Roger and saw the kind of man I'd dreamed of finding. He made me feel incredibly safe and secure.

"Okay," I said and got in.

We spent the late afternoon flying over San Francisco. The sun painted the ground below luminescent hues of gold, green, and blue. Roger showed me the redwoods to the north. He zipped by the Golden Gate Bridge. As we soared above the glistening city, I marveled at the freedom I felt. I glanced at Roger, watched him fly, steering us through the sky and then sweeping across the bay and down along the picturesque coastline, and I felt a closeness that I knew would only grow stronger.

Fortunately for us, the last day of shooting on *Once a Thief* was delayed by good weather for the next two weeks. Roger and I saw each other every day, every night, and then after his performances. We talked on the phone in the morning, then ate lunch and dinner together. One night he dropped me off at my hotel at twelve-thirty a.m., then called an hour and a half later.

"I can't stand it," he said. "I miss you so much."

"Come back over, silly," I said.

It's hard to believe that there was anything in the world left to talk about, but we talked till dawn. I already knew that someday we'd be married. I didn't know the particulars, but I knew by the third date that we had something special.

Finally, those romantic two weeks ended. I got up one morning, looked out my window, saw it was miserable outside, and went to work. We finished shooting that day. Roger still had several more days at the Hungry i and he drove me to the airport that night. Neither of us talked much in the car. We were sullen, morose, and sad.

Although we'd promised each other to get together in L.A., Roger thought our relationship was finished. He'd read about me in the movie magazines and figured that my life in Hollywood was too much for him to compete with. He thought every leading man was at my door, even though he knew me better than that and heard me tell him that all the stories were not true.

At the airport gate, Roger told me when he'd be back in L.A. and talked about setting a date to get together.

It was a tough goodbye. Roger kissed me, promised he'd call me as soon as he got into town, and then I boarded the plane.

He later told me it was raining as he drove back to the city. He turned on the car radio and listened to Tony Bennett's song "I Left My Heart in San Francisco." The lover's lament filled his hazel eyes with tears. Overhead, I stared out the plane's cloudy porthole, hoping to spot Roger's car. But all I saw as we took off were the thousands of twinkling lights of the city.

I sat there in my seat, fighting back my own tears and pondering my feelings. Roger seemed to be the man I was sure I was looking for: smart, strong, tender, handsome. Here I am, the daughter of an electrician, someone who could fix or build anything, and I can barely screw in a lightbulb. Roger, though, knew how to do everything. He flew his own airplane; he was a carpenter. He was so competent, and it was just so unbelievably reassuring to me. Roger was so much like my father in that regard. As a child, I viewed men who were strong, positive about their beliefs and had the last word: my father, my uncles, my grandfathers: all the Swedish men. Roger fulfilled that myth.

Roger never asked, "What do you want to do tonight?" He just took care of it. Moreover, he was active. He skied, and I loved to ski. He played sports, and I loved to watch sports. I admired the qualities he possessed as a person. He wasn't a Boy Scout, but he was kind. He didn't lie. He made me feel safe and protected. Yet he could be so gentle. He's always had great respect for women—their strength, intellect, sensitivity, judgment in tight situations. Roger has always said the right woman would make a great president.

Furthermore, as an actor, Roger didn't need to ask about what I did. He understood the occupation, its demands, pressures, frustrations, and the things I had to do, the problems I had, the business in which I worked. He knows every aspect of the world I'm in. We could talk endlessly about everything. I felt that if we grew old and gray together, we would still have things to discuss, that we would still be passionate about each other. At that moment, Roger seemed perfect to me.

But there were some problems. Roger had told me he was separated from his wife and was trying to get a divorce. Their marriage had come undone while he was doing *77 Sunset Strip*. Furthermore, to really complicate matters, there were three children, ages seven, six, and three. How did I feel about getting involved with a man just ending a marriage? How would I feel about his children and they about me? Would I even *meet* them? Would I see Roger again or was it all over? I had no answers that day, only happiness and lots of tears.

19

AS I WENT INTO PREPRODUCTION ON *THE CINCINNATI Kid,* I did a lot of soul-searching. Prior to San Francisco, I'd been involved with several men. Suddenly, I found myself thinking of just one. I checked the calendar daily and wondered when Roger was going to get to town and call. Being apart told me how anxious I was to see him again.

When Roger phoned, I felt like I was talking to my closest friend after a long separation. We immediately made a dinner date. Roger, who lived in a tiny apartment in the San Fernando Valley, picked me up. He stood outside my apartment, wearing blue jeans and a sport coat, his chiseled features and tall frame silhouetted against the setting sun. He brought flowers, candy, and a confession.

Roger had promised to call the day he arrived, but told me that he didn't. He'd actually returned the previous day and instead of calling he'd gone to the movies to see *Viva Las Vegas.*

"I wanted to know something about what you do," he explained. "I've read about you. And I saw you on the Academy Awards. But before yesterday, I'd never seen one of your movies."

I laughed and said, "Then I have a confession, too."

"What?"

"I've never seen *77 Sunset Strip.*"

We laughed. There was no competition between us, only understanding and comfort. It was that easiness that drew us close together in a hurry. Except for my time being limited by work on *The Cincinnati Kid,* Roger and I stepped back into the same wonderfully romantic pattern we had begun in San Francisco. Whenever I was free, we would meet for lunch, dinner, or a late-night drive. Often, we just holed up at my house, preferring to hide out from the world.

It was a wonderful period for me. I was in love and also doing a film I liked. *The Cincinnati Kid,* set in the boozy back rooms of New Orleans, focused on the world of high-stakes poker. Sam Peckinpah, the original director, had cast me in the juicy role of Melba, Karl Malden's sensuous wife, but Sam left after a difference with the producer, and Norman Jewison took over as director.

The movie boasted a remarkable cast in front of and behind the camera. Ring Lardner, Jr. and Terry Southern scripted the lines spoken by Steve McQueen, Edward G. Robinson, Joan Blondell, Tuesday Weld, Rip Torn, and Karl Malden.

It was a great time to be at MGM. In the morning I'd go to makeup and wonder which great actress I'd see in the chair beside me. However, the biggest draw was master hair stylist Sydney Guilaroff.

Already a legend, Mr. Guilaroff always dressed in a dark suit with his trademark white shirt and white tie. It didn't matter what time of the day or night it was, he looked impeccable. He performed his special talent on each woman, and then we went off to our different soundstages. It was a golden era, a stimulating, inspiring place to be.

Steve McQueen was a real tough guy, full of machismo, a man who made his own rules, but both of us got along really well. He was a truly gifted actor, insightful, sensitive, intelligent, and believable in every scene we did together. And we found common ground: our love of speed—cars and especially motorcycles. Both of us adored our motorcycles.

Then I got in hot water with the studio. My manager relayed stern orders from executives that I had to quit riding my motorcycle to work. They didn't want me doing anything risky that might cause an injury and delay the film. I couldn't ride on city streets, and certainly not on the studio lot. I objected, of course. After all, I didn't drink, smoke, or do any of the things other actors did to relieve stress.

"I like to unwind by riding my motorcycle," I argued.

Steve was the only one who took my side. He'd gone through the exact same thing.

"So what'd you do?" I asked.

"I kept riding the bike," he answered.

"What about the studio?"

"Let them worry about it. That's what they do so well."

"What do you think I should do?"

"Keep riding the bike."

Roger learned about my affection for bikes soon after we resumed our courtship. He saw my motorcycle, a new Triumph 500, and he also heard me complaining about being prohibited from riding by the studio. He'd never owned a motorcycle, but had always wanted one. One day he showed up at my house and pointed to the driveway. There was a Triumph, exactly like the one I owned. He asked if I wanted to lead him on a ride.

He still says he's fortunate to have lived to tell about that. I led him on a wild ride up Benedict Canyon, then along the dangerous curves atop Mulholland Drive as it snaked along the mountains above L.A. and the Valley. We cruised down Hollywood Boulevard and the Beverly Hills flatlands. Every so often, I'd glance back and make sure Roger was with me. He was, holding tight. Several hours later, we pulled back into my driveway. I bounced off the bike. Roger was wiped out. Much later, he admitted that while trying to keep up with me, he'd never been so scared.

"How'd you like it?" I asked.

"It was the wildest ride I've ever taken," he said gamely. "I can't wait till the next one."

I smiled. I knew we were partners.

"Neither can I," I replied with a wink.

But we had to set a date in the future. Right after that, I left for three weeks of filming exteriors and atmosphere in New Orleans. I found that while away, I missed Roger terribly. He was tied up in L.A. doing the short-lived TV series *Mr. Roberts,* and we talked on the phone for hours. One day, after a lengthy shooting session, I walked back to my trailer with Tuesday, but as soon as I opened the door, I stepped straight into a wall of Tab, my favorite diet soda at the time. Cases were stacked high, and on top there were flowers and a little note that said, "Love, Roger."

It was so nice, thoughtful, and funny. Both Tuesday and I laughed as we poured ourselves a drink.

"You really like him, don't you?" Tuesday asked.

"Yes, I do," I admitted.

Roger and I were oddballs. Although we worked in an industry that adores publicity, both of us craved privacy. Comedian Don Rickles, who used to live in my old apartment building, reacted with such surprise whenever we bumped into each other in the lobby. He'd scream, "There she is! The monk is out!" Roger preferred living as monkishly as I. Within a few months of being together, we slipped into our own reclusive world.

Roger had given his house in Los Angeles to his former wife and children, and his apartment was just a way station, he felt. So we were hermits at my house, a very feminine abode. The living room was Kelly green, lit by dark pink lightbulbs. I remember showing him the bedroom.

"That's quite a color," Roger said as he stood in the doorway and looked at the color of the walls.

"Hot pink," I smiled.

"Very hot," he said.

"It was my first idea when I moved in here."

I showed off the bathroom, which was also pink.

"How long have you been living here?"

"Oh, six months or so."

"And that bed," he commented, continuing to look around. "I don't think I've ever seen a round bed."

Elvis had given me that bed, I will now admit, and it was very special to me. Elvis knew I loved pink and had commissioned a round, pink bed in a moment of tenderness.

"I got it from a friend," I said.

Eventually the truth came out. I told Roger a little—very little—about my relationship with Elvis, glossing over how serious it was, but Roger didn't mind. He let it ride, asking questions here and there at later dates and never pushing when I, as was my habit, put my finger to my lips and smiled.

"I prefer not to talk about anybody I've dated," I said. "It makes me uncomfortable."

Roger says he liked the mystery that engendered. I was a bit of an enigma, I had secrets, and that made it all the more challenging and fascinating for him to get to know me. Roger was completely secure, another trait I liked.

Roger also knew his way around the kitchen, a room as foreign to me as Siberia. We weren't together very long before he discovered that if I prepared dinner, we either got takeout from Chicken Delight or I mixed a glass of Sego, a powdered diet drink, and called it a night. But Roger not only liked to cook, he was good at it.

Then there were the truly big nights. On January 18, 1965, I served as one of the Masters of Ceremonies at President Lyndon Johnson's Inaugural Ball, held at the National Armory in Washington, D.C. I shared the honors with Johnny Carson, Julie Andrews, Carol Channing, and Alfred Hitchcock. I was thrilled to be asked, and once again I felt as I did looking up at my name on the Radio City marquee. I couldn't believe it. I thought of sailing past the Statue of Liberty on the *Gripsholm,* an immigrant who spoke no English, and I pinched myself.

After the inaugural, I finished work on *The Cincinnati Kid* and then traveled to the Leilani Village, in Milwaukee, Wisconsin, where Roger was doing his nightclub act. I arrived in the midst of a snowstorm, which never let up the entire week. I couldn't have asked for better weather. Nothing to do and nowhere to go. Just be with Roger.

We acted like two kids. After Roger's shows, which ended well past midnight, we got into his rental car, cranked the steering wheel all the way to one side, pushed the accelerator to the floor, and did doughnuts around the icy parking lot. Although silly, I found it romantic to be by ourselves in the quiet of a nighttime snowfall. It reminded me of Valsjobyn, and inspired me to paint Roger detailed descriptions of my storybook childhood near the Arctic Circle. He'd laugh. It was so different from his desert upbringing in Arizona. And yet we were so . . .

Well, we were so serious. But there were a few obstacles, things that were more comfortably left unspoken. Actually, there were two. One was my career. Privately, Roger and Allan criticized my career as being completely off-track. I preferred to deny what was so obvious. Once, Roger attempted a question about my work and I quickly said, "Please, don't. Don't get involved." That had happened before with boyfriends and it never led to anything pleasant. The other obstacle was Roger's separation. He still wasn't divorced.

I didn't ask too many questions. It was none of my business until he wanted to make it my business.

My parents didn't look at it that way. I was their business, and they weren't exactly thrilled at Roger's credentials as an actor of dubious employment. In those days, once you were off a series, your career was often over. My parents did not see Hollywood leaping for Roger's talents, and they also sensed, as I did, that he didn't share my passion for acting. Indeed, Roger was open about this: He disliked standing around all day and being told what to do. He was feeling very sorry he had chosen acting as a profession. Then there was the problem of his three children. He wasn't, at least then, my parents' idea of Prince Charming.

Roger tried to improve matters by going to Mexico for a quickie divorce. His heart was in the right place, but that still didn't matter to my parents. They were a tough audience. I saw them nearly every day. If I didn't see them, I talked to them. They barely even mentioned his name. They barely acknowledged that he was part of my life.

In our house, we repressed our anger, held it in, and reacted with a simmering silence. However, the more the subject was avoided, the more pronounced it became. Roger didn't have to be a topic of discussion to be on our minds. My parents wanted only happiness for me, and I wanted nothing except to please them. It made for an unpleasant, tense time.

Roger saw it clearly. I was in love with him, but I also loved my parents. I wanted both. And it created great conflict.

There were two people in L.A., two fine women, whom I used to confide in. One was Lill Klaesson, a longtime friend of the family. The other was Karin Ottoson, who had a home in Inglewood. Roger always referred to her as the

Swedish gypsy, because she used to tell his fortune. Both women believed in Roger. They saw his many good qualities. They told me that ultimately I was doing the right thing by following my heart and my instincts. They knew my parents would come around.

When I decided to continue going with Roger, it was really the first time in my life I'd angered my parents. It was the toughest thing I'd ever done. It made me crazy.

Ironically, when all of us think back on that time now, Roger should've been the least of our concerns.

20

"HOW DOES IT FEEL TO BE SUED?" THE CREW MEMBER asked, thinking it was no big deal.

It was the end of March 1965, and I'd started preproduction on my next picture, *Made in Paris,* a light, romantic adventure about an American clothing buyer who travels to France and falls under the spells of three men played by Louis Jourdan, Richard Crenna, and Chad Everett.

"What do you mean?" I laughed.

"It was in this morning's paper," he said. "I just read it about half an hour ago."

What? I felt the flush of anxiety race through my body.

I'd quit reading articles about myself after an upsetting magazine profile in 1962, and I'm still reluctant today. But it was unavoidable. I got the *Times* and the trades.

I learned that Fox had filed suit against me in L.A. Superior Court, seeking to prevent me from working in any movie that would delay my appearing in their remake of *Stagecoach.* The fact that I was starting *Made in Paris* on April 19 made them concerned I'd be unable to show up for preproduction on *Stagecoach* at the end of June. They argued that an overlap would cost forty thousand dollars each week production was delayed.

"Maybe they're right," I said to my parents, trying to see both sides.

"Talk to your manager," they advised.

Roger, of course, didn't approve of how my manager was handling me. Nor did Allan, who'd predicted trouble since we met in San Francisco. But the subject was a sensitive one, one that we purposely avoided. I still trusted my manager, trusted him blindly, and ignored better judgment. I suppose this was still the good little girl in me who looked to authority figures and believed they could do no wrong. Furthermore, I put great stock in loyalty. All my life, I saw my parents being loyal to the family doctor and dentist. Once they put faith in someone, that stood, and that was how I blindly, rigidly felt about my manager. Furthermore, at that point, my parents trusted Bobby and I would never dream of opposing them.

"Well, he did a lot of things right," I argued.

With the critics turning against me and the studios suing me, it became harder to say that and believe it. In April, Fox blocked me from costarring with Marcello Mastroianni in *The Tenth Victim* for Embassy Pictures. My manager wanted me to make *The Tenth Victim,* since Embassy was offering five times as much money as Twentieth.

I hated the pressure and finally leaned on Roger.

"What am I going to do?" I cried one night when we were alone.

"What do you mean?" he said. "You have no choice."

Roger defended Fox. He reminded me that I'd put my name on a contract. Whether or not I wanted to make their movies, Fox had first right of refusal on five remaining pictures. It might've sounded good in 1961, he said, but four years later it was a bad deal. Roger and Allan were disgusted. My parents were infuriated, although they, too, were still loyal to my management.

In typical fashion, I just didn't want to get into the realities of my problems. Instead, I escaped to the romantic streets and cafés of Paris, re-created on a half-dozen MGM soundstages for the filming of *Made in Paris.* I managed to squeeze this in before the *Stagecoach* filming began. As we made the movie, I turned twenty-four on April 28. I walked into my dressing room that morning and I found a bouquet of yellow long-stem roses and a note from Roger. It was so lovely.

Then, after the first scene, I went back to my dressing room and discovered another bouquet of yellow roses from Roger. The same thing happened after the next scene, then the next scene, after lunch, and all day long. Roger sent something like twenty dozen roses, and by the final shot of the day, I couldn't even get inside my dressing room anymore.

But I had little room to breathe anyway. Four days after *Made in Paris* concluded production, I reported to work on *Stagecoach*. I played Dallas, the hooker with the heart of gold, the part created by Claire Trevor in the original *Stagecoach* directed by John Ford in 1939. Everyone I knew urged me to watch that early classic, but I steered clear so my own performance wouldn't be affected.

Our cast included Bing Crosby, Red Buttons, Slim Pickens, Van Heflin, and Alex Cord, a bunch of characters who were amused most days by watching me try to kick-start my TR 500 motorcycle. The bike didn't have a self-starter, and at five-four and one hundred six pounds, I wasn't always strong enough to kick-start it myself; then I'd have to ask one of them for help. Once they strapped a lead belt around me, and the extra weight did the trick.

That earned me special recognition. In mid-August, at the end of a long, hot day of shooting, Marty Rackin, who was producing the film, presented me with what he called the "Miss Clumsy Award." The guys gave me a nice round of applause as Marty teased, "This is for the girl who can't start her own motorcycle."

But my cycle was a big source of concern to Roger.

"What if it stalls somewhere and you get stranded?" he used to say.

"I can handle it," I'd argue.

Roger didn't want to take chances. He found someone who said he could install an electric starter on the bike. It took almost nine months, but when the mechanic finished, my Triumph was the only one in the world with a self-starter.

More and more I relied on Roger's willingness to take charge, his strength, and instinct. We secretly moved into my house together. Our relationship was no longer guarded. We attended the Oscars together. We vacationed together. Roger talked about us in newspapers. Even the press realized it was serious. My parents still remained silent.

Columnist and producer Sidney Skolsky was the first to ask if Roger was the one I planned to marry.

"You know I don't discuss my personal life," I said.
"But I will say this. When I marry, I'll put love above
everything. Whatever my man says goes."

I wanted him to come along when *Stagecoach* was filming in Denver for a few weeks, but Roger's TV show prevented him from following me. One day, Roger got a break
from his series and flew his plane out to Colorado. Flying
over the Rockies, he saw the production company set up
like a wagon train in the midst of the flatlands. I remember
we were doing a scene and a plane buzzed us, swooping
down real low, low enough so that it seemed you could
reach up and grab it.

"That's Roger!" I exclaimed.

He stayed a week, then did the same maneuver on departure. He flew low and dipped his wings. Very stylish.

Back in L.A., I started yet another picture, *The Swinger,*
a send-up of the psychedelic sixties. It proved to be some
of the most fun I'd had on a movie set in a long time, even
when I was reprimanded again by the worried studio execs
for riding my motorcycle on the lot. But Roger solved the
problem by surprising me with a custom-made gold-leafed
golf cart with my signature on the front. I tooled around
the lot just fine, and everyone had time to get out of the
way.

When the movie wrapped, I hoped that my career was
again getting "hot." Theaters were showing *Once a Thief*
and doing respectable business. *The Cincinnati Kid* pre-
miered lavishly in New Orleans to good reviews. *Made in
Paris* was due out Thanksgiving. The Motion Picture Ex-
hibitors of America honored me as their "Star of the
Year."

21

AS ROGER AND I SPENT MORE AND MORE TIME TO-
gether, it became increasingly difficult, almost absurd, that
he stay out of my business affairs. And Roger got bolder
in speaking his mind. He asked if I knew about the deals
being made for me. He asked if I knew what was happening
with the large sums of money I earned. The answer was
no.

Infuriated, Roger wanted to know if I asked any questions. Again, I said no. I never questioned people.

My mother, who was already wary of Roger, viewed his
inquiries with a skepticism that I lacked. Like me, she still
gave Bobby the benefit of the doubt, reasoning that he'd
done okay thus far. She felt reassured when Bobby warned
her about Roger's meddling. Daddy, though, relied on his
gut feelings, and said he thought Roger made sense.

Given the situation's complexity, it's amazing that Roger
and I survived. But we actually grew closer. There was no
limit to the love that had drawn us together in the first
place. If not working, we spent every hour of every day
together.

Finally, Roger felt secure enough to introduce me to his
three children. This was the element that my mother feared
most; my involvement with children that weren't mine. I
didn't have any experience with children. I'd been an only
child. I was still a child myself in some ways. Roger had
sensed much the same thing, which was why he brought
them into the picture very slowly.

Yet, when the time came, I looked forward to meeting
these kids—Tracey, Jordan, and Dallas. Roger visited them
every weekend and then told me about them at night. I later

learned from the children how nervous Roger was as he explained to them, ''There's a special lady I want you to meet.'' Then he gave them a five-minute lecture on good manners.

When I got my first glimpse of them, they were lined up outside my house as straight as the Von Trapp children in *The Sound of Music,* standing in order of age—Tracey was seven, Jordan six, and Dallas three. Roger was more nervous than they were, so much so, I'm surprised the introduction came off at all. In their Sunday best, they were all shined, polished, combed, and brushed.

We walked through the house. Many years later, Tracey told me that she eyed my pink round bed and menagerie of stuffed animals on top with the envy of a little girl who wanted to ask questions, but held back because of her daddy's instructions. Instead, she picked up one of my pet kittens. We scratched behind his ears together.

''Isn't he cute?'' I said, feeling the beginning of a bond.

Roger hovered anxiously. After a few minutes, he decided the meeting had gone smoothly enough. He didn't want me to feel pressure, which I didn't. In any event, he whisked the children away.

Later, when I told him how adorable I thought the kids were, he breathed a huge sigh of relief.

After that, Roger began to gradually include me on some of his visits with the kids. Though the children's mother at that point did most of the parenting, Roger tried to be as involved as possible. He would take them camping, or to movies and museums. Roger often invited me along, but was cautious. He didn't want me to feel his children were my responsibility. But I really liked them. I didn't much fancy camping, but I did go along for some of the movies and museums, however. And I found myself increasingly interested in the kids' problems and welfare. Roger talked to them almost every night, and I would sit and listen. I began to feel as if I were part of a new and very special family, and it felt wonderful.

Given my new attachments, it's amazing I was able to pick up and leave, but I did. In October 1965, I had received a petition from some of the soldiers in Vietnam, requesting that I come over and entertain them. The petition contained more than three thousand signatures. I didn't have to battle with myself whether or not to go. I'd been entertaining men in uniform since I was two. As soon as I heard they wanted me, I was ready. I regarded the trip as a moral responsibility, something I owed to the soldiers and to America. And you know by now my sense of duty, my moral core. Nothing could deter me.

Roger wasn't as eager for me to go. While arrangements were being made in January and February 1966, Roger and I waged our first, and fiercest, battle. He admitted to being slightly jealous of "having all those guys going crazy over me," which, I suppose, was natural. But Roger's primary concern was my safety. I wasn't going on a trip with diplomats. It was just me and the Johnny Rivers trio on the front lines for two weeks without any guarantees of safety.

Despite Roger's objections, I left in early March 1966. The fifteen-day excursion began in Saigon, which looked like a tropical vacation spot from the air. However, as soon as we landed, we were hit by the heavy, sweltering jungle air and a sense of foreboding. At the airport, I saw soldiers, guns, and body bags. I was frightened but sure I'd made the right decision.

The first show, staged at the Saigon USO, was supposed to be for two hundred people, but four hundred jammed inside and afterward the MPs told us they turned back another four hundred. We also performed on the *Yorktown,* an aircraft carrier, whose crew stood on deck in a formation spelling out "Hi Annie" as our helicopter landed. A picture of that still hangs in our office at home.

Then we moved into the countryside, an area known as the Iron Triangle. Doing two shows a day at bases around Da Nang, Phu Bai, and Chu Lai, we were constantly in danger. At one eight a.m. show, just fifty smiling soldiers watched while the rest of their unit were out on patrol. We heard shooting in the distance. In retrospect, I should have been very afraid, but I felt invincible. I thought this is where I'm supposed to be, and God would protect us all. In times like those, religion and old-time values serve you well.

One night, our helicopter was shot at going into Phu Bai. I remember the soldiers bunching against me like a human shield. This was exactly Roger's concern. But I still didn't feel concerned about my safety. I was on a mission.

I performed in black tights, a turtleneck sweater from *The Swinger,* and high-heeled leather boots. Not the best outfit to wear in the 100-degree-plus jungle heat, but I wanted to look glamorous for the soldiers. The shows left me a sight—drenched in perspiration and my makeup dripping—but afterward the guys still crowded around, talking or asking me to sign a photograph. One soldier apologized for his snapshot being ripped.

"I'm sorry, ma'am," he said. "But we've seen a lot of action lately."

I told him that if anyone was owed an apology, it was him.

"Look at my eyes," I said, laughing. "My mascara is in a lot worse shape than your photo!"

We had a good laugh. Maybe for a few seconds he forgot that he was in Vietnam. I prayed so.

There was no question on my return at the end of March that I'd done the right thing by going to Vietnam. I still get wonderful notes at shows from soldiers, telling me they saw me in Vietnam. I always say hello and tell them how happy I am that they returned alive.

Roger was ecstatic to see me after two worrisome weeks without any communication, the longest we'd ever gone without speaking. During my absence, Bobby had released me from deals at Paramount and Fox. I'd asked him to do so after Roger and Allan suggested I was making too many films. In this way, I was taking at least a small step toward letting Roger more into my business life.

Soon after I got back, we set off on a motor tour through New England, staying in bed-and-breakfasts and quaint inns. I remember lots of goose-down comforters, roaring fires, good meals, and long walks through the woods. We slept late and laughed about living in sin and it was absolutely lovely and romantic. We forgot about everything at home and slipped into our own private world.

Our last stop was New York, where Roger shared a secret he'd kept from me the whole trip. After dinner at our hotel, we commandeered a hansom cab—a horse-drawn carriage—and drove around Central Park. It was a clear, brisk night. The moon looked like a ripe melon amidst the millions of twinkling stars. It was a perfect evening.

"Ann-Margret, there's something I've been meaning to ask you," Roger said.

I looked up at him, wide-eyed, relaxed and comfortable, and with just my eyes asked, "What?"

"What do you think of the idea of us getting engaged?"

The moment took me by surprise, but I wasn't too startled. I'd given thought to our marrying, but figured we would've discussed things beforehand. After all, given my parents' feelings about Roger, our relationship was not without its difficulties. Roger was as aware of my tug-of-war as anyone.

But he was old-fashioned, impetuous, and a hard-core romantic. Aware that we weren't going to rush into any wedding plans, he later explained that he still thought it would be nice to pledge his love in some way. He wanted to give me a ring, not a friendship ring, but something more substantial.

"Well?" Roger asked.

I was speechless, scared.

"Is it necessary?" I replied, breaking my silence. "I mean, you know I love you. We're together. We'll always be together. Why do we need to change things?"

Roger knew me well and probably anticipated an answer along those lines. A simple yes or no would've been too easy. He remained calm and tried to maintain the mood. Without saying anything, he put his arm around me and stared off into the park for a few moments.

"Too bad," he finally said.

"What's too bad?" I asked.

"I don't know if I should do this to you."

"What? Do what to me?"

"Because I don't know how you're going to take it."

"Roger!" I said, exasperated. "Cut it out. Take what? What are you talking about?"

"This."

He reached into his pocket, pulled out a small black velvet box, and held it out so I could see. Such a sly man. He enjoyed teasing me, knowing that I couldn't resist the temptation. And he was right. I couldn't.

Inside the box was a five-karat diamond ring, immaculate and breathtaking. The stone was set among petals of baguettes. It glittered under the light from the streetlamps like a star, and I felt overwhelmed. I threw my arms around Roger, kissed him, forgot all about my hesitation, and said, "Yes."

Later, Roger told me he and his business manager had gone to a jeweler several weeks before we'd left on our trip. He'd purchased the diamond, which he couldn't really afford, and waited for the perfect time to give it to me.

He didn't tell me that the jeweler had pointed out a minuscule flaw in the diamond, but Roger didn't care about a microscopic blemish as much as he did about the size of the diamond. He wanted to give me something that would literally take my breath away, something that would overwhelm me. The jeweler said that nobody would be able to see the flaw and Roger agreed.

But after wearing it several days, I showed Roger the ring and asked, "What's that?"

"What's what?" Roger asked.

"Look," I said, pointing at the stone. "That tiny black mark."

"I see it," he said.

"There's something in it."

"By God, Ann-Margret," he laughed. "I thought 'Who in hell is going to be able to see that?' Now I know."

It didn't matter to me. But Roger is a perfectionist. On returning to L.A., he borrowed money from his business manager so he could purchase the same size diamond, but flawless.

Since it would've been impossible to hide the sizable ring on my finger, I broke the news to my parents as soon as we got back into town. It was one of the hardest things I'd ever had to do simply because I would've liked them to have been as happy as I was but knew they'd be just the opposite. Mother wouldn't comment. Daddy tried to show some enthusiasm by complimenting my ring. But they were as cool as a Swedish winter.

We argued. Mother and I cried. Daddy wouldn't enter the fray, but he didn't have to; their reservations hadn't changed, especially Mother's. Roger was a divorced, sometimes unemployed actor who had three kids, all of which seemed to my parents a lot of unnecessary baggage for their little girl, whose career was already giving her more than her share of trouble.

But I knew I was right. Even if I couldn't explain it to my parents, I knew in my heart that Roger was the man I was destined to wed. Over the years, I dated a lot of men, but Roger was the one who made me feel an emotional intensity.

I'd known he was special on our first date. By the third date, I knew that we'd marry some day. Over time, my intuition had proven correct. Roger had all the qualities I wanted and needed in a mate—strength, independence, respect, sensitivity, devotion. Ironically, I had found a father figure, even though my own father vehemently disapproved.

"You'll see!" I declared to my parents. "You'll change your mind about Roger. You'll see."

22

I QUIETLY ENJOYED MY RING AND MY NEW STATE AS an engaged woman on the set of *Murderers' Row,* my next movie, starring Dean Martin. Then I got into big trouble one day. I'd overslept and missed my call, a horrible embarrassment. The studio phoned my parents' house—my old number—which was all they had. Daddy answered and said that he would find out where I was.

He drove over to my house and discovered that Roger had spent the night. My mother had already exchanged words with me about this on one occasion. Neither of them thought it was proper before marriage. It was a clash of values, just one additional impediment our relationship had to survive. Daddy was a man of such honor and dignity. I hated upsetting him. I hated myself for it. But I didn't admit to wrongdoing.

Later that night Daddy and I had the worst argument in both of our lives. I ended up slamming out of the house and in the process, shattering a plate-glass door. He was angry at me and I was angry with him. It was horrible. But I didn't look back. Not even after I heard the glass break.

The problem was Daddy and I were so much alike. We weren't great communicators. We brooded. And after the fight, we refused to speak to each other for days. Mother, who disapproved of Roger even more than Daddy did, finally intervened. The family is more important, she told both of us. That was something neither of us could take exception to, and we agreed not to agree.

In retrospect, that incident precipitated a whole avalanche of troubles. During the movie, Columbia Pictures clamped down on my motorcycling to work. Since this had happened twice before on pictures, it shouldn't have upset me. But it did, and then came an even worse blow.

Mike Frankovich, the studio executive who oversaw production on *Cat Ballou,* visited the set. During a break, he pulled me aside and said he had a question to ask me.

"This has been puzzling me for years," he said. "Tell me, why didn't you want to do *Cat Ballou?*"

"What?" I said. "Why didn't I want to do it? What do you mean?"

Mike was as puzzled as I.

"Didn't you know that I wanted you for the movie?" he asked, explaining that he had expressed his interest to my manager.

"No," I said thinking back. "I saw the film. It was so funny. I would've loved to have been in it."

"I can't believe that you never heard about the offer. I'm really disappointed."

"I can't believe it, either."

From that point on, I grew wary and watchful of the way my career was handled.

A short time later, just as *Murderers' Row* wound down, Bobby asked me to meet him at a coffee shop to discuss the future. Naively, I thought that maybe he was upset at the downward spiral my career had taken and wanted to talk about parting ways. For the first time in five years, I didn't have another picture lined up after this one finished.

I couldn't have been more wrong about Bobby's plans.

"Listen, Ann-Margret," he said. "I've done a lot for you the past five years.

"Considering everything," he continued, "I don't think I'm out of line in saying that I need an increase."

"What?" I asked, confused and suddenly wishing Roger or Allan were with me.

"A raise," he said. "I've been getting fifteen percent. I'd like twenty-five."

I knew nothing about business. But twenty-five percent? That sounded high to me. Unreasonably high.

"I don't think that's unfair," he added.

Unfair? Shaken, I managed an uncertain smile and said

I had to think about it. Then I hugged him goodbye. Even in the midst of my rage, I wanted to make nice, to please Bobby, a character trait I simply couldn't shake.

I made record time to my parents' house, taking the curves of the canyon at top speed in my pink Cadillac, and poured everything out.

Later, after I explained it to Roger, he gave me a startling lesson in Hollywood arithmetic. I already paid my manager fifteen percent. Another ten percent went to my agent. Still another percentage went to my business manager. Then there was the monthly fee for my publicist.

"By the time you cash your check, it's half gone," he said disgustedly.

"But isn't it worth it?" I argued. "Look at everything that's happened. Everything I have."

"And now they want more."

"Maybe they deserve it," I said.

I also found myself confiding in George Sidney, who worked on trying to get me out of my contract. Then a friend of our family, an attorney, someone we trusted implicitly, persuaded me to let him look over my books.

Afterward, I sat in his office for three hours, listening as he read off a list of dealings that seemed to be losing propositions. I'd invested in a macadamia plantation in a part of Hawaii that got no rain and the crops had been ruined. Another large sum of money went into a housing development that failed because the property was next to March Air Force Base and drowned in the noise of constant jet traffic.

"And you know the portrait of yourself Bobby gave you as his Christmas present to you?" he asked.

"Yes," I said. "Mother hung it in the house."

"Well, look here, Ann-Margret," he said. "I'll bet he billed you for it, that *you* paid for it."

At the end, he informed me that I was several hundred thousand dollars in debt! I slid down in my chair, wishing I could disappear. No tears came to my eyes, but there was a lump in my throat the size of a baseball. I was heartbroken, primarily because my innate trusting nature had served me so poorly. I felt angry at myself, used and very shaky inside.

"What are you going to do about it?" my mother asked later that day.

"I don't know if I can do anything," I answered softly.

"What?" she screamed. "What do you mean?"

Mother had never been so furious with me. She got up from the table and chased me around the house. To her credit, Mother had been able to finally see the situation for what it was and give up her loyalty to Bobby. Loyalty was one thing. Stupidity was another.

"How dare you stick up for him!" she yelled from behind the locked door of my old bedroom.

"Mother, it's okay," I pleaded.

"It's not okay, Ann-Margret! It's a crime! Why can't you see that? Why can't you admit it?"

Eventually I had to face the truth. Unbeknownst to me, Roger was so upset by my situation that he actually had asked another attorney, his friend Daniel Gottlieb, to conduct an independent audit of my books, and he found exactly the same thing. Both Roger and my mother practically forced me to meet with my business manager, and then I asked Bobby to explain these discrepancies.

As a measure of my weakness, I was ready to forgive him. Waiting in his outer office, I just wanted him to give me a plausible answer, basically an excuse to do nothing. I waited patiently for almost half an hour, figuring he was busy, which wasn't the case. The person with whom he'd been meeting, someone I knew, came out and apologized for the delay.

"I asked Bobby if he knew you were out here," he said.

"I'm sure he did," I answered.

"Ann-Margret, I probably shouldn't tell you this," he said. "But do you know what Bobby said? When I asked if he knew you were waiting, he said, 'She's so dumb, she won't care.'"

I got so mad. But I went ahead with the meeting, which was uneasy and tense. I asked questions, made accusations, and supported everything with facts, while my manager calmly repudiated any wrongdoing. We parted without resolving anything. The next move—whatever that was—was mine to make.

"Mark my words," he said to a friend of ours. "In two years, Ann-Margret will be out of show business."

The scary part was how close that was to being true. I was offered no scripts, no prospects. The burst of heat that propelled me into multipicture deals with every studio in Hollywood was history. I felt like Cinderella. The clock had tolled midnight, the coach turned back into a pumpkin, the footmen back into mice.

I'm not totally sure why this occurred when it did. Perhaps all those bad films had finally caught up with me. I know Hollywood is cyclical, but this cycle was too fast, too soon.

And to make matters worse, I was in fairly grim financial straits. One of my business managers was now telephoning Roger and asking if there was any money he didn't know about to pay the bills that were coming in.

Pierre Cossette, Bobby's boss, had no idea what had gone on and was shattered when he discovered everything. Pierre is one of the most honest, respected, and loved men in show business. He stepped in immediately and attempted to repair things by trying to sell a TV special to a network. Roger and Allan thought that was a good idea. But too many bridges had been burned. Not even Pierre could work his magic and get the special through. And still, I refused to leave Bobby. I let Pierre do it, and Pierre and Bobby just severed their relationship. I suppose there were many complex forces at work, including my fear of conflict, my desire to please, my naive loyalty. Bobby had launched my career and somewhere deep inside I felt gratitude.

At the end of 1966, producer Joseph E. Levine got word to Roger that he wanted me for the lead in a film he was making in Italy. The offer came from nowhere, and it was the lone bright spot save for the ring on my finger.

Although the salary was a small percentage of what I was used to earning, I needed the money, and I also needed the work. Roger encouraged me to take it, and Allan believed activity bred activity. They acted as a team of unofficial coaches, trying to psyche their student back into competitive form. With *The Swinger* and *Murderers' Row* opening back-to-back in December, Roger and I flew to Rome.

Il tigre—or *The Tiger and the Pussycat*—is probably best described as a spaghetti romance, a satirical ''sexcapade'' in which a middle-aged gentleman played by actor Vittorio Gassman becomes obsessed with my character, a girl young enough to be his daughter.

The Italians were wonderful to work with, warm and admiring of American stars. But the best part of making the picture was settling down in our own apartment in Rome and for two months forgetting about the problems back home. It was the part I loved most about acting: the escape, the opportunity to slip into a life other than my own.

Allan joined us in Rome, and the three of us filled our free time with museums and sight-seeing. Periodically, Allan and Roger sent bits of news back to the gossip columns in Hollywood to keep my name in the press. But there was still no action on the TV special.

We returned home in March 1967, as I approached my twenty-sixth birthday, and I didn't know whether I was frustrated or finished. It was an incredibly painful time.

Yet I knew I was a lucky woman. Despite our differences over Roger, my parents still believed in me, loved me, and cherished me—not because of what I'd achieved and given them. I was their daughter, period.

Then there was Allan Carr, a shrewd man disguised as a preppy college kid. He had the show business acumen of someone triple his age and experience. He was as quick with a funny line as he was in analyzing a situation. Careers were about momentum and perception, he said. Momentum and perception. He repeated it like a mantra.

And of course there was Roger, always patiently at my side. He and I had never talked about setting a date to marry. He had adopted my attitude that we were engaged and it worked. Why rock the boat? We knew all too well that show business marriages rarely worked, and we feared a wedding would be the beginning of the end.

So we continued to live together without much thought to the future. It's curious, given my very traditional upbringing, that I was willing to drift on and on in an engagement with no wedding in sight. I had been so shaken by the Burt Sugarman experience, by the fear of hurting my parents with a wedding they disapproved of, that I couldn't risk it again. Meanwhile, Roger and Allan made it clear that they not only were willing to, but wanted to assume management of my career. Although I continually refused, there was no doubt that, as one mess led to another, Roger and Allan were the only ones I trusted in business.

One weekend we flew to Las Vegas and saw Eddie Fisher at the Riviera Hotel. Halfway through his act, Eddie slid from the stage and sang from the audience, moving like a cat. One minute here, then there, and then, to our surprise, he jumped on top of our table. Eddie and I had parted good friends and I knew he was happy to have me there. I also sensed the excitement, the high that Eddie felt, moving among an adoring crowd, and I knew I wanted to share that.

"One of these days I'm going to have a show of my own," I told Roger later that night.

"A nightclub act?" he asked.

"Sure," I said. "That's how I started out."

Roger didn't even wait.

"Let's do it," he said.

I hadn't expected that response. I quickly withdrew my offer.

"I can't," I said.

"What do you mean? You're a performer, aren't you? That's what you've done all your life. You're happiest when you're singing, dancing, being on stage, right? So why do you say you can't?"

"Because," I replied softly, "I'm frightened."

That wasn't the real me talking, the person who could take a TR 500 around a corner at high speeds, and Roger knew it. He brought up a nightclub act in what seemed like every conversation we had. I always refused. Earlier in my career, I had adored performing before a live audience. I could still feel the visceral thrill of my days with the Suttletones. But now, I clenched. This was the first of certain recurrent fears that emerged as I grew older, and they would come and go. One moment, I would be reticent and the next fine. I sensed the capriciousness of the profession that I thought my happiness depended on. I didn't want to be hurt.

It seemed as if I'd been the one who always said no in our relationship—engagement, wedding, nightclub act. But shortly after we returned from Las Vegas, we were at the table enjoying the nice dinner Roger had prepared.

"You know we've been going out three years now," I said.

"Ah-huh," he said. "So?"

"I've got this notion," I continued. "Three years is the cutoff."

"What do you mean?" he asked.

"After three years, you make a decision—either split or get married." I wish I could analyze what made me take this sudden leap forward, to transform passive into active, but I can't. Suddenly, some inner clock told me the time was right. Instinct. Intuition. The same forces that always guided me were again at work.

Roger looked up, surprised.

"We're going to have to talk about it," he said, scrambling for an answer.

"What do you mean?" I asked.

"I mean I want to marry you," he said. "But I think there are a few things we have to talk about first."

I could see Roger regaining his balance. He'd done his share of thinking, too.

"I don't have any things," I said.

"Well, I do," he answered.

Roger explained that he loved me deeply. He wanted to marry me. He had no hesitation when it came to pledging his love forever. But there was a problem. He didn't want to take our relationship to the next step unless I severed my relationship with the people involved in my career—from my manager on down. Everyone who'd had anything to do with getting me in the situation I was struggling to escape. Roger was a very strong-willed man, one who had a deep sense of right and wrong. He perceived what I was doing with my career as being very wrong and he simply couldn't condone it, as much as he loved me. At least that was how he felt then.

"Let Allan and me run things," he said. "Because I can't be married to you and have that person screwing things up more."

"I can't," I said.

"Even though you know what he's done to you?" he argued.

"I can't," I repeated.

"Even though Allan and I are already involved?"

"I just can't."

"You're not going to do anything about it?" he asked.

"I can't," I cried once more, sounding like a broken record.

By then, Roger had grown weary of acting. He knew he didn't have the fierce ambition you need to succeed in this business, and he was far more interested in my career than his. He felt I was the one with the real talent as a performer, and his role was to help me.

Finally, Roger got angry, and rightly so. I cried. The disagreement quickly escalated into a horrible argument, the worst in the nearly three years we'd been together. We were both proud and neither of us would back down. Roger stalked out of the house and got into his car to leave. I followed.

"Then we can't get married," he said.

I stood beside his car as Roger looked at me, expecting me to answer. My face was wet from tears. Without saying a word, I slipped off the engagement ring, handed it to him, and walked back into the house.

23

OUR BREAKUP WAS CHRONICLED IN THE NEXT DAY'S edition of the *Los Angeles Times*. The story, dated March 28, 1966, began, "One of Hollywood's most colorful romances of recent years hit the rocks. . . ." To this day, Roger and I have no idea where or how they got the story, and seeing it in print only made things worse.

I was proud and angry and I made up my mind that I wasn't going to sit home and sulk. I would show Roger I didn't care.

During that first week, I went to dinner with my former fiancé Burt Sugarman, and saw Bobby Darin. But no matter how hard I tried to distract myself, I couldn't shake my feelings for Roger, and that just aggravated my misery.

Throughout this time I had no contact with Roger, but Allan, who knew everything through his extensive network of contacts, informed him of my activities. Allan also told Roger that Pierre had booked me into the Riviera Hotel for a salary that was hard to turn down.

Although I agreed to the booking, I was very ambivalent. Part of me didn't want to think about doing a nightclub act without Roger in my life. All the while, I could hear Allan's voice in the background saying, "Ann-Margret, activity breeds activity. Until you start another film, this is going to keep the momentum going."

Meanwhile, Roger spent the first week we were apart sitting by the phone. He was convinced I'd call. When it didn't ring, he worried. When he heard that I'd gone out with several of the men I'd dated before him, he worried even more. When he heard about the Riviera, he worried—

but this time he worried *for* me. He knew how scared I felt about a live show.

About two weeks later he sent me a letter. I hesitated before opening the envelope, fearful of getting hurt all over again. If Roger had something to tell me, I thought, why didn't he just call?

Then I read the handwritten note and realized that sometimes the heart speaks better on paper. I reread it several times, and then had to wipe my eyes. In straightforward prose that read like poetry, Roger simply said that he missed me, he loved me till his heart ached from exertion, loved me beyond rational thought, and he had been wrong to push me to do something I didn't want to do.

Roger reiterated that he thought it was a grave mistake for me to stay with my management, but he confessed that he'd rather have it that way than lose the special love both of us had for each other. He didn't care what happened to my career, he said. He cared only about me. When my career hit bottom, as he predicted it would, we'd at least have each other.

"And even if you don't think you need me," he wrote, "I need you."

At the end of the letter, Roger asked me to call. As soon as I composed myself, I dialed his number.

"I love you," I said upon hearing his voice. "The letter—it was beautiful."

"I missed you so much," he said. "I worried that I wouldn't hear from you again. That you wouldn't call."

"You're right. But I love you so much."

"Let's make a date," Roger said.

"I'm free now, tonight, and later on," I replied.

"No, a date to get married," he said. "Let's set a date, and the next time we see each other it'll be to get married."

"Agreed."

I'd always imagined a storybook wedding for myself. A white dress, lots of family. Perhaps the ceremony would be at the little white church in Hotagen. Or perhaps it would be just a beautiful garden-style wedding. But never in my wildest dreams did I think it would be a family catastrophe.

May 8, 1967, should've been the happiest day of my life

but it turned out to be one of the worst. I stared out the window, waiting for Roger and determined to exchange vows that day no matter what. But of course that "no matter what" part bothered me. I was torn between being a good, obedient daughter, a daughter committed to never displeasing her parents; and an adult, an independent woman. As I waited, Daddy brooded in a dark silence and Mother locked herself in the bedroom.

Roger picked me up, drove to the airport, and flew us to Las Vegas in his plane. Soaring through the cloudless sky was the highlight of the day. The world and all its troubles were far below.

Roger had arranged for a suite at the Riviera, and the management was happy to help, since I was booked there and it would be good publicity. Except we wanted everything to be kept quiet. We felt there was enough tension without having to deal with the press. A friend helped Roger make the secret arrangements—a marriage license was readied at City Hall, a minister hired, a wedding cake ordered.

After landing, we took care of the papers at City Hall, where several reporters routinely hung out, waiting for just such an occasion. We hurried to the hotel before word spread too far. But as we pulled in front of the Riviera, we saw a giant banner that said, WELCOME ANN-MARGRET AND ROGER.

We went directly to our room. Traveling in my wedding outfit, a white piqué micro-miniskirt and matching piqué fluffy short shorts (after all, this was the sixties), I went to apply my makeup and lipstick, but my hand trembled so violently from nerves I could barely do it. My face was puffy and my eyes swollen from crying so hard. As I struggled, there was a knock on the door.

"Could you please hurry," a strange voice said.

"Is something the matter?" I asked.

"Well, the minister has another wedding to do right after yours."

When I walked into the adjoining suite, where the ceremony was to take place, I was engulfed by smoke. Looking through the gray cloud, I saw the room was completely full. A throng of reporters and photographers in their shirt-sleeves stood around, talking and smoking. Why not? It was just another workday for them. But not for me. I'd always vowed that I'd have just one wedding in my life. This wasn't the church wedding I'd envisioned, in Sweden with friends and relatives, but for better or worse, this was it. Yet I could barely see my soon-to-be husband through the crowd.

I felt tears coming. The poor minister, a nice man, had no idea what hit him. As he readied the service, I started to cry. A few moments later, I really lost control. The minister stopped, picked up a napkin from a buffet table that had been set up, and handed it to me. By the time the short ceremony ended, my makeup was completely smeared. Then the newsmen surrounded me. And I sobbed uncontrollably that this was how my wedding day had turned out. We left the food, cake, and whatever else had been arranged to the crowd in the room, and flew back to L.A.

Roger phoned the kids and told them we were married. I think he felt that because we had done this in such a hurry and because my parents were so upset, it was best not to make a big deal, alerting the kids in advance. He knew they loved me and would be thrilled.

"Great, Daddy!" was their response.

Were I to do it over, I would have had them there at our side and my parents, and Roger's mother, too. But we felt it was a time for us alone, right or wrong.

We spent our wedding night at our house, and for a moment I felt our relationship would return to normal. However, the next night I freaked out and left Roger. We had spent about fifteen hours as a married couple. Then I moved back in with my parents in a fit of confusion and panic. I suppose I was acting out the conflicted emotions I simply couldn't resolve—whether to be a grown-up or a child, a wife or a daughter. Marriage represented one side of the argument. Moving back in with my folks the other. I felt a terrible pull I could neither understand nor articulate.

With me, nothing was simple. I spent the daytime with Roger, but then disappeared around dinnertime and went back to my parents. I wanted to apologize to my parents in some way—my mother in particular—for hurting them by going through with the wedding, and also to show them that even though I'd married Roger, I was still their little girl. I was trying to convince all of us that our bond was as strong as ever. For a while, my mother quietly watched this. Privately, she was appalled. I had made my bed, so I should lie in it. Roger was now my husband and it was, she felt, my duty to be with him.

Of course, living in two different places at once created a huge mess—literally. My clothes were strewn across the floor of my parents' house. The rest of my things were tossed around the house Roger and I shared. I didn't know whether I was coming or going.

Then one day Roger phoned my mother. This was unprecedented. They rarely spoke on good days.

"Mrs. Olsson," he said, "I guess you know that Ann-Margret is not living with me now."

"Yes, I do," Mother answered. "What's going on?"

"I was hoping you could tell me that," Roger said.

"Well, I don't know what's going on."

They discussed the situation for a while, and that call became a bridge over troubled water. Mother was able to articulate to Roger why she had been against the marriage.

"I have one child, and you have three children from your previous marriage. I wonder if my kid, who's been sheltered all her life, can take that. I'm afraid. That's all. I have nothing against you, Roger," she told him.

And that opened the gates. They were able to talk better, and Roger was able to tell her it would be okay, that we would make it. He told her what I meant to him and that he was committed to making the marriage work.

Finally, Mother and Roger had something in common. Both of them were completely bewildered by my behavior and unsure of what to do; this forced them to talk to each other. They compared notes, tried analyzing me, and in the process took preliminary steps toward becoming the close friends they are today.

One night I sat down beside Mother and had the sort of long talk we used to have when I was a girl. I told her my basic problem: I feared marriage would pull me away from her and Daddy.

"Is that what you really feel will happen?" she asked.

"No," I said.

"Then why is that a worry?"

"I've heard about husbands like that," I said. "I've read it in magazines and seen it on television. They keep their wives wrapped in chains." I know now how ridiculous I was sounding, but I had to offer some response.

"How long have you been seeing Roger?" she asked.

"Three years," I said.

"Is that what he's like? I don't think so. So what's the problem, Ann-Margret?"

"You don't like him," I said.

"I didn't like him, I'll admit that. I had my doubts, and I may still have some," she said. "I'll be honest. He's not the husband I dreamed about you marrying. But lately Roger and I have been talking, and—"

"And?" I interrupted, suddenly aware there'd been communication I didn't know about.

"And I'm warming up to him," she said.

"So what do you think about him?"

"What do I think? I think he's your husband. I think that being married isn't always easy. And I think you should pack your belongings and go home to your husband."

The next morning I did that. I had received the parental blessing I craved, and something unlocked for me psychologically. I was in love with Roger and I loved my parents. I wanted to please both, and now I could. I was released, in some degree, from my childhood and ready to be a married woman. Roger and I stayed together that night, and every night since then.

24

WHATEVER INHIBITIONS I HAD FELT ABOUT DOING A nightclub act also lessened. I was still nervous, but I was capable of performing. And because there was less than a month before opening night at the Riviera, the pressure to put together an act was intense. As I perspired and ached through grueling twelve-hour days, six days a week, I realized that I was more comfortable working on songs and learning how to tango than doing anything else in the world. What had been the fear?

I was surrounded by terrific people. Bob Wells produced and scripted. David Winters, with whom I'd worked on several movies, choreographed. My friend Maggie Banks assisted. One day a reporter from the *Times* watched rehearsals, and I overheard him ask Maggie if I was nervous about returning to Las Vegas. A little, Maggie answered, but Ann-Margret "never throws tantrums. She just stares at you and then gets sick to her stomach."

I wanted everything perfect. In movies I'd played different characters, hiding behind costumes, hair colors, and various fictional situations, but a live stage show was something else altogether. When the audience determined whether or not they liked my nightclub act, they'd be basing their judgment not on a character, not on the product of a writer's imagination and a good director's vision, but on me.

It had been a long time since I had danced with George Burns. I had been so natural, unaffected, and I hoped I still was.

For opening night, June 7, 1967, friends and fans turned out in full force. George Burns gave me a good-luck kiss backstage. Elvis sent a huge bouquet of flowers shaped like a guitar, something he'd do every opening night from then on. I always felt a wonderfully warm glow when I saw them.

Andy Williams, Virginia Mayo, Frankie Avalon, Lorne Green, Gene Barry, Rona Barrett, and Clint Walker filled the best tables. Sick to my stomach with nerves, it was hard for me to enjoy the excitement.

My mother came to my side moments before the curtain went up and said, "Ann-Margret, *'tre sparkar!'* " It was a reminder. Suddenly I was a little girl again. I turned around and she gave me my three Swedish good-luck kicks. I was ready.

There was no subtlety to my arrival on stage. Amid a shower of psychedelic lights, I rode to the center of the stage on a Harley Davidson, flanked on each side by six dancers who were also on bikes.

It was a production that didn't let up for ninety minutes. We threw in a bit of everything from *Birdie*'s "A Lot of Living to Do" to the Swedish folk song "Violets for Mother," which I'd learned as a child. In between, I sang "Yesterday," go-go danced in a cage, parodied Ruby Keeler, and finished with a smoking rendition of Aretha Franklin's "Respect." And that was what I hoped to reclaim after my abrupt decline.

Afterward, a crowd that included Johnny Carson gathered in the dressing room to celebrate. It reminded me of what I already knew—that there's no substitute for performing in front of a live audience. The feeling of triumph was a welcome boost to my bruised ego.

I was overwhelmed by the reviews, which Roger and Allan read out loud so I couldn't avoid them. The *Los Angeles Times* was really terrific, saying that since "this is her first time as a stage headliner, the girl with the svelte figure, vibrant youth and boundless energy came up with aces and joins that select group of performers who can enchant an audience for ninety minutes."

Toward the end of the five-week engagement, I received another compliment. Elvis, his father, and a couple of the guys came to see the show. Knowing the hassles he went through going out in public, I was really touched that he went to the trouble. Afterward, the entourage visited the dressing room. At one point, I was by myself in front of the makeup mirror in the innermost room of the backstage chamber when Elvis walked inside. I turned and smiled. He shut the door. Our eyes met and suddenly the old connection burned as brightly and strong as it had years earlier.

Elvis complimented me on the show. Coming from him, it meant the world. I started to thank him. But Elvis interrupted. It should be the other way around, he said. His smile faded and his eyes lost their playfulness and turned serious. He started thanking me for the happiness I'd given him. All of a sudden he wanted to remember the times we'd shared, how happy we'd been, and how happy *he* had been.

Elvis then stepped forward and dropped to one knee. He took my hands in his. I felt the heat in both of our bodies. In a soft, gentle voice weighted by seriousness, he told me exactly how he still felt about me, which I intuitively knew, but was very touched to hear.

When the five-week engagement was up and we returned to L.A., we faced the same frustration as before. The networks still weren't interested in a TV special and the studios weren't sending any scripts.

Roger and Allan made a strong appeal to take over management of my career. By then, Roger had made his last movie, *Rogue's Gallery,* and was really disappointed with his work. He knew he had lost the desire to perform and was willing to devote himself to me and my career. He and Allan argued that nothing was working. I needed a change. I knew they were right, but I couldn't make that decision. I didn't have the guts. I didn't have the self-worth.

But I did have the sense that my life had changed in the subtle ways that mark the ascension of adulthood. It was more attitude than event, more the gradual assimilation of everything I'd experienced the past year—the criticism, managerial troubles, financial difficulties, my engagement, breakup, and the decision to marry. Playing Las Vegas, too, helped.

With that shift in perspective, Roger and I sat down to

dinner one night and he poured himself a glass of wine. He
knew better than to offer me one. We'd had that discussion
before and I'd always refused, claiming that I didn't like
the taste of alcohol—liquor, beer, wine, it didn't matter.
Roger understood, never pushed.

But a glass of wine back then was a symbol of sophis-
tication, something that enhanced the enjoyment of a meal,
and being a gourmet, someone who appreciated good food,
he wanted me to share that pleasure. He had no idea of my
father's history with alcoholism. I had felt this was a private
matter between Daddy and me. Nor was I aware of the
genetic disposition of the disease. Then Roger brought a
bottle of Boone's Apple Valley wine.

"You might want to try a glass of this," he said.

"It's wine?" I asked.

"Yeah, but it tastes like punch," he said. "A little glass
with dinner. You'll like it."

I suppose I was feeling happy and confident after returning from Las Vegas. Moreover, Roger had likened it to
punch. I was able to shrug off my past refusals of any
alcoholic beverage and let Roger pour me some wine in a
glass full of ice. He was right.

"This tastes great!" I beamed.

The first glass went straight to my head. I felt a wonderful warm feeling through my body. I relaxed. Everything
was well with the world. Midway through the second glass,
I was happy, carefree, warm throughout my body, cracking
jokes, and brimming with confidence. I was certainly not
myself. In fact, I was surely more *fun* than myself.

Or so I thought. Little did I realize that the wine set off
a chemical reaction in my brain. Then I had wine with
several other dinners. And within a couple weeks, I was
drinking scotch, and had progressed from teetotaler to
eighty proof. The warning signs were there; I didn't rec-
ognize them, and Roger had no reason to. I suppose he
thought the alcohol relaxed me and was harmless. Little did
we know.

As I relished the new sensations of alcohol, my career
began to improve. Although I still had no offers in the U.S.,
The Tiger and the Pussycat was a hit in Europe. The pic-

My mother and father (Anna and Gustav Olsson) with me in Stockholm, 1941.

With my grandmother (whom I called Mooma) on the main road of Valsjobyn, the tiny town in northern Sweden, where I lived until I was six.

My favorite childhood picture, on the road in Valsjobyn, at age five. This photo brings back so many wonderful memories. (Neal Peters Collection)

Performing "Cuanto Le Gusta" at age seven. Mom made *all* my costumes! (Neal Peters Collection)

My first trip back to Sweden in 1951, experiencing my first motorcycle ride on the back of Uncle Calle's bike. It started my love affair with motorcycles that continues even today.

Cheerleading at New Trier High School in Winnetka, Illinois.
(Neal Peters Collection)

December 1960. Backstage, opening night, with George Burns at the Sahara Hotel, Las Vegas. This was my first big break, thanks to Mr. Burns. (Neal Peters Collection)

Filming my first major television appearance, *The Jack Benny Show*, February 1961. (Neal Peters Collection)

"Twisting" with my dad in our new California home, as Mom watches. June 1961. (Neal Peters Collection)

With Bobby Darin, on his opening night at the Flamingo Hotel, Las Vegas, February 4, 1962. We had just made *State Fair* together. (Neal Peters Collection)

Singing "Bachelor in Paradise" at the 1962 Oscars telecast. (Neal Peters Collection)

My third film, and what a fun one it was! (Neal Peters Collection)

My character, Ann-Margrock, on *The Flintstones*. (Hanna-Barbera/Neal Peters Collection)

One of my favorite dance numbers in *Viva Las Vegas* called "C'mon Everybody." (Neal Peters Collection)

With Elvis, on a break, during the 1963 filming of *Viva Las Vegas*. (Neal Peters Collection)

A rare, private shot of Elvis and myself, at a birthday party for my then landlady, Mrs. Jorgensen.

A scene from *The Cincinnati Kid* with Steve McQueen in 1965. (Neal Peters Collection)

Performing for our troops in Vietnam, 1966. (Neal Peters Collection)

A surprise party at the home of my friend Lill Klaesson, to celebrate my engagement to Roger Smith in 1966. (Lill Klaesson)

May 8, 1967. Roger set the timer on his camera to get this picture of us "crossing the threshold" on our wedding day.

The Smith kids, Jordan, Dallas, and Tracey, at about the time when I first met them.

At home, by the pool, with the children.

My first Las Vegas show, as a headliner, in July 1967. This was the opening number, "Big Time." (Neal Peters Collection)

Lucille Ball was a much-loved guest on my second television special, "From Hollywood with Love," which aired in December 1969. (Neal Peters Collection)

An intense, emotional bedroom scene with Jack Nicholson from the 1971 film *Carnal Knowledge*. (Neal Peters Collection)

Duke always had me laughing on the set of *The Train Robbers*. He was an extraordinary man. (Neal Peters Collection)

At home in October 1972, recovering from a major accident. Five weeks before, I had fallen twenty-two feet from a platform above a Lake Tahoe stage. (Delmar Watson/Hollywood Archive)

Returning to my stage show, just ten weeks after my fall. This was in November 1972, and my father was very ill. I really wanted to show him that I was okay. (Neal Peters Collection)

That same night, backstage with Roger. The flowers are from Elvis, a guitar-shaped arrangement that was his constant opening-night gift. (Santiago Rodriguez/Neal Peters)

A ceremony was held on July 11, 1973, to unveil my star on Hollywood Boulevard. (Delmar Watson/Hollywood Archive)

One of my husband's innovative production numbers for the Vegas show. Three separately filmed screen images served as my "backup" singers, all timed and choreographed to precise synchronization. (Neal Peters Collection)

Dancing with Bob Hope on his television special in 1974. (Neal Peters Collection)

A birthday party was given for me during the filming of *Tommy*, at London's White Elephant restaurant. Allan Carr was with Roger and me.

Thrilled to win the Foreign Press Association's Golden Globe as Best Actress of 1975 for *Tommy*. (Neal Peters Collection)

On my 1975 television special, "Ann-Margret Olsson," I performed a medley ("Nutbush City Limits," "Proud Mary," and "Honky Tonk Woman") with my friend the dynamic Tina Turner. (Neal Peters Collection)

Doing "The Bump" with Roger at an Allan Carr party aboard producer Robert Stigwood's yacht in Cannes.

Rehearsing in 1977 with Minnie Pearl, Bob Hope, and Perry Como at the Grand Ole Opry in Nashville, for a television special called "Rhinestone Cowgirl." (Neal Peters Collection)

This picture sums up my relationship with Johnny Carson—he always kept me laughing. (Neal Peters Collection)

A lighthearted meeting with King Carl XVI Gustaf and Queen Silvia of Sweden in Minneapolis, Minnesota, in November 1982.

Portraying the real-life Lucile Fray, a cancer-stricken woman who must find homes for her ten children, in the ABC television movie *Who Will Love My Children?* (Neal Peters Collection)

A wonderful closing moment in concert. (Ron Aliano/Neal Peters)

One of my most challenging roles, portraying Blanche DuBois, in the television miniseries of Tennessee Williams's *A Streetcar Named Desire.* (ABC TV)

With the wonderful Claudette Colbert in the 1987 miniseries *The Two Mrs. Grenvilles,* based on my friend Dominick Dunne's bestselling novel. (Neal Peters Collection)

Gene Hackman and me in a scene from the film *Twice in a Lifetime.* (Neal Peters Collection)

Skiing with Roger in Aspen, Colorado, near our new winter home.

Our family in 1993 when Jordan *(lower left)* married Robyn *(lower left)*. On the right is Dallas, and below him is Tracey. Next to me, of course, is Roger.

With two of Hollywood's greats: Jack Lemmon and Walter Matthau, for the feature film *Grumpy Old Men*. (Ron Phillips/Warner Bros.)

At home with my mother and our dog, Sugar, who jumps through my arms, her only trick! (Neal Preston)

In the kitchen at our house. Roger must have just made some comment about my lack of culinary skills. I don't cook. And I don't care. (Neal Preston)

At home, on our front steps. (Neal Preston)

Today. (Harry Langdon)

ture's producer, Joseph E. Levine, signed me to two more movies. As soon as the scripts were ready, Roger and I flew to Italy, where I teamed up again with Vittorio Gassman and director Dino Risi in *The Prophet,* the story of a man who reenters civilization after a long exile and falls for a young girl.

For the first time, I was outside the mainstream. Although the Italians themselves were a delight, the working conditions were different from Hollywood productions. The budget was tight, the schedule taxing. The perks that made twelve- and fifteen-hour days tolerable were nonexistent. But I adapted.

How I adapted was questionable. Without realizing it, I found myself looking forward to the half-bottle of white wine that was automatically included in each day's lunch basket. I thought, How great. It always made long afternoons so serene and didn't seem to affect my work.

We spent the Christmas holidays at home with the kids. Then after they returned to their mother, we traveled to Argentina to shoot the romantic thriller *Criminal Affair,* which costarred Rossano Brazzi. As far as filmmaking went, this was an emotional low. Schedules changed every day, as did equipment. The production company operated on such a shoestring that there weren't even any dressing rooms. I rushed back to my hotel between scenes to change. I had only two outfits.

If I was unhappy, Roger was miserable during the shoot. He didn't mince words, either.

"Everyone wanted you," he said. "You could've done one big movie a year, but that damn manager kept selling you into mediocre pictures, with no script approval. And now look at us: No dressing room, sharing a bathroom with strangers."

After a miserable month of filming, we flew to Beirut, the location of my next picture, *Rebus.* Beirut in those days was lovely, cosmopolitan, peaceful, with fine French boutiques, casinos, and some of the most gorgeous beaches we'd ever seen. However, as we confronted endless script changes, equipment breakdowns, and delays, the movie was another trial.

25

I GAVE THE BEST I COULD IN BEIRUT, BUT I WORKED
in a state of numbness—guided by instinct, protected by an
emotional detachment that was purely a matter of self-
preservation.

In the midst of the production I became incredibly disgusted with myself. It had nothing to do with the film, but
everything to do with how I felt about myself. I was furious
that I had allowed myself to have been taken advantage of
to such a degree, and I was miserable. I was overweight,
having gained more than I care to say. I drank too much
at night. Both were symptoms of how badly I wanted to
blot out the anger and hurt.

I walked, talked, sang, danced, acted—I did whatever I
had to. The only thing I couldn't do was express myself to
Roger. I was silent and morose.

"Ann-Margret, what's the matter?" Roger asked.

"Nothing."

"Tell me," he insisted.

"I can't," I cried. "I'm stubborn. I'm stoic. I don't want
to."

In reality, I didn't know how to tell Roger how bruised,
hurt, and battered I felt. I had never learned to really express my inner thoughts because that wasn't my way. And
my reticence only frustrated both of us all the more.

Finally, after one dismal workday, I got so angry that
the depth of my emotion scared me. I didn't want to make
movies that no one saw; I didn't want to be exiled from
the mainstream. I was so upset I knew something had to
give or else I would destroy myself.

Long ago, when my father hurt his back, my mother

consoled me by explaining that God never gave people more than they could handle. If that was true, I realized it was up to me to at least try to change things.

I couldn't sleep that night. I watched the sun rise over Beirut, and I waited for Roger to wake up.

"Please, you take over," I said to him that morning. "Okay?"

"What do you mean?" he asked.

"Everything," I explained. "You and Allan. Just take over. Make things better. Will you?"

"Yes, I will," he said.

Roger then held me very tight and finally I felt serene and not nervous for the first time in a long while.

Roger and Allan soon met with Pierre, who'd quickly severed his relationship with Bobby, and worked out the details of extricating me from my old management contract. Then, within a month of taking over, Roger and Allan did the impossible: They had heard that Canada Dry was interested in sponsoring a variety special. Realizing that my act from the Riviera could easily be adapted, Canada Dry bought the show as a television special. Although this helped me get out of debt, money wasn't as important as self-esteem. The special gave us the opportunity we wanted—to repackage me to the public and erase the perception that I was nothing but a tarnished actress.

Once we had firmed up the deal, Roger and Allan knew what to do. We put together a new album, *The Cowboy and the Lady,* and that plus news of my Canada Dry deal got me mentioned in the columns and some chances to go on the talk-show circuit. You could see Allan's philosophy at work: Activity breeds activity. Meanwhile, Roger supported him, watched, and learned.

"I can feel the momentum building," he told me.

In the spirit of starting over, Roger and I shopped for a new house. In November, we found our dream home, a beautiful white Cape Cod–style house on a ten-acre spread in one of the canyons. "HEDGEROW," as it was called, had once been owned by Hedy Lamarr and Gene Rowland. Humphrey Bogart and Lauren Bacall had also lived there, but they moved because of the rattlesnakes that often slithered up the hills. That was the reason, I later learned, that former President Reagan and his wife Nancy had passed on the house when they were shopping for a place to raise their children.

Roger and I had our own history with the house. I'd actually looked at it in 1962 when I was buying a home for my parents. However, by the time I got up the long driveway, the realtor came out and told me the owners had changed their minds and didn't want to sell. Roger had also noticed it whenever he drove in from the Valley, and fantasized of the day when he could buy a home like that.

We didn't negotiate. The owners had a history of pulling the house off the market during negotiations. We simply gave them their price and moved in.

Before we purchased the home, Roger would occasionally take his children on camping trips to Big Bear so they could see animals. The most they ever saw was a squirrel. At night, he'd set out some strips of bacon, wait until the kids went to sleep, then get rid of the bacon. When the kids woke up in the morning, he'd tell them bears had come! But on our new property there were deer, coyotes, bobcats, possums, raccoons, quail, owls, snakes, and more—and this was in Beverly Hills! We loved all the wildlife, and just made sure we stayed in our protected backyard.

Late one night, well past midnight, we heard someone outside our bedroom window. It was raining hard, but there was definitely a strange sound, and we were sure it was burglars. In a loud voice, Roger said, ''Well, I guess I'll go out and get another bottle of champagne.'' He got out of bed and crept outside. Holding an empty champagne bottle, Roger jumped around the corner and screamed.

''What?'' I asked when he came back inside, dripping wet.

''Well, after I yelled, a deer jumped five feet in the air and leaped over the fence!''

Another time I went shopping and asked Roger to make sure that my favorite gray kitty at the time was brought inside by late afternoon so the predators in the hills couldn't get her. Shortly before I got home, while working in the yard, Roger happened to look up and see an owl flying across the sky with something gray in its talons. Figuring it was the cat, he worried how I would react. Acting quickly, he then threw out the cat's bed and feeder and whatever else he thought might remind me of it. It was the old adage—out of sight, out of mind. Then Roger got out his shotgun and went looking for the owl to seek revenge. Instead of finding the owl, he found the kitten, very much alive. Roger fished the cat's belongings out of the trash and put them back in the house minutes before I pulled up the driveway.

We worried—needlessly, it turned out—about how my special would fare when it aired on December 1, 1968. This hour-long razzle-dazzle of song and dance spotlighted all the different sides of my personality. I opened riding a motorcycle along the beach, singing "Big Town," included an intimate personalized video tour through parts of Sweden, a tongue-in-cheek rendition of "Somebody's in my Orchard," and also comedy sketches with Bob Hope, Jack Benny, Danny Thomas, and Carol Burnett.

The next day the critics who'd run me out of town showed a reversal of opinion. "A bomb-load of talent exploded on the tube last night," *The Hollywood Reporter* announced, adding that what was more noticeable was "the manner in which [Ann-Margret] appeared to be enjoying herself while doing something she likes." That part made me particularly happy, because it was true.

Afterward, though, I stepped straight into a more serious role, rehearsing with Bob Hope for his annual Christmas show in Vietnam. In size and scope, this was completely unlike my first trip in Southeast Asia. The production was mammoth, a Broadway production in scope. We also had elaborate security. We opened in Saigon before an audience of twenty-thousand.

We might've been shielded from the bullets, but not their effect. I walked through combat hospitals and visited with the wounded soldiers, smiling, thanking the bandaged guys lying in bed, hoping they couldn't see how upset I was for them. I remember asking about soldiers whom I'd met the previous day, and finding out they'd been killed in combat hours after we'd shaken hands.

It was an emotionally numbing experience. I held on tightly to Roger. After returning home, I suffered nightmares for six months, thinking about what those brave men and women endured. I have a pain in my heart to this day— and always will.

26

ROGER AND ALLAN, FIRMLY IN CONTROL AS MY MANagers, felt it was time to shed my old agent. So I signed on Sue Mengers, a smart, ambitious woman who was then well on her way to becoming a force in the industry. Sue gained my confidence with her clear understanding of my career drive and belief in my ability. She sympathized with what I'd been through and offered a vision of the future. She also had a strong supporter in Jack Gilardi, my dear friend, who offered to help.

"That'd be great," Sue told Jack. "She'd like you not to forget to bring a corsage to the prom."

Was there going to be a prom again? Sue certainly thought so. Allan and Roger did, too. But they didn't hide the fact that things were going to be done differently. This time around I wasn't the new fresh face everyone wanted for their movie. This time around I was going to have to do things I hadn't done before. I was going to have to prove myself.

"TV specials are one thing," Sue said. "Your show was terrific. But movies are another ball game. I don't know if you've ever auditioned, or when the last time was, but you're gonna have to do it. You're gonna have to put everything on the line."

No one's ever forced me to do anything. I wouldn't have been in Sue's office if I wasn't willing to do just that.

Meanwhile, Roger took care of every detail of our lives, shielding me from everything that didn't include performing. He answered calls, dealt with agents, read the scripts, and oversaw the shows. He made sure situations were comfortable for me, by prepping me. During shows, he always watched from behind the curtain. He was totally, wonderfully willing to do anything to make me happy and advance my career. I felt sheltered and very lucky. I didn't have to worry about anything except doing my best.

Nor could Roger take anything for granted, which meant I didn't either. After we performed at the Riviera in February, Roger accepted a lucrative offer to play the Orient, something we wouldn't have agreed to if not for the money. The tour featured just two dancers, including Walter Painter, who was plucked from the chorus of the Riviera show and made choreographer, my conductor, Lenny Stack, and Roger as emcee.

The tour was a bumpy ride. In Singapore, Roger's old series *77 Sunset Strip* still played weekly and his popularity was so overwhelming we drafted him into the show. After dusting off bits from his old Hungry i days, we dueted on ''Little Green Apples,'' which has turned out to be the only time we've performed together over the years.

On the flight to Seoul, I became deathly ill with food poisoning. A female army doctor injected me with something that generated a miraculous recovery and allowed me to do the show that night. But there was no such shot in Manila, where we played a small bar that catered to a military base, and we lost out to the Happy Hour.

Somehow, we were able to laugh about all this long after we returned home and began work on my second TV special, which featured both Dean Martin and Lucille Ball as guests. I'd been a big admirer of Dean's and Lucy's for years.

Lucy was as expected—funny, warm, helpful, and just plain fun. Lucy and I did a song-and-dance number called ''Autograph Annie and Celebrity Lu,'' a parody of autograph hounds. Afterward, we had to go into the recording studio and dub the vocals. Lucy was scheduled first; we wanted to be as respectful of her time as possible. She didn't need long, a few takes. We thanked her and said she didn't have to stick around any longer. But she sat down and lit a cigarette.

''I'm not going anywhere,'' she announced. ''I'm just

going to sit and wait and see how long it takes Junior to do this.''

Then Lucy flashed me a big grin. A friendly challenge.

"Okay," I said, and then I did my part and luckily I nailed it in just one take.

"The kid's all right!" Lucy said.

We laughed then and shared quite a few laughs over the years. About a month before she passed away in 1989, Roger made a videotape of "Autograph Annie and Celebrity Lu" as a present. I called her to see if I could bring it to her personally. When I arrived, she'd just washed her hair, which prompted a spate of jokes about redheads. We reminisced for a while, then as I left, Lucy stopped me in my tracks with a risqué remark about one of the men I'd dated before Roger.

"Lucy!" I said aghast. "I'm shocked. I can't believe you said that."

"At my stage in the game, I can say anything I want," she said laughing, and then she walked back inside, smiling to herself.

The special, which aired December 6, 1969, scored well in the ratings and earned great reviews. It also generated a certain buzz. Then Sue Mengers heard that Stanley Kramer, who'd directed classics like *On the Beach, Judgment at Nuremberg,* and *Guess Who's Coming to Dinner,* was about to begin a picture, *R.P.M.,* with Anthony Quinn. But the female lead had yet to be cast. Stanley, though, was somewhat hesitant about seeing me until our mutual friend Jack Gilardi persuaded him otherwise. And, once Stanley heard me read, he gave me the part, which turned out to be a mixed blessing.

My role called for partial nudity, which, by 1970, was hardly unusual in the movies. I had certainly been told in advance that in one scene I would have to stroll across the room in a sweater that was pretty see-through, and that in another I would perform a partially nude scene with Tony Quinn. I felt comfortable that these scenes made sense, and weren't needless sensational peeks, and, I must admit, I agreed to them. For one thing, I accepted this as a norm in filmmaking. But rational thought didn't matter once the filming started.

In fact, I decided to fight. Nudity, I argued to the director, wasn't as sexy to me as a man and a woman wearing something suggestive, something that hinted at sensuality but maintained the mystery and allure that generated the passion. It's not necessary, I debated, to show it *all* to deliver the message.

Nobody bought my argument, and I found myself at a crossroads. People who saw the performer astride a motorcycle on stage, hair wild, body contorting, could not have envisioned the shy woman inside. By now, I had reconciled myself to the two Ann-Margrets, and I had resolved not to overanalyze the situation. The outside world, however, figured I was a seductress, an extrovert with few inhibitions, and who could blame them? No one could have imagined that undressing was a big deal to me, but it was. Given my strict upbringing, it was a *very* big deal. And I made that point clear to Stanley and Roger, both of whom saw my stress level rise.

I promptly took the edge off my nerves with alcohol, just as my father used to take a drink at night to relax after suffering his stroke. Neither of us realized what we were doing to ourselves. Furthermore, for me there was a subtle, psychological change under way. Whereas at first I'd liked the confidence alcohol had given me, now I began to anticipate my drink at lunch or with dinner as if it were medicine. Perhaps I had begun to perceive my drinking as wrong, but I still couldn't stop myself.

Stanley Kramer dealt with my fear and hesitancy like a coach. He constantly questioned me, needled, prodded, dug, poked, and searched for psychological pressure points in me, until he knew exactly how to trigger whatever emotional response he wanted. Stanley delved into my background, upbringing, family, relationships, always goading and spurring me, building up to what he referred to as "Number One."

Both of us knew the scenes *that* referred to. I spent the night before and the morning of the nudity takes trying to prepare for the ordeal. Roger assured everyone I was okay, but two hours before the scenes, I balked. I worried about what my family would think when they saw the film. Finally, I told Roger I wasn't going to do it.

"That's not an option," he said.

"But I can't," I said trembling.

Roger prodded, but didn't push. He knew that he just had to hold firm.

"Ann-Margret, we've had this talk before. This picture is important for you to do, and from the start you knew it required partial nudity and you agreed. Isn't that true?"

"Yes."

"So what are you going to do?"

It was the last day. Stanley had purposely saved the most sensitive scene for last. The set was closed. Stanley primed my emotions by reminding me of the one and only bad fight I'd had with my father many years before. My tears flowed, and I forgot about my inhibitions and got into the character. As I walked around the set, partially nude, Anthony Quinn was totally professional. We did the scene several times before Stanley was happy, and somehow I got through it. But the moment Stanley yelled cut, I covered myself and disappeared into my dressing room, relieved that it was over. I supposed I had achieved some psychological milestone and I should have felt pleased. But I will never shake my innate reserve and prudishness no matter what I do.

Eighteen days after *R.P.M.* wrapped, I began working on another feature, *C.C. and Company,* the story of a New York fashion designer who becomes involved with a gang of motorcycle outlaws. On paper, it sounded like the kind of exploitative film I was trying to avoid. With one big exception.

The movie had been Allan's idea and Roger wrote the script. Furthermore, Roger and Allan's newly formed company, Rogallan, was producing. "The name of our game is star!" Allan chirped to a reporter during the production. In other words, they'd created this film as a vehicle for me, a throwback to Hollywood's golden days when studios developed projects for specific personalities.

Roger and Allan were not total neophytes at this. During

one of my Italian movies, Roger had passed the time by writing a script, and then Allan had helped sell it to Clint Eastwood without ever revealing the writer's name. Later, Allan bought a coming-of-age script about three boys who fall in love with a prostitute, and he asked Roger to fix it. The rewrite, titled *The First Time,* starred Jacqueline Bisset.

For two guys without any significant experience when they began managing me, they learned quickly, resonating with ideas and acting forcefully. When they produced *The First Time,* they joked about Roger having previous experience as a producer. As a child, he'd created animal shows in his backyard and then staged acts in high school. With *C.C. and Company,* though, Roger and Allan entered the big time. They generated lots of attention when they got the New York Jets superstar quarterback Joe Namath to costar in the movie.

"He's so hot now," Allan enthused.

"But can he act?" Roger wondered.

"Sure. He's a natural, really charismatic," Allan said. "The combination of Joe and Ann-Margret is going to be terrific."

"The chemistry is perfect," Roger agreed.

That's what I mean about them; they had enthusiasm, trust, and absolute faith they could pull off anything they planned through quintessential teamwork. Once we started production, which took place in Tucson, where Roger had gone to college, their passion translated into pure fun. Allan threw parties at the drop of a hat. The sun's come up? Great, let's sit by the pool and party. It's cooling off, we've got to celebrate. Joe was unrelentingly cheerful, and many of his Jets teammates visited the set and treated the shoot like a party.

One day a real gang of bikers crashed the set. I hid in my dressing room until Roger escorted me out.

"It's okay, honey," he said with a half laugh. "All they want is your autograph. They came to meet you."

When it came time for me to do the scene in which Joe and I make love on a living-room floor, it wasn't any easier than it had been in *R.P.M.*; it was *never* easy for me. With Joe, who was so kind and understanding, and my friend

Seymour Robbie, a director who had worked with Roger when he was acting in *Mr. Roberts,* I got through it. Instead of torturing myself for days before the scene, I needed only four hours of coaxing from Roger.

Roger came under a lot of criticism then for having written a nude scene for his wife. Oddly enough, at the time, I saw that the scene was important to the film and we didn't argue about it. Of course, that doesn't mean we always agreed. Our relationship was sometimes complicated by the various roles we played. I'd have to discern if his opinions were said as my manager, producer, or husband. If I felt he was putting my personal needs aside for commercial reasons, I would protest. But, generally, I felt that Roger tried hard to do the right thing as a husband and as my professional lifeline. He was able to put his own needs, his own acting career aside and care only for mine. And that is rather remarkable. I needed that and wanted it. I was very old-fashioned in those days, despite all the news about feminism. I preferred my man strong and in charge. I suppose that sounds rather weak, but I was then. I wanted to be in a protected world or I couldn't function.

When *C.C. and Company* finished, Roger and I returned to our home. I had worked too hard and drunk too much. In fact, my drinking was becoming habitual. Not that it interfered with my performance or other activities. But in retrospect I'd begun using alcohol as a crutch to numb the tingling I felt inside, the fear.

Did it have a noticeable effect on my behavior? Not yet. But it would, pretty soon.

27

I MANAGED A BRIEF RESPITE BEFORE MY AGENT AN-
nounced she had another project waiting. Sue wanted to put
me in a Western that was being cast with lots of big-name
stars. Roger admired the script and liked the actors who'd
already committed, but his instinct told him not to accept.
R.P.M. had earned me good notices and reminded mainstream audiences I was still out there. *C.C. and Company*
was due out in October. He believed in the work and
wanted to see the reaction.

Sue thought he was making a big mistake. She warned
him not to wait too long and urged him to be practical.

"Look," she said with annoyance. "Mike Nichols isn't
exactly calling with an offer."

That admonition was a blessing in disguise. A week
later—to the day—Mike Nichols called Sue with an offer.
More like a half offer. But it turned out to be the break
we'd hoped for.

Carnal Knowledge chronicled the romantic intimacies of
two men as they matured from college through adulthood.
It was a brutal, tragic dissection of sexual attitudes and
relationships.

Written by Jules Feiffer, with Mike Nichols directing, it
was an actor's dream, and three of the four parts had already been cast: Jack Nicholson, Candice Bergen, and Art
Garfunkel. Mike had been stymied in his search for an actress to play Bobbie Templeton, a sexpot betrayed by her
sensuality and her men. He'd already considered eighteen
actresses; then Kathleen Tynan, the wife of theater critic
Kenneth Tynan, suggested me to Mike over lunch one day.

Mike called Sue Mengers and sent her a script with one

caveat. He wasn't going to send me a ticket to New York to audition. But if I happened to be there, he'd be very interested in meeting with me. Roger booked a flight immediately.

The script for *Carnal Knowledge* was one of the best I'd ever read—riveting, devastating, tragic, emotional, and at least for me, terrifying because of what giving life to Bobbie would require. I'm not a technical actress. I can't turn it on and off. I'm all raw emotion and nerves. I literally become the person I'm playing. Bobbie Templeton was a case.

At my first meeting with Mike, he told me that he remembered liking me in *Kitten with a Whip*. A nice way to begin, it immediately buoyed my confidence. He asked Laurence Luckinbill, a wonderfully talented New York actor married to Lucie Arnaz, to read with me, and we worked on two scenes. Mike listened carefully, noticing everything. He suggested several different ways that I could play Bobbie, and afterward said, "You did fine. I'd like you to test."

We stayed in New York another week, and for the test, I performed one scene three times. Again Mike asked me to give Bobbie's character several twists, creating a new personality each time. The test was long, challenging, taxing, and stimulating, and when I finished, I was thoroughly exhausted. Mike complimented my work, which I took as an encouraging sign.

I was changing in my dressing room when there was a knock on the door. Mike entered, with something to discuss. He had been impressed with my test, though I did not learn that until later. He told me he realized how hypersensitive I was, how frail I could be, how exposed and fragile I was compared to most people. He also knew the depth to which I'd have to reach into my soul in order to play Bobbie. I'd have to expose myself—emotionally *and* physically. He wondered how far I was willing to go. If I was up for the challenge. He'd come to my dressing room to issue another test, a test of a different nature that would help answer a few of his questions.

"You know what's required of this part?" he asked.

"Yes," I said. "It's frightening."

I knew what he was hinting at, and I didn't mind side-stepping the issue. But he got to the point.

"Ann-Margret, you're going to have to reveal yourself—take off your clothing—in the movie. You've read the script. Obviously, nudity is integral to playing Bobbie. Will you be able to do that?"

"If I get the part—yes," I answered.

We shared a cab back to my hotel, where he wished me luck as I got out. Three days later I was in the suite while Roger and Allan were at meetings, when there was a knock on the door. A delivery man handed me a dazzling bouquet of flowers and a nice bottle of chilled champagne. For some reason I assumed this gift was a surprise diversion from Roger and Allan to relieve the incredible suspense of waiting to hear from Mike. But then I opened the card and read: "Jules loves you, I love you, you have a job . . . Mike Nichols."

My scream filled the room. I wished I had someone with whom I could share this exceptional news. Then the phone rang. My friend Billy Friedkin, the director, heard I was in town and called to say hi. The timing was too unbelievable.

"Billy, guess what just happened?" I squealed.

"What?" he asked confused.

"Mike Nichols just sent a note! I got the role in his new film *Carnal Knowledge!*" I was ecstatic, jumping up and down. "I'm so excited."

"That's great! I was just calling to say hi to you and Roger and Allan. I'm thrilled for you. Congratulations."

After we returned home, I anticipated a restful couple of months before *Carnal Knowledge* began. However, I couldn't rest. The strain of going nonstop, of being on a treadmill, of juggling one project after another as well as the pressure finally started catching up to me. I wasn't even aware of it. Who had the time to notice? I signed a lucrative contract to do eight weeks at the International Hotel in Vegas, and in preparation Allan exercised his extravagant creative vision by taking over production tasks for what would be one of my most spectacular, lavish shows. It was scheduled to open right after *Carnal* finished. I had another TV special to think about. It was a lot to handle.

For the first time since I'd taken my first sip of wine, my drinking became a topic of discussion between me and Roger. He had observed my escalating alcohol consumption over the years, but had chosen not to make an issue of it, since it seemed to make me braver and more outgoing, and because it never affected my work. But now he expressed some concern, which I ignored. I might've even taken offense. But I drank more often than before, chasing after that feeling of confidence and relief alcohol had originally given me, in those early champagne days. Yet now I felt only melancholy and angst, and nothing was more frustrating. The more I craved the comfort, warmth, and security I'd once been able to get with a drink or two, the more unattainable that feeling became, and the more irritable I got. I wasn't me.

I avoided my parents, who were the foundation of my existence, and the talks Mother and I had on a daily basis dwindled to sporadic conversations. She knew something was different, something was being hidden from her, but she didn't know what.

Roger and I argued a lot—something that just didn't happen before this stressful period. Arguments would erupt over small things, nothing in particular. Often it was something precipitated by my drinking. Roger would question me. I'd feel backed into a corner. I didn't know how to fight. I didn't know how to express anger because I had grown up learning to suppress hostile feelings.

So at a certain point I'd bolt out the door, hop on my Harley, and roar down the driveway, even if it was three a.m., and it often was. I'd leave Roger's protestations behind, drowned by the deafening roar of my bike. I'd speed along Mulholland Drive going as fast as I could, exhilarated by the wind in my face and the sheer speed. I wanted to escape, to return to the simpler, happier moments in life. I'm sure what I was doing was quite self-destructive. I often roared off with a good quantity of alcohol in my bloodstream and I'm sure I must have been affected by it, though I can't honestly say I ever felt drunk or confused on the road. I just felt sad and melancholy, while Roger waited at home, terrified that I would crash.

Such was my state of mind when work began on *Carnal Knowledge* in late November 1970. I read and reread the script on the flight to Vancouver, aware that I would be emotionally taxed and drained by the task of playing Bobbie. During the three weeks of rehearsal that followed, we sat around a table—Jack, Art, Candice, me, Mike, and Jules—and experimented with the scenes, reading them one way, then another. By the end of rehearsals, I knew I was Bobbie.

I'd met women like Bobbie Templeton, sensuous and fragile. Bobbie wants to marry and have children, but the man she is obsessed with, Jonathan, turns into a madman at the thought of surrendering his freedom.

By the time shooting began, I'd crossed the psychological line that separated fantasy from reality. I became Bobbie—this pitiful woman, this doormat for abuse, who'd spent her life attracted to the wrong kind of man. I wanted to appear full and blowsy, so I put on weight; I appeared puffier, fuller. Unable to sleep at night, I took pills to knock me out. I returned from the set, wrapped myself in Roger's bathrobe, and didn't leave the hotel room until I was needed on the set. Sometimes that was days.

My life assumed an eerie parallel to the movie. At one point Bobbie despairs that she can no longer continue solely as a receptacle for Jonathan's needs, despairs over the time she spends in bed, warning, ''I'm already up to fifteen hours a day. Pretty soon it's gonna be twenty-four.'' By that time, I'd capitulated to the character. I spent hours at night pacing the bathroom, depressed, teetering on the brink of a breakdown, and hoping I made it through the movie. This was part of the metamorphosis I had to go through in order to play Bobbie. Roger and I had long ago discussed the possible changes that would ensue, the alteration of my personality. He knew that to play a character as complex as Bobbie I had to feel like her. Be her.

Roger saw himself in a support role. He had two different attitudes when it came to my work. If we were doing a stage show, he was there every second. But on a movie, he stayed away and respected that it was a dialogue between the actor and director and no place for a spouse.

During *Carnal Knowledge,* Roger saw his job was to keep me sane and happy and stable. He had a tremendous respect for what I did. I was the submissive one, the one who wanted a strong shoulder to lean on, a strong man to lead me through life. But Roger knew the type of freedom I needed as an actress, and he gave it to me. He was there to be leaned on, but not to intrude.

The others realized my sensitivity and paid special attention. I remember doing a scene in which Bobbie can't stop crying. For some reason, I couldn't force myself to cry. I couldn't connect. Then, abruptly, Jack turned on me. From behind the camera, he became Jonathan and started screaming insults, horrible things about Bobbie that caused me to burst into tears instantly.

Sometimes I needed only a nudge. In one bedroom scene, I sat on the edge of the bed with a glass of fake scotch beside me. I felt exposed and jittery. My breathing was heavy as I waited for Mike to get everything set up to his liking. He walked beside me, studied me for a moment, then put his hand very gently on top of my head and held it there for an instant—a simple, comforting gesture.

It was exactly what my father used to do when I was young and troubled by something. He might not have known what to say; however, that light touch let me know there was nothing to worry about because he was there. I tried to hold back the tears, as we hadn't discussed doing that particular scene with me crying, but I couldn't help it and sobbed softly. Mike noticed and called, "Action."

Roger monitored me with the utmost concern. *Carnal Knowledge* left me in a depressive stupor fueled by pills and alcohol.

After *Carnal* wrapped, I had less than a week to switch gears before the most ambitious, grandiose show I'd ever undertaken opened at the International Hotel in Las Vegas. I'm surprised that after three months of living as Bobbie, I could make such a change. Fortunately, I did. It had to do with control, control over Bobbie.

I told myself that I was through playing her. What I couldn't predict was that she wasn't through with me.

28

IN RETROSPECT, I THINK THE CHALLENGE OF SHIFTING from playing Bobbie to being a nightclub star once again gave me a temporary respite from my inner demons. By now, I was programmed to perform, and I was particularly excited by this new act. Allan and Ron Field, of *Cabaret* fame, came up with the idea for a show we called "AM/PM." True to their vivid imagination, "AM/PM," which debuted at the International in spring of 1971, was the most ambitious act ever staged in Vegas up to that time, with elaborate costumes and sets raising the cost to a staggering amount of money each week. We hired Ron to choreograph and direct.

It was actually a show within a show, beginning with a group of people around a piano, including Steve Martin, then an unknown comic, acting as if they were the producer, director, choreographer, and writer. They talked about what sort of a production it should be. Then I entered.

"So they want me to play the International," I said. "What're we going to do?"

Suggestions flew. With each mention of a song, such as "Side by Side by Side," one or more dancers would join me and we'd perform a snippet of the music, then ask for an opinion. We did a variety of numbers, without actually finishing an entire song. A lot of bang for the buck.

The show's second half was a musical *tour de force* through modern history. Utilizing lavish sets, eighty thousand dollars' worth of costumes, and innovative video clips, I opened as Elsie Janis singing for troops in World War I, then Dillinger's Lady in Red, Rosie the Riveter, Marilyn Monroe, and so on till I played a robot representing 1970.

Reaction to "AM/PM" was mixed. The critics loved it that we tried to pull off something totally new and different. "It was the most innovative stage performance Vegas had seen," Las Vegas critic Mark Tan wrote, "and carried off with such flair and theatrical style, it is, if anything, too much show and too much happening for an average audience to absorb, savor, and appreciate at once." But the International's management had reservations. They thought it was too Broadway and not enough nightclub.

For me, it was plain exhausting. As soon as the International engagement finished at the end of March, my body gave out. The strain of shifting from movie to nightclub act finally took its toll. In a weakened state when we left Vegas for home, I collapsed with a virus and had to be hospitalized. It was as if the dam broke. My body couldn't hold up under the stress anymore.

While in the hospital, I went through a withdrawal of sorts—no drinking or sleeping pills. It was the first time in months that I had thought of anything but work, and I got scared. I was without energy. I didn't feel like me. I wondered if I'd pushed myself too hard and too fast.

While lying in bed, I remember having a few early stirrings of motherhood. Actually, I wondered what it would be like to give birth and to raise a child. The schedule I'd been keeping was exacting a toll. Surely there was something else, something more completely fulfilling than this constant push and pressure of performing. I mentioned having a child to Roger and to my family. Roger would have been thrilled to have another child, but he knew how obsessed I was with work.

"But I'll quit," I said. "This was my final tour, my goodbye tour. You know I'm only going to work till I'm thirty-nine."

Somehow I got it into my head that I'd quit then. In those days, there wasn't much work for actresses of a certain age.

"You've said that before," he nodded.

"This time I'm serious."

I talked this way when I was tired, and now I was exhausted. I was drained of my desire.

But Roger knew me better than I did sometimes. He listened to me talk about slowing down and knew I couldn't stop. In time, despite my thoughts in the hospital, habit and temperament prevailed, and I soon plunged back into my work with the same intensity. I would worry about a child later. I was only twenty-nine, and I figured I had plenty of time. I had no idea then that I would spend many agonizing years undergoing all kinds of fertility treatments, trying to conceive. Nor did I consider what effect, if any, all the pills and alcohol would have. Like so many women, I was caught up in my own needs of the moment. I simply couldn't envision any problems later.

With *Carnal Knowledge* and my hospitalization a memory, we were back on stage, surrounded by excitement and glitter. In such a familiar setting, I was my old self, as if nothing had happened.

In April, we opened at the Fontainebleau in Miami Beach with a new show. Few places could compare to the Fontainebleau back then. The showroom held 1,000 people, and we sold out fourteen shows each week over a two-week period, shattering house records. Roger and I still can't decide which was better about our Miami stays—the wonderful audiences or eating at Joe's Stone Crab.

A funny thing happened one afternoon. While we slept in, my friend Norma looked up from the book she was reading beside the swimming pool and saw smoke billowing from the roof. It was coming from over our room. She asked the hotel operator to ring our room but was told there was a "Do Not Disturb" request on the line. So she decided to tell us herself.

Roger and I both heard the banging on the door. I rolled over and let him handle it.

"Who is it?" Roger asked groggily.

"Norma."

"What do you want?"

With smoke seeping into the hallway, Norma worried that if she yelled "Fire!" she would alarm me. Yet there was no denying the urgency.

"Come here," she said, trying not to show the panic she felt.

Roger, half asleep, wanted to know why. Finally, Norma couldn't stand it any longer and screamed, "THE HOTEL'S ON FIRE!" Well, there wasn't any mistaking that. Roger was up in a flash. As for me . . .

I never go anywhere without making sure I look presentable. Even with my husband, my friend Norma, Alan Margulies, then the entertainment director of the hotel, and a handful of firemen staring at me with mounting anxiety through a door and a hallway filling up with smoke, I have my standards. First things first, I had to put on my makeup!

We got out just fine. The fire turned out to be smoldering mattresses in a nearby storage room. And I looked great for an exhausted woman forced out of bed.

During May and June, we tackled my next TV special, *Dames at Sea*. Then on June 28, 1971, *Carnal Knowledge* opened, and I was "hot" again.

The movie, banned in Georgia, sold out in New York, and hailed in Hollywood, generated an extraordinary amount of debate among filmgoers for its raw, graphic, and unsettling script. My performance, it seemed, generated nearly as much discussion and shock. I was featured on umpteen magazine covers, including a second appearance on *Life*'s. Even the critics were kind: "It was like watching Minnie Mouse play Ophelia—brilliantly. Nobody could believe that Ann-Margret, the Swedish meatball, the thirty-year-old high school cheerleader, was actually acting," said one. Proclaimed another, "Ann-Margret acts! And the movie-going public has not been so astonished since Garbo talked!"

For me, it was very heady stuff, particularly after my recent ignominious experiences. Yet, I tried to react calmly, to take it all with a grain of salt. I was determined now to keep Hollywood in the proper perspective and not let it affect my moods. Mostly, I was happy for my parents, Roger, Allan, my friends, and everyone else who'd stuck by when the critics weren't so kind. I fell back on my typical stance, ingrained since childhood; don't boast, don't enjoy, just keep on working.

In truth, I was too busy to really focus on this shift in my fortunes. After *Carnal Knowledge* opened, I performed at the Concord Hotel in upstate New York, then did a small tour of the Playboy resorts. By the time we got back home, I wanted to disappear into my bedroom and sleep for the rest of the season. But Roger begged me to do one last interview.

"It's with CBS TV," he said. "They want to ask about making *Carnal Knowledge* and working with Mike Nichols."

Even as we got off the elevator at CBS's Television City, I was griping, "If this wasn't for Mike."

Oddly, though I didn't think about it at the time, I walked straight into a longtime fan of mine, Patsy Ng, who'd been writing me beautiful letters for years. I chalked it up to coincidence. A moment later, Ralph Edwards, the host of *This is Your Life,* introduced himself and said that he was going to interview me.

"What an interesting choice for an interviewer," I whispered to Roger.

As we walked into the studio, I never once suspected anything unusual might happen. I just wanted to do a good job and get it over with. Then Ralph Edwards came in. I switched my brain to interview mode.

"Ann-Margret?" he asked, with a sly smile.

"Yes?"

Then he paused, held out a large book, which I should've noticed earlier but didn't, and in a strong, enthusiastic, excited voice declared, "Ann-Margret Olsson Smith, *this* is your life!"

For the next half hour, I struggled to maintain my composure as the people who'd been closest and dearest to me were paraded in front of me: my mother; Uncle Calle, who'd flown in from Valsjobyn, amused at how the show's producers had tracked him down in a sauna; my godparents, Gus and Helen Randall; Holly Fitzgerald, one of my best girlfriends since elementary school; Dr. Peterman; and George Sidney, whose words echoed a faith in me that others were discovering.

After telling Mr. Edwards that the show represented only

"Part One" of my life, Mr. Sidney referred to my career and said, "I don't think it's even started. She's going to go to real great, great heights."

Maybe so. But I was also going to go to some real great lows.

29

ROGER AND I CHERISHED OUR RECLUSIVE LIFESTYLE.
Although we cover it up well, both of us are shy, private
people, soul mates who are in the limelight almost in de-
fiance of our nature. We rarely ventured out to restaurants
and almost never to Hollywood parties. Hence, few people
outside of a trusted group of friends even had a clue of our
fights over my drinking. People didn't associate Roger and
me with raised voices, slamming doors, sudden volatility.
Neither did we.

But I wasn't myself, and that changed both of us. Roger
was horrified by my drinking, by the effects alcohol had
on me. I became frightened and inconsolable at home. If
someone looked at me, I might disappear into my bedroom.
I was hurtful to those I loved, including Roger and my
mother. Roger begged me to stop drinking. One night, in
pained desperation, I screamed at Roger, "Please, don't
buy any more for the house." After one binge, I became
so sick that Roger rushed me to our physician's house. He
didn't even examine me, just let me sit until my panic dis-
sipated. Then he expressed sincere concern.

"Listen," he said. "I know a woman. She's a friend of
mine. I'd like you to meet her."

"Why?" I asked.

"For your drinking," he said.

"I don't want to meet her," I replied firmly, defiantly.
"I'm happy and healthy."

"Well, if you change your mind," he said. "Call me."

It was easy for me to fool myself. Although emotionally
out of whack, I still functioned normally. I was able to do
yet another show at the International. Roger always pos-

sessed a keen eye and even sharper instincts, and he used them to his advantage by promoting Walter Painter, who'd choreographed our Far East excursion, to director-choreographer. It was Walter's first big job. He's since won three Emmys. Roger was the company's anchor, its Rock of Gibraltar. Everyone flew around like crazy people, their imaginations soaring. Roger remained the calm center. Walter used to marvel at him and say, "When I grow up, I want to be Roger."

Marvin Hamlisch, who'd been my rehearsal pianist, took over the music, and both he and Roger wanted me to get more comfortable talking to the audience. I'd always made a few comments, but never had the confidence to engage in unscripted chit-chat. Marvin added the song "Take a Little One-Step," from *No, No, Nanette* and Walter choreographed it so that I sang from the audience and stepped from table to table talking with people.

One night, as I went from table to table, I spotted some of Elvis's guys. I thought, "How nice, they came to see my show." I worked my way back toward a booth and suddenly I knew exactly who I'd find sitting there. Sure enough, he stood and the spotlight caught his famous grin.

"Ladies and gentlemen," I said. "I'm sure you know who this is."

As the audience screamed and clapped, Elvis then improvised a short dance with me. But deliberately he threw me off track, so I whispered, "I'm going to get you for this." Elvis, though, wasn't through. As I made my way back to the front, he somehow got backstage and as I finished up, he ran on and slid halfway across the stage, stopping right at my feet. The audience went wild. Pretending it was nothing extraordinary, I said, "I didn't know you could do a knee slide." Elvis laughed harder than anyone.

Another time Roger and I arrived in Las Vegas a few days prior to an engagement and Elvis invited us to a party. When we arrived, there were about one hundred people in his enormous suite. Elvis was entertaining a few people off to the side of the living room with a sample of his karate moves. He had studied martial arts for many years and was excellent at it.

As soon as he spotted me, he got that familiar mischievous look in his eye. He knew he could have some fun.

"Hey Rusty, come over here," he called.

"Sure," I said gamely. "What do you want to do?"

Flashing his crooked grin, Elvis explained that he wanted me to stand perfectly still while he threw several karate chops my direction and showed how close he could come to my face without touching or hurting me. A mistake of a mere millimeter could kill me, injure me severely, at the least. But I trusted him implicitly.

"Now, don't move," he warned. "Don't even flinch."

"I won't," I said.

Elvis stepped back, faced me and bowed slightly, and then with lightning speed, reeled off several punches. They happened so fast I couldn't see them, although I did feel a slight breeze touch my face. Afterward, he shook his head in amazement.

"You know, you're crazy," he marveled.

"So are you," I smiled.

Roger might have been more nervous than I was, but he was amazed as well. It's a funny thing. One of the traits I love about my husband is that he was never jealous of the friendship I shared with Elvis. If it had been another old boyfriend who periodically appeared in my life, bearing flowers and gifts, I don't think he would have been as understanding. But Elvis was different, he was special, and like everyone else, Roger put Elvis in a category all his own. He knew that we had a unique understanding of each other, a bond that would never be broken, and he didn't try. In fact, he and Elvis always got on well. It allowed all of us to enjoy the few times when our lives intersected and we could amuse each other.

Toward the end of the engagement, the enormous marquee outside the hotel, which Don Rickles called "the Eye Test," advertised my appearance in giant red letters. But one day the letter P in the word PRESENT slipped off, making the sign read:

ROGER SMITH AND ALLAN CARR

resent

ANN-MARGRET

The truth was anything but. The three of us had become a cohesive team, a family. They had a right to boast, to trumpet the good job they'd done with my career, a career no one wanted to touch when they assumed control. Roger remembered one person warning him, "Look, Roger, you're in love with her. But she's just not as talented as you think!"

After *Carnal Knowledge,* though, suddenly, I was "talented" again. In January, Hollywood's Foreign Press awarded me a Golden Globe for Best Supporting Actress for the film. *Photoplay* magazine named me their "Star of the Year." Then, in February, during my regular stint at the Fontainebleau, I received a call that everyone around me said I'd get, but one that I'd never expected.

"Are you sitting down?" Warren Cowan, the president of Rogers and Cowan, my PR firm, said.

"Yes."

"You got it!"

I screamed and started to cry. Roger took the receiver.

"Congratulations. She got it. Ann-Margret was nominated for an Academy Award for *Carnal Knowledge.*"

Roger and Allan were ecstatic for all the obvious reasons. An Oscar nomination meant vindication—vindication from everyone who'd criticized me, who'd refused to answer their calls, who'd said I had no talent.

The joy I felt was very pure. I remembered how as a younger girl I'd seen the names and pictures of the nominees listed in papers and mentioned on the news. When I opened the Miami papers the next morning and saw my name up for Best Supporting Actress, I felt as if I were living out one more fabulous fantasy.

But I had little time to savor all the excitement. I jumped right into *The Train Robbers,* a fairly traditional cowboy picture starring John Wayne. When I was ten, a horse had tried to bite me at a carnival and I was scared of horses ever since. In fact, I'd never ridden again. But *The Train Robbers* was an honest-to-goodness Western and I had to ride; there was no way around it.

For three weeks before filming I received riding lessons from Chuck Heyward, an excellent horseman who'd worked as a stuntman with Duke for twenty-three years. By the time I got in front of the camera in Durango, Mexico, I felt pretty brave. But then the horse they gave me to ride wasn't the one I'd practiced on, and my confidence disappeared.

The very first shot was at midnight. We had to gallop across a patch of desert, then halt on a specific mark. By the time director Burt Kennedy yelled "action," I'd worked myself into a state, though I thought no one could tell. I was wrong. Duke rode up beside me, sipping a bottle of mineral water, as calm and at home as could be. He winked.

"Are you okay, little lady?" he asked.

Now, I'd already become acquainted with Duke—well enough to feel comfortable calling him Duke. But how do you tell John Wayne you're scared to ride? I smiled, and he offered me a sip from his water bottle; I think he noticed my hand shake while taking a drink.

"What's wrong?" he asked again.

"Well," I said, "I'm a little afraid of horses."

It was late at night. The only sounds were the muffled grunts of the horses, insect chirps, and John Wayne chuckling.

"Don't worry," he said. "Nothing's going to happen, I'll see to that."

Despite having had a cancerous lung removed earlier, Duke was still a strong, rugged, formidable man, larger-than-life and incredibly personable. He was a big teddy bear, and we got along famously. Duke gave me the confidence I lacked.

We had a very special relationship. He once told a reporter, "When I'm dead, at my funeral, I want that little lady to dance on my coffin. Because if I don't get up, then you'll know I'm really dead." Several years later, he became seriously ill. One afternoon I heard a report that he'd passed away. Instantly, I called his office and asked his secretary if it was true. She said there'd been other calls like mine.

"He just walked in," she laughed. "Would you like to talk to him?"

At Academy Awards time, April 10, 1972, we were still filming *The Train Robbers* in Durango. I wasn't the only actor working on *The Train Robbers* up for an Oscar. Ben Johnson had also been nominated in the Best Supporting category for his work in Peter Bogdanovich's *The Last Picture Show*. Duke put both of us on his private jet and wished us good luck.

I didn't expect to win. As a blanket rule, I never expect to win anything.

I said as much to the army of reporters who shoved microphones at me as Roger, Allan, and I arrived in a long, black limousine, waved to fans, then walked past the spotlights and up the red carpet. Inside, I was sick with nerves. Smiling, I clutched Roger tightly as we entered and hoped my legs didn't give out.

I had additional things to worry about. Not only was I one of the nominees, I also copresented the Cinematography Award with Screen Actors Guild President John Gavin. We had scripted lines, but when John got to the podium he picked me up and ad-libbed, "I'd like to thank the Academy for this trophy."

When Gene Hackman and Raquel Welch read the names of the nominees for Best Supporting Actress—Cloris Leachman and Ellen Burstyn, both for *The Last Picture Show;* Barbara Harris for *Who Is Harry Kellerman and Why Is He Saying Those Terrible Things About Me?;* and Margaret Leighton for *The Go-Between*—every second seemed to last an hour.

I gave myself little to no chance. Even so, every muscle in my body tightened as the envelope was opened.

"And the winner is," she said, pausing, "Cloris Leachman." I squeezed Roger's arm and put on a brave smile. Sure, I had wanted to win, but all that training in Swedish stoicism helped me through. I felt let down, but okay.

The next day, we flew back to the set. Ben had won, and I was so happy for him. Duke congratulated both of us. I don't know what he said to Ben. But later, he took me aside, wrapped his big, strong arms around me, smothering me in his bearlike clasp, and put the whole thing in perspective.

"The hell with those trophies," he said, looking directly into my eyes. "Little lady, you've got something more special than an award. You've got the ability to make people happy. That tells me you're going to be around a long time."

"Thank you," I smiled.

"It took me forty-one years to get a goddamned Academy Award," he continued. "You've got plenty of time. So what do you say we go back and finish making this movie?"

30

THE PHONE CALL CAME WHILE I WAS IN A MOTEL room doing a scene for *The Outside Man,* a French-American thriller. Standing in a silk jersey minidress and stark white-blond wig, which made me feel anything but myself, I had the impression—a fleeting impression—that I was dreaming the call, that my mother would call back with completely different news. But I couldn't sustain that for long. The truth was that my father had cancer, and that it had already spread.

I broke into tears after hanging up. Roger tried to console me, and makeup artist George Masters paced nervously, wishing he could do something more to help me than reapply my makeup. Director Jacques Deray suggested putting off the scene for several days to let me devote attention to Daddy. I thanked him, but declined. I knew about budgets and schedules. I didn't want to be responsible for any delays.

Somehow I finished out the day, then rushed to St. Vincent's Hospital without changing out of my costume. Daddy was still groggy. Lying in bed, he did a pretty good job at covering up his anger and disappointment over his biopsy results.

"What happened to your hair?" he asked, unable to take his eyes off my white-blond wig.

As I stared at my father and tried to make conversation, I knew I couldn't deal with the reality of his illness. Mother might've been the source of most of the wisdom in my life, but Daddy was my rock, my anchor, the root of my strength. I'd inherited good and bad from him. Even though I was married, I still considered him central to the way I related to the world. He was my father and I was his little girl.

Roger and I made the drive home in silence while I replayed memories I had of Daddy: spotting him on the pier after the *Gripsholm* docked in New York; going to Radio City Music Hall that night; recuperating from his fall; driving five hundred miles to my first singing job at the Muehlebach Hotel in Kansas City; admitting, despite Mother's contrary opinion, that Roger might just be an okay man . . .

In the days that followed I vowed not to give up hope, not to let myself think about Daddy not being there. I tried concentrating on work. Roger and Allan had thought *The Outside Man* would be another chance to grow as an actress, but I barely made it through the picture. I literally pulled the lines out of me, forced myself to perform, but everyone knew how sad and depressed I was.

In private, I felt myself losing control. Roger didn't know what to do with me. I reached a point where my days and nights blended into one continuous, foggy state of inebriation. I'd drink a fifth of scotch, pass out, wake up, drink some more, and pass out again. I suffered periods that I couldn't remember.

One night I came out of the bedroom in a desperate search for Roger. I didn't know why. It was an impulse. I urgently needed to see him but couldn't explain why. My clothes were disheveled, my hair a mess. I heard his voice, and then found him in the living room. But I couldn't get myself to enter the room. Instead, I peered around the corner, frightened and embarrassed. In my own house, I didn't want anybody to see me for fear they might see into me.

"Ann-Margret?" he asked.

I didn't answer; I couldn't. Roger looked at me with concern and fear. I looked at him with just one emotion—terror. A moment later, I fled back to the bedroom. For a short while, the bedroom became my private hideout, and I was afraid to go out.

In summer 1972, I made a trip to Durango to promote *The Train Robbers*. Needless to say, I didn't want to, preferring to remain in my bedroom. My arm rarely left my husband's side. If I was shaky at home, I was ten times shakier outside that comfort zone. At the hotel, I got sick.

The hotel's doctor examined me. He thought it might be the flu or some such virus. Nothing serious. Roger called our personal physician at home just to be on the safe side and filled him in. The next day I called our doctor, described how I felt and then stopped in mid-sentence. I quit pretending.

"Remember that friend you once told me about?" I asked in a little girl's soft voice I could summon when I wanted.

"Yes," he said.

"Well, I think I'd like to meet her."

"Here's her number," he said. "You make the call."

But I didn't. Not right away. Several days passed. We returned home and, once again, I locked myself into the bedroom. Usually, I liked to unpack our luggage right away, never entrusting it to anyone else. But this time it stayed in the entry hall, unopened, for four days.

I can't remember what made me finally look up the phone number and call. Self-preservation, I think. I detested the thought of becoming a victim.

"Kathleen?" I asked in a tentative, shaky whisper.

Roger looked on proudly. He never believed that I was going to make that call. He'd figured an accident would have to precipitate it. Either that or something worse. He didn't think I'd ever wake from the stupor.

"Yes?" Kathleen, this stranger, answered.

"This is Ann-Margret Smith," I said. "We have a mutual doctor friend and he told me to call you?"

Everything was a question.

"I know," she said. "I'd love to meet you."

"Yes, that would be good," I said. "We'll arrange a time that is good for both of us?"

"That would be great," she said. "Just tell me how to get to your house."

I gave directions up the canyon, then hung up. I'd neglected to set an exact day and time with her, but thought, Oh, well, I'll call back. We'll get together in a few days. Imagine, then, my surprise when less than two hours later, two women, Kathleen and her friend Muriel, pulled into the driveway and introduced themselves to Roger, who was standing outside with Steven Gottlieb, our attorney's brother. Roger was grateful to see Kathleen and Muriel. But he took one look at them, these two very proper women, elegantly dressed, and said to himself, "There's no way Ann-Margret's going to listen to them."

Kathleen had her own doubts, she confided in me later. She thought, "Here's this woman who has a beautiful house, a loving husband, and a career that's going better than ever. She's doing just fine. How am I going to tell her that her life is unmanageable?"

Then she walked into the house. She saw our unopened luggage, the disarray. Next, she met me, staring at her with fear. As Kathleen recalls, she looked into my eyes and thought, "They're dead. Her life *is* unmanageable."

For the next few hours, the three of us talked and sipped tea in the living room. Kathleen had a comforting presence. She made several insightful observations that immediately put me at ease. She let me know that I wasn't a "bad person." In fact, by telling me about her own experiences as a recovering alcoholic, I realized she understood what I was going through, the powerlessness and the shame that I felt. I identified with so much.

"You don't have to live this way anymore," she said in her soft, but firm voice. "There is a better way."

She saw the inquisitive look in my eyes, a look that revealed a glimmer of hope that life could be good again.

Kathleen mentioned that she and a group of people were meeting the following night at the home of another one of her friends, and she, Kathleen, was going to speak.

"Yes?" I said. "About what?"

"My life, some experiences I've had," she said. "I think you might find it interesting."

"Really?"

"Why don't you join us," she said without the inflection of a question.

I was nailed. Kathleen sensed how much I wanted help and knew how powerless I was to do anything about it.

The following evening I went to hear Kathleen speak. It was the first time I had been to such a gathering, and I sat in the back, shaking and embarrassed. I wore a black dress and black wig, and tied a black scarf around my head. I slipped on a pair of dark shades. Everyone was so nice and understanding and sympathetic, especially when it was my turn to introduce myself.

"Hi," I said. "I'm Ruth."

Everyone replied, "Hi, Ruth."

I left that meeting realizing that I did, as Kathleen had said, have a choice. All my life, I have had the enthusiasm of a child, the strength and determination of an ox, but also an undiluted innocence. I have always been a happy person. I could continue being miserable and hurting everyone that I loved, or I could finally make a decision to stop. It wasn't that hard a choice to make.

Two days later I went to another meeting, this time without camouflaging myself in black clothing. I felt no need. I'd already admitted I was powerless over my addiction. I'd made steps toward discarding my life of denial. And I'd accepted that, although my battles weren't finished, I could at least mount a different fight.

Those few days were a private nightmare. I went cold turkey, and for four days and nights my nerves rattled against the surface of my skin. Ordinarily when people detoxify their system from alcohol or drugs, they're put in the hospital and brought down slowly. But Kathleen wanted me to experience the really awful shock of my body returning to normal, and I did. I got sick. I was on edge. I endured the shakes and sweats. I didn't sleep for four days or nights. Kathleen, her husband, who is a physician, and Roger supported and tried to comfort me around the clock. Kathleen told me that when my body was tired enough, I would sleep, and finally, mercifully, I did.

It was slightly better, but not much, when I woke. It was all extremely difficult. But eventually I said, "Hey, if I can do this, if I can say no, there's nothing I can't do. Nothing in the world." What if something frightens me? "Big deal," I say. "I'll just take it one step at a time . . . one day, one hour, one moment."

Whatever it takes. If it doesn't kill me, it can only make me stronger.

31

I HAD STOPPED DRINKING, AND I FELT STRONG AND IN control. My eyes were clear for the first time in months, and I was trim and happy. Roger and I had stopped fighting and I was sure I had conquered my problem, which turned out to be false confidence. And I was ready to give my all to helping Daddy.

At first, I tried taking care of him at our house. We got hospital equipment and set up everything he needed. We hired a full-time nurse. I was determined to do everything in my power to return him to health, and failing that, to make him as comfortable as possible.

Mother and I took turns being with Daddy. I kept up nonstop conversation, sang him songs and talked about shows, movies, relatives, anything I could think of that might alleviate the pain he suffered or at least distract him. But after several months, we transferred him to a convalescent home. Daddy was getting worse and needed more care than I could give him.

I felt guilty, as if I'd failed. But even from his bed, Daddy remained strong, a voice of reason.

"You can't worry every second," he told me. "You've done everything possible. It will be better."

At the same time, I plunged into rehearsals for a totally new nightclub act, which was the best possible distraction for me. Although "AM/PM" received critical acclaim, and it was a show I loved to do, it was not a financial success for us. Roger then started producing all of my stage shows, and found he had a real talent for it. My nightclub career now became extremely profitable.

Marvin Hamlisch, who coproduced with Roger, selected

a batch of new songs—"I'll Get By," "You'll Never Know," "Time After Time," and "Someone to Watch Over Me"—and had us work out the arrangements at his apartment. Then we put in the dances.

Everyone worked so hard to make this show great. Marvin and Walter and costume designer Bob Mackie and the cast of seemingly thousands who appeared in the show all talked about making this the quintessential nightclub act, the production by which all others would be measured. The effort, combined with the glitz of the show itself, generated incredible excitement.

I remember someone saying, "Ann-Margret, we want to make you the Queen of Las Vegas."

There was no question I would rise to new heights with the innovative opener Roger had dreamt up by fashioning the stage as a carnival. The dancers wore masks that turned their faces into bizarre animals and creatures of the night. A giant harlequin was positioned at the side of the stage, its hand a platform that would lower me from twenty-two feet above the ground while I sang Eric Clapton's "After Midnight."

We tested the stunning effect a number of times prior to the show's debut at the Sahara Hotel in Lake Tahoe September 1972. Then, Roger coached the hotel's stagehands, making sure they understood how the platform operated, which was actually quite simple. Both ends of the platform were attached by guide wires to a single pipe above the stage and raised and lowered like scenery.

It worked without a hitch during rehearsals and several performances. During one show, Roger observed the platform rocking a bit as it was raised. It bumped some wires on each side, but it didn't interfere with anything. Nor did it pose a danger. He pointed it out to several stagehands, but only so they'd be aware.

Up to that point, the most difficult part of the engagement had been trying to help our children get ready for school. Jordan happened to be with us, in Tahoe, vacationing. Dallas was camping in the area. Back home, Tracey was about to start a new private school and was nervous about the change. Roger wanted to accompany her that first day.

"I'll fly out tomorrow," he said. "I'll be back the next morning."

That was on September 9, 1972.

"Okay," I said.

"But that means I'm going to miss one show. I'm not going to be here. How do you feel about that?"

Roger had never missed one of my performances, or giving me my three Swedish good-luck kicks before every performance, then waited stage left. Despite all my superstitions about routines, I didn't mind. Family came first. It was more important for him to assist Tracey.

After he left for L.A., I spent the rest of the day resting, preserving my voice, visiting with friends, and then going downstairs to my dressing room, applying makeup, getting dressed, and just preparing mentally for the performances.

The early show was as smooth as all the others. Yet without anyone telling me, somebody changed the rigging on my platform between shows. They put the front of the platform on one pipe, the back on another. Instead of one pipe, there were now two. They believed that would eliminate a minor sway, make it work better, and help them raise the platform more smoothly.

As I stepped onto the platform in preparation for the twelve-thirty show, I heard our friends Mitzi McCall and Charlie Brill, the comedy team who opened for me, go into their final bit. All around me, the dancers and musicians took their positions. I nodded to the stagehands and they grabbed their guide wires and took me up into the air.

I got up about twenty-two feet into the air—almost to the top. The curtain parted slightly as Charlie and Mitzi left the stage. Mitzi, whose zipper had broken, was easing off so no one could see the back of her dress. At that moment, the pipe balancing the front part of the harlequin's hand went out of synch with the one in back. Suddenly, the platform tipped, wobbled, bounced, and flipped upside down. All I remember is the start of the fall and seeing the floor coming toward me. Whatever else I know of the incident is what people have told me.

Charlie remembers hearing a crack, then a scream that

came from one of my singers who saw me fall and hit the stage.

Walter Painter, seated in the audience, heard her say, "Oh my God, she fell," and thought how silly for her to be standing so close to a live mike.

Jordan, who was downstairs in my dressing room, heard it and immediately knew who it was.

Then there was an announcement over the house PA: "Is there a doctor in the house?"

Unconscious, I was sprawled out under the fabric of my yellow chiffon dress, lying facedown, crumpled and broken. Walter, realizing something was dreadfully amiss, streaked backstage and hovered over me. A pool of blood formed under my head and flowed onto the stage. The hotel nurse appeared. Then a doctor materialized from the audience. Walter asked what we should do and the doctor said to turn me over.

"Are you sure you're a doctor?" he asked emphatically. "Are you sure? Because I'm going to do what you say, and you better know what you are talking about."

"Turn her over," he said.

The nurse rolled me over and took my pulse.

"We're losing her!" she screamed. "We're losing her!"

For several moments, people thought I was going to die. Walter's assistant, Bobby Thompson, dashed into the huddle, having remembered there was a wire hanger in the hood of my cape, and pulled it off my neck. My foot moved.

"It's coming back," the nurse said. "I feel her pulse getting stronger."

"Somebody get scissors," another person yelled, figuring they should cut the hanger away entirely.

One of my dancers took off and jumped down ten stairs to get scissors and in the process broke his leg.

While we waited for an ambulance, my friend Marcia sprinted to a phone and called Roger at home in L.A. He happened to be with her then husband, Daniel Gottlieb, our lawyer. At first, Roger thought she was joking when she said that I'd had a terrible fall.

"Don't kid around," he snapped.

Marcia burst into tears, and he realized it really was a true emergency.

"I don't know what's wrong," she said, sobbing. "She's on the stage. Not moving. Blood's coming out of her mouth, her ears. It's horrible. You have to get up here and do something."

It was almost one a.m., which was too late for Roger to catch a commercial flight. It was also too late to rent a plane. Neither Roger nor Daniel had any idea of what to do, but both knew they had to get to Lake Tahoe right away. Roger still occasionally flew his own planes, renting them from an airfield at the Burbank Airport, so he and Daniel rushed there, only to find it closed. But Roger knew it was possible to start some small planes without a key; all you needed was an unlocked door. With a light rain coming down, they climbed a chain-link fence, made it over barbed wire, and frantically checked planes until they found one that was both open and filled with gas.

As they took off, neither Roger nor Daniel thought about the fact that they were stealing a plane. They didn't care. Roger flew most of the way under heavy clouds, dangerously low, without any help from air-traffic control, until he found an opening. He gambled there'd be a clearing above Lake Tahoe. Luckily, there was, and the moon's reflection on the water guided him in.

On the ground, they sped to the hospital and corralled the doctors who were treating me.

"She's still unconscious," the doctor informed them. "She's in a coma."

"I want to see her," Roger said.

Though briefed on my condition, he still wasn't prepared for what he saw in intensive care. My face was collapsed and swollen beyond recognition. Numerous bones in my face and above my eye were either broken or fractured. My jaw was broken in two places. My left arm was broken and looked terrible. There was a huge gash on my knee, which had split open, like a splattered tomato. The doctors feared I'd never dance again—*if* I survived.

"What can you do? What are you going to do?" Roger asked them, holding back tears.

First they needed to stabilize me, then they'd start repairing the broken bones in my face. Roger and Daniel gazed at me while listening to the doctors. Roger was ready to say okay, just fix everything, and make her better. But then Daniel interrupted. Noticing that somehow the skin on my face was unbroken, he asked if the surgery they planned would leave scars, and, if so, was it possible to go through my mouth.

"In other words," he said, "do the surgery without cutting her cheek. Leaving the skin unmarked."

They said no.

Daniel looked at Roger, one of those lawyerly looks suggesting they take a step backward and think before reacting solely on emotion. Daniel remembered an article he'd read on facial surgery that had mentioned going through the mouth. He and Roger talked and decided to call their physicians to find the names of plastic surgeons who could do the surgery without slicing my cheek.

Though it was after three a.m., they started calling doctors in New York and L.A. Two names kept coming up. Dr. Tom Rees in New York and Dr. Frank Ashley, at UCLA. Somehow they got ahold of Dr. Ashley, told him what had happened, explained what they wanted, and he said, yes, he could do the operation through the mouth.

"You get ready," Roger told him. "I'll get Ann-Margret back to Burbank and have an ambulance meet us."

The Lake Tahoe doctors objected when Roger told them that he'd hired an ambulance plane to take me back to L.A. They told him flat out that he was jeopardizing my life by moving me. I was unconscious. What did they think the changing pressure of an airplane was going to do?

"She could die," they told him. "And you'll be responsible for her death."

One of the doctors called the owner of the ambulance plane Roger had hired and explained the situation. He scared them, warning that they'd be liable, and they canceled the plane.

Roger, infuriated, decided to proceed anyway. Despite doctors' warnings that he was going to kill me before I left the hospital, he and Daniel picked me up, ignoring the protests of the nurses, slowly carried me out to a car, and then drove to the airport where they'd parked their stolen plane, a six-seater, small and cramped. In order to fit me in, they ripped out five of the seats, tossing them on the tarmac, and then gingerly placed me on the floor. They immobilized me as best they could by packing each side with sleeping bags borrowed from Jordan and Dallas.

Just as they finished, a doctor sprinted onto the airfield to make a final, futile plea to stop. Roger started the engines, screamed at him to get out of the way, and taxied onto the runway, while Daniel sat on the floor holding my head as still as possible.

Both men were scared out of their minds. They knew the risky nature of the flight, but they were determined to get me to UCLA Medical Center. Because of the bad weather, the flight was bumpy and Roger changed altitudes more often than he would've if the air had been clear. He didn't even want to think about what the air pressure was doing to me in this unpressurized cabin. Roger looked back at Daniel, who held me gently, and saw tears running down his face. I remained motionless, oblivious to everything.

An ambulance waited on the runway as Roger landed the plane. He taxied right to it, and the attendants lifted me out and in seconds sped off.

As the ambulance disappeared, Roger and Daniel watched. They hoped they'd done the right thing. Daniel contacted the plane's owner and told him what happened. Until then, he hadn't even known the plane was missing. Though shocked, he seemed grateful that he could contribute something to this terrible drama. Roger then set off for the hospital. Earlier, he'd informed my mother of the accident and told her not to worry, that I'd be just fine. As he drove to meet me, he prayed that he was right.

32

FOR TWO DAYS, I LAY BANDAGED AND UNCONSCIOUS at UCLA Medical Center as Dr. Ashley took X rays and pondered the best course of action. Then, in an operation lasting five hours, he reconstructed my shattered cheekbone, fitting the fifty small bone fragments around a tiny ball of string that had been coated with penicillin and stuck inside my cheek. A small piece of the string hung out my mouth, so it could be removed later.

From the moment I arrived at the hospital, Roger had stayed beside my bed. My mother didn't know where to go, alternating between me and Daddy, who was in a different hospital. She couldn't bear to look at me, bandaged, swollen, and broken, but she wouldn't let herself cry in my room. In the hall, however, she broke down. The kids were devastated, calling constantly to see how I was. I can only imagine how horrible it must have been for them.

Even while unconscious, I had shown glimmers of my usual self. Until Dr. Ashley had wired my jaws shut, I mumbled sentences that were understandable. Somehow I knew that the show had been canceled and I wondered if my dancers had been paid. I wondered about the audience. Did they get their money back?

Then I woke up the day after surgery. I had no idea what had happened, where I was, or why I couldn't move or speak. I wanted to speak. I wanted to ask questions. But now I couldn't talk at all. I got angry and I was confused. Then I looked up and saw Roger.

"Don't worry," he said, putting his hand on top of mine. "Everything'll be okay. You'll be as good as new."

I had a thousand questions, but couldn't ask one. I motioned toward the mirror, but Roger shook his head no. He explained what had happened and where I was.

I couldn't talk, Roger explained, because I'd broken my jaw in two places and it had been wired shut. I felt the wire. It reminded me of a piece of fence. Dr. Ashley put braces on my teeth and laced my jaw shut with wires. A piece of cartilage is still missing from my jaw, which to this day causes a weird noise whenever I open and close my mouth.

That wasn't all. My left arm was in a cast and my leg, which had a large gash, was covered by a huge bandage.

I suddenly had a team of doctors—a plastic surgeon, an orthopedic surgeon, a neurosurgeon, a dentist, and others. They were patient and encouraging, but guarded. It wasn't long before I was able to communicate by mouthing words through my clenched jaws. Everyone asked if I felt pain.

"No," I said. "I feel great."

It might've looked quite different, but that's the truth. I was on so much pain medication, I felt wonderful.

"Just explain everything to me," I said. "As long as I can understand what's going on, I'll be okay."

My friends were wonderful. Nancy Sinatra and her mother paid me a visit. So did my friend Norma Collins and her daughter Cathy, who later became Bo Derek. I hobbled down the hallway holding onto Walter and a nurse, singing "Take a Little One-Step," and I took my first walk around the hospital grounds holding onto Marvin Hamlisch.

One day Roger boosted my recovery with a small box containing something with magical healing powers. With my one good hand, I opened it up. Inside was an enormous diamond ring—twenty karats! I thought, that's big! As soon as Roger slipped it on my finger the pain stopped. Okay, maybe that's a slight exaggeration. But ever since, I've sworn that diamonds *are* better than Darvon.

I never felt sorry for myself. For what reason? I was alive. I knew I'd recover. Others might have understandably succumbed to a "Why me?" position, but I think I was once again protected by my upbringing, by the sentiment ingrained in me that God only sends us what we can handle.

I did have questions, though, since everything the doctors

told me was clouded by uncertainty—they only knew so much. But during my second week in the hospital, Mother arrived for her daily visit and mentioned for the first time that my father was very worried about me.

Daddy was in the hospital with terminal cancer, and he was worried about me! I was outraged—outraged at myself for adding to my father's burdens. He had more important concerns than worrying about me. I knew what I had to do: I resolved right then to stage the fastest recovery on record and show that he had no reason to be concerned about me.

After eleven days, I was finally released from the hospital. It took two trucks to take home all the beautiful flowers that people—people I knew and many wonderful, caring souls whom I'd never met—sent to sweeten my recovery. Roger transformed the den into a makeshift hospital room and hired round-the-clock nurses. I also had twenty-four-hour visitors: Allan, Bobby Darin, Marvin, Sue Mengers, Warren Cowan and Paul Bloch, my publicity experts and dear friends, Kathleen and many more.

I never had any doubts that I'd bounce back to normal—even better than normal. I only had to look at my husband for an example. In 1960, long before we met, he'd had an accident that caused a blood vessel to burst in his head. Over the next five months, he suffered seizures and lost normal neurological functions. His doctors thought he was having a breakdown. Then a specialist noticed he was afflicted only on his right side, performed an angiogram and then an emergency operation for what he diagnosed as a subdural hematoma.

For the month before and after the operation, Roger could neither speak, read, nor understand what people said to him. Doctors said he'd never regain all of his functions. But Roger, like me, refused to give up on a life that held so much promise. Rather than believe the doctors, he willed himself better and then vowed to live each day so that if it happened again, he wouldn't feel sorry about the things he hadn't done.

Me, too.

The first big event in my recovery was the day Roger decided to let me look in a mirror. Until then, he'd prohibited it. Every mirror in the house had been covered. My nurse, Carlene, fixed my hair in pigtails and let me put on some jewelry and makeup. Then, amid fanfare provided by Roger and my mother, I inspected the damages myself. My arm was in a cast, my eyes black and blue, my jaw wired shut, the whole left side of my face resembling the worst case of mumps in history. In fact, the skin on my face stretched so tight it shined.

But I smiled, and through clenched jaws, muttered, "I think I lost weight. All right!"

Everyone laughed.

There were also some dark moments. I heard horrible stories about Roger. People blamed him for my accident, saying he pushed me too hard. That made me so mad. He didn't ever make me do anything I didn't want to do. I worked as hard as I did because I wanted to. I worked because I loved it.

I also heard the rumors that I had fallen because I was drunk. The truth is I had no alcohol in me when I went up on that platform that night. I had stopped drinking. Period. Yes, I would break my sobriety, but it wasn't for a long time afterward.

When it became clear to Mother that my spirits were returning, she told me that our old family friend Gus Randall had gone into the hospital with cancer. As soon as I was able, Carlene took me to the hospital so I could see him. He drifted in and out of consciousness the day I showed up, but his eyes opened and he knew it was me. We smiled.

He lived only a few more days, and I was heartbroken. Gus was as close to me as family. Naturally, I thought of my own father, bedridden with the same awful disease. But at least Daddy had more time.

Roger concentrated on lifting my spirits. One day he talked about vacationing someplace exotic over Thanksgiving. He asked if there was anywhere I wanted to go, anywhere in the world. I thought for a moment. Thanksgiving. Weren't we already doing something? Wasn't I supposed to open at the Hilton in Las Vegas on November 28?

"You can't be serious," he said. "I'm canceling that."

"Why?" I asked in a muffled voice.

"Just look at you," he said. "You're barely out of bed. You walk with a cane. Your mouth is wired tight as a drum."

"So?"

"You're telling me not to cancel?"

"Yes!"

My goal was simple. I wanted to show Daddy that I was back to normal and he didn't have to worry. I realized the only way he'd believe that I was back to normal was if I did my stage show again—soon. Roger put the subject aside, but I think he knew how emphatically I felt about this.

One day I asked my nurse, Carlene, for a pain pill and she said no.

"But I think I have some pain—"

"Where?" she asked.

I still suffered a little pain, but it wasn't as excruciating as it had been early on, and Carlene knew I no longer needed the medicine. My brain didn't know, though. It'd grown quite fond of the painkillers. Carlene delivered the message.

"No more," she said emphatically.

And that was it. No more pain medication. Cold turkey.

Then my appetite returned. Up till then, my nourishment had consisted solely of juices—apple, carrot, tomato, and orange juices—anything I could suck from a giant syringe. Suddenly, though, I craved everything I'd eaten before— steak, chops, pizza, potatoes, and desserts. The frustration got to me one day as I watched Roger and Jordan eat a cake my mother had baked.

"Cake!" I whimpered through my wired jaws. "I'd love to have some cake."

In a moment of inspiration, Roger got out the liquefier that he used to make my juices, dumped in a big slab of cake, and switched it on. The machine whirred, the cake tossed around the container, and then, seconds later, it was a white liquid. We marveled at the sight. Roger dipped his finger in, tasted it, and loaded it in my syringe.

Cake juice! That started Roger on a craze. He liquefied everything—pizzas, roast beef, Caesar salads, cookies, sandwiches, cake, and ice cream. Having my jaws wired changed my life in other ways, too. If I left the house—say, to go shopping—I gave a pair of heavy-duty wire cutters to whoever was with me to cut the wires in case I got sick and had to spill my cookies. When I phoned people, they immediately knew it was me. But who else talked with their mouth shut?

After six weeks, Dr. Ashley felt I'd healed on schedule. He pulled the string out of my mouth and then clipped the wires holding my jaws shut. I'd expected to be back to normal; I wasn't. Despite removal of the wires, I couldn't open my mouth. Evidently my concern was apparent. Dr. Ashley explained that I had lockjaw, an expected complication.

"You're going to have to work at it," he advised. "Little by little, you'll be able to open it."

From Dr. Ashley's office, Roger drove me directly to Daddy's hospital. I made it a point to show him every little bit of progress I made in my recovery. First, I'd hobbled into his room, using my cane to show him that I wasn't bed-bound. Then I'd walked in without it and announced that I was going back to work in November. Daddy'd asked me if that wasn't too soon, but I'd told him it wasn't soon enough.

Then I smiled for him. He saw that I'd gotten the wires off and his eyes lit up. I still couldn't open my mouth, but I made him laugh by using my hands to pry my jaws apart and explained how with a little work they'd loosen up.

Other parts of me needed work, too. My right hand trembled as a result of neurological damage and my muscles needed lots of strengthening. But I only had to see Daddy smile at my progress to summon the courage and determination needed to push through physical therapy at a furious pace. All I thought about was my father, and proving to my father that I could get back on stage by Thanksgiving.

Several weeks later I made the leap from rehab to rehearsals, though it was still a big hurdle. Walter had me try a simple turn; I got dizzy and had to sit down. I was okay doing my first lift. The guys began calling me "Slugger."

Each day I got a little stronger, a little better at opening
my mouth, a little more confident that I was going to make
a full recovery and perform as scheduled. I also felt an inner
strength, because I wasn't falling back on alcohol to sustain
me. I hadn't had a drink since six months before the accident, and I felt I had at least that under control.

The show stayed pretty much as before, with one major
difference: I entered from ground level instead of riding
down on the harlequin's hand.

After each rehearsal, I visited Daddy and sang and
danced the song on which I'd worked. I felt like a beginner
again. I wasn't performing just because I wanted to, I was
also doing it because I *had* to for Daddy. Each day I
showed him something new.

"Look, Daddy," I said. "Look how my mouth opens
this wide—almost like before the accident."

"That's good! Very good!" he replied.

"And I can kick. Watch this!"

"Don't hurt yourself."

"Don't worry."

The most frightening part of the show was when I
climbed atop a giant drum and on a specific beat fell backward into the arms of my waiting dancers. It was a blind
fall. I had to have complete faith in the people who were
catching me, which I did. We rehearsed this last.

"Don't you want to change this part?" Walter Painter
asked.

"No way," I said.

I knew that I couldn't run from my fears. I'd already
learned my lessons about that from my battle to stay sober.
I'd decided that if something doesn't kill you, it only makes
you stronger, and that was certainly true with this stunt.

The dance steps came automatically, so much so that I
found myself on top of the drum without so much as a
minor hesitation. Then came the cue. I took a deep breath.
I had total confidence in my dancers. As for the courage I
needed to fall backward? Well, I thought, It's now or never,
and then yielded to what I knew would be the outcome.
Everyone clapped.

"Okay, we got that out of the way," I said. "Now let's try it again."

The week before Thanksgiving, I staged a dress rehearsal at the Paul De Rolf dance studio in the Valley. Although it was in preparation for opening at the Hilton, I considered it a command performance for Daddy. He was too sick to attend the show in Las Vegas. As a result, I decided to stage the entire act with all the costumes and motorcycles just for him.

Mother pushed his wheelchair into the studio. A nurse pushed Daddy's roommate from the home beside him. He was a white-haired, eighty-five-year-old cancer patient whose bright blue eyes didn't miss a trick. They'd watched my progress in their hospital room, but this was their first time seeing the show in its entirety.

I'd never pushed myself harder in any dress rehearsal, but I'd never had more to prove. Daddy's cancer had drained him of his strength, but he clapped and smiled after each number. As a surprise, I finished with "When You're Smiling," Daddy's favorite song. Daddy couldn't get up, but his whole face brightened. A big grin unfolded and tears filled his eyes. He blushed. Tears drenched my own eyes. After, I set the microphone down and kissed him on the cheek.

"See, Daddy, I told you I'm fine," I said.

I was struck by how little had changed in thirty-one years. I was still very much the small girl singing and dancing to entertain my parents and win their approval. However, I only had to look at Daddy in the wheelchair, a shadow of himself, to understand that nothing had stayed the same. Except for one very important thing, which I whispered to Daddy.

"I love you."

33

WHEN ROGER AND I LEFT OUR L.A. HOME AFTER
Thanksgiving 1972, and headed for the Las Vegas Hilton,
we were consumed by the anxiety and press attention sur-
rounding my comeback. We arrived at the hotel several
days early in order to settle in before opening night on
November 28. Elvis happened to be the headliner when we
checked in, and was ensconced in the performer's suite atop
the hotel. We were in a suite a few floors below. I regarded
Elvis's presence as an extra bonus. I was pleased to know
he was nearby, and I hoped we could connect somehow.

After the accident, I'd received flowers from him, but
we'd yet to discuss the ordeal. I knew he was concerned.
I obviously would've been if the situation was reversed.
However, our schedules made it almost impossible to get
together in any normal fashion. But late one night as Roger
and I entertained friends in our suite, Elvis and a few of
the guys came by unexpectedly.

Despite the crowd, Elvis managed to get me alone at one
end of the living room, where we conducted a conversation
in hushed voices. It was kind of funny. I was worried about
talking to him while not being rude to my other guests, but
he wanted to get personal. Suddenly, he wanted to play
catch-up. He wanted to know all about the accident, my
recovery, Daddy.

It was so easy for us to lapse into the closeness we'd
always shared, but it was clear from some of Elvis's comments that he really missed having me in his life. He missed
having a friend, someone who understood him as well as
someone he trusted. Neither of us noticed that Roger re-
peatedly walked by and tinkered with the thermostat on the

wall in an effort to eavesdrop. We laughed about it afterward.

I eventually told Elvis all I could and then had to go back to our guests. He also had to prepare for his show. I knew that I'd hear from him again, though. And I did.

Late that night the phone rang in our bedroom. I knew who was on the other end, and I was pleased that Roger was in the living room next door. If he had answered the telephone, I supposed Elvis would have hung up, just like in the movies.

Elvis told me how great it had been seeing me earlier. I looked wonderful. His prayers for my recovery had been answered. But then his tone changed. Saying he was lonely, he asked if he could see me. It was a question I'd anticipated since afternoon but hoped that he wouldn't really ask.

"You know I can't."

"I know," he said. "But I just want you to know that I still feel the same."

By opening night, I'd put that backstage drama out of mind and moved to another place, emotionally and otherwise.

As soon as the curtain rose, the crowd welcomed me with a standing ovation. The response touched and embarrassed me. I tried to inject a bit of perspective by reading a telegram Don Rickles sent. "Since when do you do a high-wire act? Have booked you into Circus-Circus with the Flying Wallendas. Next time use a net, dummy!"

As the show moved along, I didn't think I'd finish. Near the end, my right hand trembled noticeably and weakened. My knees started to wobble. I struggled to remain on my feet. I walked to the piano and held on. If I'd ever felt like this before the accident, I wouldn't have finished, but there was no way that I was leaving that stage.

Though I tried hiding the shaking, I think the audience knew what I was going through because they didn't seem to want to leave either. We'd all shared in my triumphant return to the stage, and it was a fabulous, glowing feeling. Yet, I was so drained, so trembly, it was hard to sustain the mood.

But I was determined to keep going and to grow stronger.

I knew now how much my accident had affected me, and I wanted to surmount it. After a Christmas break, we started rehearsals for a new TV special. In the middle, Daddy's illness worsened. He never complained, especially about the excruciating pain caused by the cancer. Till the end, he stayed true to form, a man who walked gently and bravely through life.

He passed away very quietly on February 7.

Mother was with him. Roger and I were asleep when she called with the news. I couldn't even speak.

Even though doctors had warned of this for months, and even though I'd watched my father deteriorate physically over time, I still couldn't handle it. I wouldn't accept his death. I couldn't. He was one of the three centers of my world—Daddy, Mother, and Roger.

With the news, something inside me snapped. I withdrew deeper into myself than ever. Roger got scared. I didn't know how to communicate the despair, loss, and grief inside.

I don't know how I got through Daddy's funeral. Seated between Mother and Roger, I couldn't get my body to stop shaking violently. I held on to them tightly for support as well as for dear life. I couldn't—wouldn't—look at Daddy lying there. I wanted to remember him alive. Our dear friend Seth Riggs filled the church with "The Lord's Prayer," his voice painting the room with a love and dignity and strength that reminded us of Daddy.

I knew he was listening from above. God bless his soul.

Afterward, friends expressed grave concern about my state of mind and kept a round-the-clock watch over me. There was no messing around. People were direct: If Roger wasn't with me, one of my friends was. I'd fallen into such a deep depression that they rightfully feared I'd do something desperate.

They were right. One evening while Roger was doing some project around the house, I remembered a bottle of painkillers I'd shoved in a drawer after my accident. I was in pain—a horrible, twisted emotional pain. I didn't think I could stand it and sought the pills.

I locked the bathroom door and dumped the bottle of

pills onto the counter. I stared at them for a moment, imagining the relief they'd bring, and then I read the label. Take one every eight hours and then discontinue after the pain ceased. I wondered if there could be an end to such pain.

No, it was impossible. The wound was too deep. His absence irreplaceable. I filled a cup with water and swallowed a pill, even though I knew that one wasn't going to be enough. I studied my tear-streaked face in the mirror. Quickly, I gulped the remainder.

Was I trying to commit suicide? I never once wanted to end my life, because even in that miserable despair, I knew how much I had to live for. Very simply, I didn't want to be in any more pain.

As soon as I began to experience the tingling sensation in my fingers and back caused by the pills, I panicked. I found Roger and told him that I had to go see Kathleen. Then I got in my car and drove to her home in Santa Monica. It was stupid to be driving in that condition, but God must've watched over me. Somehow I made it. When I got there, I didn't mince words; I told Kathleen and her physician husband, Carl, what I'd done.

"I don't want to go to a hospital," I pleaded. "Please, help me."

They neither scolded me nor expressed sympathy. Carl asked me what I'd taken, then forced me to drink something, I don't know what, that immediately made me vomit up the pills and cleaned out my stomach. Then he warned me.

"I'm never going to do this again," he said.

"This is serious, Ann-Margret," Kathleen added. "Do you know what could've happened to you? Do you want to die?"

"No," I cried. "No, no, I don't."

"Then why'd you do this?"

"I just don't know how to handle the pain," I confessed.

"That's what we're here for," she said. "If you can't handle something, call us. We'll help you."

Which they did. After calling Roger, who was beside himself, they stayed up with me the entire night. We drank coffee and discussed the tangle of deep, confused emotions that had caused me to take such drastic, possibly fatal action. What I really wanted and needed was to reach out and be comforted and understood. In the morning, they drove me to rehearsal.

The ups and downs continued without letup. At the end of February, I made a highly emotional return to the Sahara in Lake Tahoe, the site of my accident. Although five months had passed, I could still close my eyes and clearly picture the stage speeding toward me as I tumbled to the ground. Part of me shuddered at the thought of getting back on that stage, but the fighter in me could hardly wait. I did request, however, that they forgo the platform.

Except for my initial entrance, the show remained the same as before—from my dancers to my yellow chiffon dress, now cleaned and puffed and free of any blood stains. No one talked about the significance of the date. I tried lessening the tension by gathering all the musicians, singers, and dancers backstage and sharing my thoughts.

"I know what's on everybody's mind," I said. "Part of me is terrified about doing this show. Scared out of my mind. But I want to do this. Otherwise I'm never going to set foot on a stage again."

At the end of the show, I could tell the audience shared my sense of triumph. It was as if they'd participated in the performance. All night I felt how they'd imagined my fears, then watched me conquer them. We were in this together, and when it was all through we shared in the magic. They didn't want to leave, and neither did I.

But nothing filled the emptiness created by my loss of Daddy. Mother and I grieved together, trying to help each other as best we could. We talked about him all the time, just as we'd done when I was a little girl in Valsjobyn waiting, hoping, anticipating the day when I would be reunited with my daddy who was in Chicago. Yet there was no reunion to which I could look forward.

At thirty-two years old, I realized I needed some deep soul-searching and did something I'd never done: I took a sabbatical, six months off to regroup. Friends told me that the only way I could fill the void was to grow inside, and they were right. I had to take the time to develop myself as a person, not as a performer.

So Roger and I bought a house on the beach in Malibu. I ran on the sand. We hiked in the hills and went on picnics. I knew such enforced leisure was hard on Roger, who had been so totally immersed in my career. Sure, he had plenty of business meetings, screened scripts, ran all the household matters, and kept up with life in general, yet I know he wasn't as content as I was. I took Spanish and French lessons. I played volleyball. I tried to knit and sew, but did so unsuccessfully. I even attempted to bake chocolate-chip cookies once, but forgot the chocolate chips. Okay, so some things didn't change.

But the most important things did. I relearned how to have fun. I regenerated my soul.

And indeed, I emerged stronger. We were able to spend plenty of time with the kids during this period, swimming and hiking, and I realized more than ever the importance of family. I now knew how badly I wanted a child of my own. We'd tried before, but now I was really determined. The loss of one very important person in my life made me want to add another. I felt the maternal instinct more powerfully than ever. I had so much to offer—love, understanding, companionship, discovering all the mysteries of life, chasing butterflies . . .

Every month I'd hope, then every month I'd be disappointed and buoy myself for another attempt. I heard jokes about how much fun it was to try, but that was still no consolation. The more conception eluded us, the stronger I felt the biologic pull. Each month, when I realized I wasn't pregnant, I would call my mother, distraught.

For a year, Roger and I tried natural methods. With three children by his first marriage, he didn't worry that there might be a problem with him. At the same time, he showed great sensitivity in making sure that I didn't think it was my fault either. But maybe it was.

I had umpteen blood tests. My hormones were checked; Roger was examined. I asked whether my accident could've affected anything. Roger had his own questions, but the doctors couldn't find anything wrong with either of us.

Neither of us blamed ourselves or each other. What good

would that do? We were too practical, too much in love, too sensitive and respectful of one another. We hoped and prayed and remained fairly philosophical that if we were meant to have a child together it would eventually happen.

In the meantime, our involvement with Roger's children was increasing. Tracey, fourteen, Jordan, thirteen, and Dallas, nine, had been spending more and more time with us. There were many difficult, confused months as we sorted out changes in the family relationships, and all the other adjustments that needed to be made. Roger wanted to do what was best for the children, and it was clear they were happy being with us.

Roger and the children's mother, who had custody of them, couldn't reach an agreement on permanent visitation rights and ended up letting a judge decide for them.

I'll never forget the day Roger returned from court. I'd decided not to go with him, too nervous to be of help and too worried about attracting attention. When he came home he was white as a sheet, his hair was disheveled, and he looked distressed.

"You lost, didn't you?" I asked, concerned.

He took a deep breath and put his hand on my shoulder.

"I think you better sit down," he said.

"You didn't get visitation, did you?"

"No, not exactly," he replied.

"The judge took Tracey and Jordan away, too?"

"No, not exactly."

"Then, what?"

Roger explained that the judge, weighing all the facts at his disposal, decided to give him sole custody of all three kids and visitation rights to their mother.

"What? When?" I asked Roger.

"That's right. Starting tomorrow we're the parents of three teenagers."

I didn't know how to react. I was happy, excited, scared, and confused. Yet I honestly didn't know how I felt.

But I had always loved Roger's children, and had never felt any of the negativism some women feel about caring for stepchildren. I met them when they were so young, and I had spent so much time with them. They were a part of me, just as Roger was. Here I'd been fretting over having one child, a baby, and then he came home and told me we were getting three teenagers. It sounded like the plot of a Bob Hope–Lucille Ball movie.

Even though the decision had already been handed down, Roger continually asked me how I felt about the situation. He was attempting to iron out his own feelings on the subject as well. Both of us were surprised. I responded the way any decent, unprepared woman with no domestic skills would—I sprinted inside the house and called my mother.

"You will do okay," she said. "The children, they already love you so much."

"And I love them," I said.

"So what's the problem? There is nothing you can't work out with a lot of love and patience."

I followed those words of wisdom with a call to Kathleen. She also assured me that I could manage.

"It's not going to slow you down," she said. "You can't look at it like that. With three children, your life is suddenly fuller, richer. Every day will present a new experience. It's an adventure."

And like all adventures, ours began by setting up camp. Our house was a three-bedroom, not designed for kids, so we figured out the logistics of adding three new members of the household, three teenagers. We built a guest house that became Tracey's room, an apartment above the garage for Jordan, and Dallas was given the housekeeper's room. For the year we remodeled, Jordan insisted on sleeping in the backyard in a tent.

It wasn't a traditional setup, but there was a coziness and spirit to the arrangement. We called our house "Camp Smith," and it worked for us.

All three kids were now enrolled in boarding schools, but they came home frequently. We made sure there was always a housekeeper to take care of their physical needs, and we tried to be there for them emotionally, even if we were away on tour. We flew home at every given moment, even if only for an afternoon or a day, to let Tracey, Jordan, and Dallas know we were available for a chat, a hug, a walk in the woods, or a family dinner. We also scheduled family vacations to Europe or Hawaii.

We tried to be good sports, to let them be kids. All three knew they could invite plenty of friends over to play tennis, swim, or hike around our hilly property, and believe me, they did. Some mornings, I stepped around so many sleeping bags I thought an army had decamped.

The kid in me loved all this. One day, the boys were seeing who could swim the most laps underwater holding their breath. One of their friends boasted he could do three laps and no one could beat him. So I jumped in and topped his record, though it almost killed me.

In terms of discipline, Roger and I were opposites. He was easy-going, dutiful, but sometimes too lenient. I referred to myself as "the wicked stepmother of the west." I cracked down on homework and tried to apply the same rules my parents had used with me: children didn't speak unless spoken to; they respected their elders; they studied diligently; they said "please" and "thank you."

But times and the rules had changed and the kids simply couldn't accept what they regarded as my old-fashioned Swedish concepts. They did try hard to at least adhere a bit, and I soon learned to be a little looser. We tested each other and had our share of fights. But on the whole, we felt like a real family. It required learning and adjustment on all our parts.

I just remembered my mother's advice: There is nothing you can't work out with a lot of love and patience.

That summer we sent the kids to camp. One day Roger opened a letter from Jordan, in which he wrote of the many hours he'd spent contemplating our new situation. He felt comfortable about things, he said. But he had one question. "Do you think it would be okay with Ann-Margret if I called her 'Mom'?"

Roger showed me the letter. I read it over several times. I couldn't recall having read anything so sweet, heartfelt, and sincere.

"Mom," I said out loud. "I love it."

I treasured three stepchildren, but I still wanted a baby of my own. Month after month we tried and there were days when I felt so sad and empty, and so inadequate, even though I had promised myself I wouldn't assign blame. I managed to get through all those dark times without grabbing for a bottle, and for that I felt gratified. It was also helpful that I had my career back on track. Professional self-esteem could do a fair amount to quiet my inner turmoils. I felt ready for a new career challenge, and soon I would get it.

34

FOLLOWING A VACATION IN MEXICO, ALLAN PICKED us up at the airport, and drove about ten minutes before pulling over to the side with good news.

"You just got the part of Nora!" he said. "In *Tommy!*"

"What?" I asked.

"It's the rock opera. By the Who. It's the hottest script in town. Everybody's in it—Jack Nicholson, Elton John, Eric Clapton, Oliver Reed."

Allan told us he had recommended me for the part to his friend Robert Stigwood, who was producing *Tommy*. Stigwood then screened *Carnal Knowledge* for director Ken Russell, who admired the movie and remarked, "And she can sing, too?"

I'd only heard a couple of songs from the Who's album and I wasn't aware that the band had staged it as a play. But Marvin Hamlisch knew everything about *Tommy*, and gave me the album. If we were near a piano, he'd say, "Listen to this," and then play "Pinball Wizard" or one of the other songs. He filled me in on the genius of Pete Townshend and the rest of the band.

And of course he was right about everything.

In February 1974, we went to London to record the soundtrack of the movie. I learned all eleven songs on the plane, which reminded me of the time I learned a dozen new songs while driving to my first job at the Muehlebach Hotel in Kansas City. With score sheets in hand, I spent two ten-hour days in the recording studio with Pete. One day Roger Daltrey, the Who's lead singer, came by the studio, heard me sing, and admitted, "I didn't know you could do that, too."

"Yeah, a little," I smiled.

I could tell we were going to have fun when we started shooting in April. First, we returned home and squeezed in my regular nightclub dates and one additional special evening that I wouldn't have missed for anything.

On April 2, just days before I had to leave town, we attended the Academy Awards. Marvin's work on the films *The Sting* and *The Way We Were* had earned him nominations for Best Song Score, Dramatic Score, and Song. With Burt Bacharach, I presented the Oscar for Best Song, which went to Marvin for "The Way We Were" and turned out to be his third of the night. Just three years earlier, Marvin had flown out from New York to write dance charts for my "AM/PM" show, and as a bonus ended up playing piano during rehearsals. In no time, Marvin was offering Roger suggestions, so much so that Roger joked about avoiding his whispers. But he admitted, "You know, that kid playing piano has always got something to say about everything. But damn, if he isn't always right."

Then it was back to London, where Allan arranged for us to rent Michael Caine's flat. I spent the first few days of production on *Tommy* trailing Pete, asking him questions about my character Nora. Since I'd never done a film remotely like *Tommy,* which was as wild and exaggerated as a hallucination, I wrote reams of notes and studied them before every scene.

Everyone else involved in the movie tried to be spontaneous. Imagine the cast of freewheeling spirits: Elton John, Eric Clapton, Tina Turner, Oliver Reed, Jack Nicholson, the Who's bassist, John Entwistle, and their drummer, Keith Moon. Keith was so loose he once slipped a diamond ring off his finger and gave it to me simply because I admired it. Clapton seemed to fill the background with blues, and somebody was always ready to jam.

Director Ken Russell added an exhilarating, inspiring creativity. He was wild, indulgent, kind, and funny, always pushing for more. He didn't think anything of doing twenty-five or thirty takes on a single scene. In fact, that was normal.

During one of the early takes, I smashed a TV screen

with a champagne bottle to show Nora's frustration. In the next take, my hand went into the TV screen and the cut glass sliced into it. Dripping with blood, I was quickly wrapped in a blanket, carried off the set, and then rushed to the hospital, where doctors took twenty-seven stitches to close the wound.

The next day, I showed up on the set, ready for work. In fact, I shot a scene with my arm hidden under a table. Later, Ken decided not to risk any further injury by shooting around me and instructed me to take a few days off. I wouldn't have, if he hadn't insisted.

Taking advantage of the unscheduled vacation, Roger and I sent for our children, who were already waiting for us in London, and we traveled to the Greek Isles. By the time we got back, my bandages were off.

I've always admired the talent of Tina Turner, an immensely gifted, intelligent, and proud woman. I'd seen her in clubs several times, but during *Tommy* we got to know each other well.

After the film ended, Roger arranged for us to stay in London and shoot my next TV special there. Tina flew back home to California. A few days later, we called and asked her to come back and guest on the show. She returned immediately, with only the clothes on her back. That's when I learned how little money she had, and the extent of the rough time she had gone through before leaving Ike Turner.

Later, when we returned to L.A., we spent more time together. She and her assistant, Rhonda, came to our house many times for dinner; Roger and I went to hers. She once admired a dress Bob Mackie had made for one of my specials, and I gave it to her. Roger and I truly believed in Tina as a person and a performer, and we wanted to do anything to help restore her self-confidence and self-esteem. We've remained friends ever since.

After the show aired, both Roger and I felt it was time for another reprieve. I decided to take him home to Valsjobyn. In almost ten years together, he'd certainly heard about my hometown but had never been there until the little seaplane we rented in Stockholm landed beside the lake.

"Finally," he said with a big grin.

With my mother, who met us in Stockholm, we stepped out of the plane and walked into town. Mother and I pointed out sights and people and tried to encapsulate a lifetime of memories. There was one store, some homes, the bridge, the rivers, and a few more houses in the distance. I'll never forget what happened next. After spending several minutes in town, Mother and I debated where to go next—the shop (a combination gas station–grocery and drugstore and post office) or one of our relatives' homes.

"Where's the town?" Roger asked

We stopped talking, turned and looked at him as if he'd lost his mind.

"This is it," Mother said. "This is Valsjobyn."

At that moment, I realized that much of my success, and certainly many of my troubles, stemmed from the fact that I've never been anything more than a village girl struggling to survive in a big city. Reconciling this very simple background with the pressures and public exposure of show business has always been very tough for me. I always felt I had one foot in two places, a tenuous balance at best. More than ever, I felt the presence of the two Ann-Margrets, and so, I think, did Roger.

35

ALLAN EXCLAIMED THAT THE PARTY FOR *TOMMY*'S world premiere was going to be the biggest ever, and he wasn't kidding. Invitations etched in white on black Plexiglas went out by messenger to the screening at New York City's Ziegfeld Theater on March 18, 1975, and the celebration afterward.

Following the screening, guests descended to the 57th Street subway station, where producer Robert Stigwood and Allan had turned the brand-new, three-block-long space into a spectacle. The six hundred guests waded past a jungle of trees, fauna, and flowers to tables overflowing with food: artichokes stuffed with truffled chicken mousse, lobsters, octopus, crab, roast beef, salmon, oysters, smoked turkey. By the entrance, three thousand cherry tomatoes spelled "Tommy."

One thousand people turned out to view the party from outside. I ate dinner with Roger, Allan, and Tina, danced with Elton, and listened as gossip columnist Earl Wilson told me New York City had never witnessed an event this lavish, and I believed him.

After New York City, Roger and I attended *Tommy* galas in L.A., London, and Chicago, where the city's mayor—with many of my relatives and friends present—proclaimed it "Ann-Margret Day." All in all, I'd say *Tommy* was a real high point for us, a glittering, exciting time. We felt we were part of a spectacle and the dawn of a new movie tradition.

None of the attention would have meant the same without Roger sharing it with me. After eleven years together, we were still in love, still spent every day with each other, still had a million thoughts and ideas to share. Our greatest pleasure was that the success belonged to both of us. Since I had stopped drinking, the fighting had also disappeared. Sure, we had our disagreements, but they were never mean and hurtful, as they had been, and we also had developed a surefire way to prevent them from becoming so: As soon as Roger became a little too inflamed, I would stick out my tongue, blow him raspberries, and make a funny face. That would defuse things. A little odd perhaps, but it works for us.

About then, Roger began creating effects in my nightclub act that were years ahead of his time. During the show, for instance, three film screens came down and three different images of me were projected onto them. In effect, I was able to sing backup for myself, as well as trade dance steps. Then, as I changed costumes, one of my dancers came out and also danced with the different screen images. Long before MTV, this was a really sensational effect.

Despite our penchant for privacy, Roger and I weren't afraid to exploit our personal lives on TV, which is one of the many reasons I believe those specials were so popular. I knew that I could shape the personal parts as I wanted them to appear, and thus I felt open and honest, knowing there would not be distortions of the truth. I could laugh at myself and also put situations that had once seemed threatening into perspective.

My sixth special, *Ann-Margret Smith,* which we taped in London, was a good example. Over the years Roger had been accused of being a Svengali: Hence, the special opened with him at the typewriter, banging out a scene for the show. Our marriage had once generated considerable dissension in my family: so, in one scene I played my mother and, with a heavy Swedish accent, ranted about Roger's shortcomings.

On the special, we indulged our fantasies by rewriting history a bit and having the wedding I'd always imagined. For the ceremony, Roger wore a morning suit and I finally looked like a resplendent bride in a gorgeous wedding gown. Sid Caesar married us. Afterward, we roared off on a motorcycle with a "Just Married" sign on the back and tin cans dragging behind.

Though it seemed as if the pursuit of a career occupied all our waking moments, we devoted an equal, if not greater, portion of time to having a family life. I have always talked to my mother at least once a day, and I also tried to see her as often as possible. She had settled in a house near us in the San Fernando Valley, and seemed to have handled Daddy's death with her usual quiet resolve. We helped each other through periods of loneliness, but I'm sure it was tough on her in ways I wasn't able to understand.

Not surprisingly, though, Mother did not shrink from the world. Over the years, I was more than surprised to see a strong, independent woman emerge. Here was my mother, and suddenly I was discovering, and admiring, a whole new person who allowed herself to experience adventure and new relationships and the joys of being carefree.

I also grew closer and closer to my stepchildren. I helped Tracey through different boyfriends and tried to take her side when she felt the three guys in the family were ganging up against her. I also helped her with fashion and makeup. As my mother had done with me, I prohibited her from wearing a black dress until she was seventeen. No need to grow up too fast, I felt.

And somehow, it worked out. We stayed close. At nineteen, she got her first American Express card and came to me soon after for help.

"Ann-Margret, please take it away from me. I can't control myself." So I did.

When Dallas began keeping a pet snake in his room, and described during mealtimes how he fed it live mice, I refused to go near that part of the house.

I thought I knew men. But the boys were different. Even as the years passed, Roger continued to be more permissive while I refused to lower my standards, the same ones that I'd been raised on. Take table manners. Try teaching two active, hungry, mischievous teenage boys table manners. They'd rather plow through a meal like wild animals breaking a fast. I kept at them and kept at them. We reached a point where they didn't want to come to the table anymore, fearing their wicked stepmother's rules.

But we got through it. Not too long ago, both boys came to me and said they were grateful I taught them properly, because there've been many times when they've gone somewhere and needed those impeccable manners. It made me cry.

Normal, right?

Okay, so Roger might've installed a custom-made whirlpool bath that was made from pink marble flown in from Italy, and filled with hot water at the flick of a switch. Reporters loved that. But what few people ever knew was that soon after it was completed, our cats took it over as a resting spot and eating area. We rarely used it.

Material things provide only so much comfort. I stepped up my efforts to conceive, and would've gladly traded anything for success. We'd been trying for years now. When carefully timed efforts didn't produce results, I underwent all sorts of examinations, tests, X rays, and even several laparoscopies. But doctors still could find nothing wrong.

I tried to shut my feelings out, to put my energies into Tracey, Jordan, and Dallas. They continually pushed for independence, as I still struggled to instill some of those old-fashioned standards. There were also the inevitable clashes over marijuana. Once, I remember, a guest lit up a joint in front of one of the children as we talked in the living room. Although Roger ignored it, I jumped right up and asked our friend if I could speak to him in private.

"What you do away from here is your business," I said. "But please don't ever do that again in front of my children."

Raising children was hard, much harder than doing an hour-and-a-half show in front of an audience. While on the road, we listened to their problems over the phone, and plunged into them as soon as we got back, if the kids happened to be home from school for a vacation or weekend. The firm stepmother in me always wanted to exercise control over the kids. The hardest lesson was mine—giving them the space to learn on their own.

My friend actress Nancy Walker, who often helped me

rehearse sketches, introduced me to a gifted psychologist, Dr. Lu. Before Dr. Lu, I didn't fully deal with the pressure or feelings that were a part of my hectic life. Sure, I had managed to stop drinking, but I had never really examined all the deep-seated problems that were within. I suppressed everything. If a situation cropped up, I discovered that I really didn't know how I felt or how to react. I just wanted to please others. I'm sure some of this repressive behavior created a monster. I was often anxious and taut inside, a coiled spring. I had unwound dangerously after my father died, and I feared I would do it again if I didn't get some help.

Dr. Lu knew how to turn me inward. One day she asked, "But what about you?" What about that? With her help, I began the process of learning about this woman named Ann-Margret.

Between therapy and regular meetings with my friend Kathleen, I developed a strong, dependable, and healthy support system. I can't imagine not having had it. That network kept me from self-destructing. I learned it's okay to seek help without compromising an iota of my stubborn Swedish pride or privacy. I grew more reasonable, I think, more willing to compromise with the children. Instead of saying a firm no to their plans at times, I tried to at least hear them out and offer alternatives if I couldn't say yes. All of us matured together—the children grew older and I much wiser.

Consequently, I was better equipped to juggle the stresses of managing both a family and career, which heated up dramatically with the new year. In January 1976, I won a Golden Globe for Best Actress for my work in *Tommy*. Several weeks later, I appeared on the cover of *People* magazine. Both were shades of 1961—the year I won a Golden Globe as Newcomer of the Year and editor Richard Stolley had helped me onto the cover of *Life* magazine; now my old friend Richard was in charge of *People*.

By February, I'd started getting in shape for a new nightclub act that was scheduled to open at the Hilton in March. On the morning of February 17, the day the Academy Award nominations were handed out, Roger decided to avoid all news and phone calls in order to keep up with our tight schedule. We'd come home from jogging up the canyon when the phone started ringing. We ignored it. Seth Riggs, my voice coach, showed up for a lesson and we got started. Then the phone rang again.

"Don't answer it," Roger said.

But Seth wanted to know and picked up the receiver. I knew by his smile what was being said. Then he handed it to me.

"Ann-Margret?" It was my publicist.

"Oh, hi," I said.

"I just heard on the radio!"

"Oh, my God!" I screamed, knowing I had been nominated for Best Actress in *Tommy.*

A few minutes later, my publicist again called and told me the news all over again. It doesn't matter how many times you're told, there's nothing like hearing the words, "You've been nominated for an Academy Award." I screamed even louder. Seth gave me a look of reproval.

"I'm sorry," I said. "I know it's bad for my voice. But—"

"You don't have to explain."

The other nominees were Louise Fletcher for *One Flew Over the Cuckoo's Nest;* Isabelle Adjani for *The Story of Adéle H.;* Glenda Jackson for *Hedda;* and Carol Kane for *Hester Street.*

With this second nomination, I had no reason to doubt myself as an entertainer again, although I don't think I'll ever feel total confidence. I had no reason to doubt myself as a person, period. I knew how close I'd come to giving up, to losing my way in a haze of drink and depression, and that certainly was not the solution. I finally felt secure in the fact that I had something special to share with people, and I knew it came from inside me. I was still here, still kicking, a survivor, and it felt good. I called my mother and told her the good news, and told my father, too. I figured he was listening.

36

DURING THE SPRING OF 1976, ROGER AND I LIVED IN A seventeenth-century English manor house outside Stow-on-the-Wold, a secluded village in the Cotswolds, while I played Lady Booby, a peasant who'd married well, in the restoration comedy *Joseph Andrews.*

Perceptions had definitely changed. After the heavy drama of *Carnal Knowledge* and the flamboyance of *Tommy,* somehow I'd escaped another decade of typecasting by moving into comedy. I inflated Lady Booby to such outlandishly comic proportions, including an English Restoration accent, that I amused even myself. It was hard to find the real Ann-Margret in that character, and I loved that freedom.

Even at this new level of career comfort, I still pushed as if it was 1966 and not 1976. Following *Joseph Andrews,* we hit the Fontainebleau Hotel for one of our biggest, most successful nightclub productions. Then it was back to England for Marty Feldman's *The Last Remake of Beau Geste.* Right after, I played breathy Romanian sexpot Jezebel Desire in Neil Simon's *The Cheap Detective.*

In March of 1977, I taped my next TV special, *Rhinestone Cowgirl,* in Nashville. Since I was so close to Memphis, I half-expected to hear from Elvis. Someone had told me he'd canceled a recent tour because of illness and was at Graceland. Even when we didn't see each other for stretches of time, there was always a flow of messages: "Hi. How ya doing?" Stuff like that. Elvis kept in touch through mutual acquaintances like Joe Esposito and Nancy Sinatra. Roger and I once had a slot machine made up to give to Elvis on his birthday—instead of three bars, you won with three guitars.

Lately, I'd been very worried about him. During my last stint in Vegas, while performing at the Tropicana, Joe came to the show and I questioned him about Elvis's health. I'd heard things that troubled me and wanted to investigate for myself. I never came right out and asked Joe about specific problems, but I hinted at things and made myself clear. I'm sure of that.

"Don't worry," he told me. "Everything's fine. There're a few problems, but we're taking care of them."

I looked Esposito straight in the eye. I knew he was covering up for Elvis, and he knew that I knew. But neither of us said anything. If he would've come forward about the difficulties Elvis was having, I would've been there in a second to intervene. But the matter was kept private.

When I opened at the Hilton on August 15, 1977, there was, for the first time since I began doing my nightclub act, no guitar-shaped flower arrangement from Elvis. He hadn't missed an opening in ten years. No flowers, no telegram, no message. It was strange. I did two shows that night, but not without worrying in the back of my mind that something was wrong, and I had to make some phone calls the next day.

I got off stage sometime after midnight, and Roger and I didn't get to sleep until the middle of the night. On the morning of August 16—despite a "Do Not Disturb" order at the switchboard—our phone rang, and Roger answered. It was Shirley Dieu, Joe Esposito's girlfriend. They spoke briefly, but as they did Roger looked at me and I could see the grief building in his eyes.

"It's Shirley," he said.

"Something's wrong," I blurted in a panic. "It's Elvis, isn't it?"

I got on the phone and Shirley told me as many of the awful details as she knew. I turned ice-cold. Elvis was dead. I couldn't speak. I started to weep and handed the phone to Roger, who finished up and left word for Joe to call when he had the chance.

Soon after, Joe himself called back. I was so distraught,

I could barely hold the phone. Joe told me the funeral was taking place on the eighteenth, but said he didn't expect us to be there.

"It's going to be a madhouse," he said. "You don't have to come."

I knew I had to go and say goodbye in person. If I'd been the first to die, he would've been there for me.

"We're coming," I said.

"Okay, I'll have a car pick you up at the airport."

I was a basket case. Roger asked the Hilton, which was also where Elvis performed, to cancel the two performances that evening, but they didn't. I was outraged by this insensitivity.

Backstage, everyone was under strict orders from Roger to watch every move I made. Roger even warned my dancers to keep an eye on me during the show. He watched from the wings and carried me back to my dressing room after the show. I can't imagine how I managed to get through it without falling apart.

We flew to Memphis early the next morning aboard the Hilton's private jet with passengers Joe Gercio, who conducted the orchestra for both Elvis and for me, and Dr. Elias Ghanem, my and Elvis's Las Vegas physician. The entire city of Memphis seemed in a state of mourning. Some twenty-five thousand people had filed past Elvis's coffin the day before as it lay in state at Graceland, and another seventy-five thousand stood outside the gate about the time Roger and I entered the house.

The funeral took place in Graceland's opulent living room, and I remember a surrealness to the scene. Flowers of every color and kind, of such sweet fragrance filled the room from floor to ceiling. Yet those flowers were so sad, so incredibly sad, and the only way I made it through that service was by clinging to Roger and by telling myself, as I did when I was a child living in a funeral home, that God was with us, watching.

Elvis's father, Vernon, and I held each other for a long, long time. There was so much to say, to recount. But instead, we cried.

"Why, oh why?" he sobbed. "How could this have happened?"

I held him tighter. I wanted to somehow make it better, make the pain less, but knew I couldn't.

"He was so proud of you," Mr. Presley whispered.

It was equally emotional with all of Elvis's guys. We hugged each other and cried.

At Memphis's Forest Hill cemetery, I could barely bring myself to bid farewell to Elvis. I managed only a glance at the casket, which was covered with flowers. It was too much for me, and I let Roger lead me away.

Three months later, Colonel Tom Parker, Elvis's longtime manager, and Mr. Presley asked me to host *Memories of Elvis,* a two-hour NBC tribute that combined footage from his 1968 and 1973 televised performances. To this day, it's remained one of the most difficult, wrenching jobs I've ever undertaken. In introducing the different parts of the show, I was supposed to be somewhat upbeat, at least celebratory of Elvis's contributions, but I had a particularly hard time fighting the tears. The footage was truly extraordinary; but I was just horribly sad.

Roger attempted to coax me through the dialogue, but without much success. As the segment, totaling just fifteen minutes, went into its sixth hour of taping, Esposito finally talked me into calming down.

"Now, Rusty," he said, calling me by my character's name from *Viva Las Vegas,* "you know that he's up there, laughing away, saying, 'Look at 'em all, making such a big fuss over me. And she can't even say the words.'"

I smiled. He was right.

"Elvis and I made a movie together called *Viva Las Vegas,* and we remained close friends after that," I began. "I cherish the memory of that friendship. He was a good man. He was kind. Very respectful. A gentleman.

"But I'm not just here tonight as someone who knew him or worked with him. I'm here as you are . . . a fan."

I will never recover from Elvis's death. He is a part of me, of my happiness and my sorrow, and that will never go away. Elvis and I crossed paths at a time when we were both young, passionate, vulnerable, and idealistic. I treasure the time we were together, and I feel lucky and fulfilled that we were able to sustain such a long, loving, and caring friendship. It's rare to have such a friend as Elvis, rare to have such a soul mate.

37

ROGER WATCHED ME CLOSELY DURING THE PERIOD after Elvis's death, knowing how thinly balanced I was. He also knew that the best distraction for me was work. So, he encouraged me to do *Magic,* starring Anthony Hopkins as a whacked-out ventriloquist controlled by his dummy and thwarted in his effort to romance his old high school sweetheart. Writer William Goldman, who'd based the screenplay on his own novel, told me that I myself had inspired the story when we met several years earlier at a birthday party for Allan at Regine's nightclub in Paris.

We discovered that he and I had attended rival high schools in Illinois—New Trier and Highland Park. I admitted having been a cheerleader, and after that night he started working on a story about a cheerleader named Peggy Ann Snow, a reversion of Ann-Margret (Peggy). After Bill explained this, I was, needless to say, greatly amused.

Before the year got too old, Allan and Roger decided on an amicable parting of ways. While Roger was content to manage only my career, Allan wanted to branch out into other areas of the business. Really, there was no holding him back, and as we predicted, he produced the motion picture *Grease* and the Broadway show *La Cage Aux Folles,* both gigantic successes, and became one of the most respected producers in Hollywood.

Meanwhile, we carried on. We spruced up my nightclub show by hiring Lester Wilson, who had choreographed John Travolta's fancy footwork in *Saturday Night Fever.*

Lester created one of my all-time favorites, a number titled "Lil's Place," which began with ten mannequins

dressed like me on stage. Then ten guys in trenchcoats
came out and danced with them. Enter Ann-Margret and
the mannequins were discarded in favor of the real me.

This brilliant man choreographed my nightclub act for
the next fifteen years. Our company was nearly a second
family. Some dancers, such as Wade Collings and Tommy
Peel, stayed with us for almost twenty years, as did my
conductor, Donn Trenner. We worked hard on stage and
played hard off. At least once a week, Roger staged a big
party after the show, showing homemade videos he taped
of all of us that week, and serving delicious food.

Steve Martin, Marvin Hamlisch, and many others enliv-
ened our parties with outlandish silliness, impromptu
dances, skits, and songs. Once, the dancers arrived wearing
their leather motorcycle costumes and pretended they were
a real biker gang. Without breaking character, they attacked
Roger, wrestled him to the ground and threatened worse
before they left. Later, the guys returned as themselves and
never mentioned the incident.

Between gigs we spent as much time as possible with
our children. Roger would fly the whole family up to Big
Bear for camping trips. We also did a lot of skiing. We
vacationed in Hawaii, where we all rented motorcycles and
zipped around the tropical wilderness.

And I continued trying to get pregnant, but managed to
be more philosophical. After all these years of trying and
failing, I couldn't sink into depressions each month or I
would cease to function. In a funny way, you grow immune
to disappointment, or at least you try to.

Both Roger and I tried to make things better by pursuing
more fun in our lives. If a script or a show didn't sound
really good and fun, we said no. I finally understood what
Roger meant years earlier when he criticized my first manager for accepting everything instead of waiting for only
the best projects. Now we were in that position.

In September 1978, we went to New York for the taping
of *Rockette,* a two-hour celebration of the Radio City's five-
decade history as told through one of its world-famous
Rockettes—the part I played. I didn't have to act in order

to express my feelings about Radio City. Nor was I alone among the guests who told of personal ties to the landmark showplace. Greer Garson had starred in the two movies that boasted Radio City's longest runs, *Random Harvest* and *Mrs. Miniver.* Beverly Sills, Ben Vereen, and Alan King all performed there. Gregory Peck, who hosted the show, had once worked as an usher and proved it by reciting the tour speech he had memorized as a teenager.

The special, which aired two weeks before Christmas, allowed me to live out one of my fantasies: I joined the actual Rockettes in their chorus line. I sang a song called ''How Do You Get to Be a Rockette,'' preceded by my confession to the audience that I had always wanted to perform on that stage.

A few months after that incredible high, in January, I received word that Elvis's father, Vernon, had become seriously ill in Memphis. I had always felt close to Mr. Presley, so I chartered a jet and paid him a visit.

Charlie Hodge, one of Elvis's guys, met me at the airport and took me to see him at Graceland. I couldn't tell how sick he was, though he'd certainly lost the color of good health. It was heartbreaking to talk about all the wonderful times and to realize that they were in a past that was sailing further away.

We had a good visit, though, laughing and crying and trading stories. He told me how much he missed his son, and I said that I missed him, too.

Periodically, I called Mr. Presley to offer kind words and to hear how he was feeling, in the hope that my familiar voice would add comfort to his days. I later heard that he'd occasionally ask if I'd called or wonder what I was doing, always describing me to his nurse as a ''real nice girl.'' When he died on June 26, 1979, I knew that at least I'd been in his thoughts.

At that time, Roger and I were in Toronto and wondering if we might be pushing ourselves too hard. During the day, I worked on the film *Middle Age Crazy,* with Bruce Dern, a New Trier alum. At night, I recorded ''Love Rush,'' a disco LP written and produced by my friend Paul Sabu, the son of Sabu, the Elephant Boy. I'd work on the album until one or two in the morning, and then I'd get up at five a.m. the next day for makeup and hair. Once, I came to the set, delivered my first line of the day, and nothing came out—nothing but a scratchy facsimile of my voice. Somewhere between the studio and the set, I'd come down with laryngitis. It was a warning.

I wished Roger and I had recognized that we were working too hard, tackling too much, but we didn't. Whenever I was on a set or making a record, Roger was there at my side, handling all the details, solving all the problems. He did it all effortlessly, but I knew he worked as hard as I did.

In July of 1979 came the premiere of *The Villain,* a Western spoof costarring Kirk Douglas I had filmed the previous winter. I also gave a mini-concert for the *Billboard* convention at Roseland in New York. Over Christmas and New Year's, I played Caesars Palace—where Alan Margulies, our friend from the Fontainebleau, was head of entertainment.

In February, the *Love Rush* album came out and hit the eighth spot on the dance charts. In March, I picked up the Jimmy Durante Award as best female entertainer at the Las Vegas Entertainer Awards. And in May, my TV special *Hollywood Movie Girls* aired. It was one thing after another.

Roger and I were so caught up in all this activity that it was easy for us to brush aside the subtle warning signs that we might've been going too fast for our own good. Except for my accident, neither of us had been sick since we'd begun dating in 1964. Yet, since Toronto, Roger had been complaining of fatigue.

The fatigue came and went with unpredictable severity, which made us brush it off as a virus. However, as I began working on *Lookin' to Get Out,* he stayed relatively stable while I slipped into more immediate danger.

When you break your sobriety it's not like all of a sudden you say, "Ah-ha, I'm going to have a drink today." It's much more deceptive, much trickier than that. Your mind plays games. One day the thought enters your mind like an intruder. It lurks about, plays a sneaky game of hide and seek, waiting for a sign of weakness.

During production, I continued an acupuncture program I'd started earlier after someone recommended it as a way to increase the chances of getting pregnant. And it seemed to work. Three different times—twice during the movie— I truly believed I was pregnant.

But each high was followed by a horrible low. The pregnancies all turned out to be false. I really thought that I'd finally gotten pregnant, as I'm told some women do, after all I had been through. Then when it turned out not to be true, I became incredibly distraught. I was in real pain, and the thought of a drink, which had been in my mind for months, took hold.

I drank champagne. I knew I was going to regret it and I knew it wasn't going to alleviate the pain. In fact, chances were it was going to increase the amount of suffering I had to go through. But you don't think logically in that circumstance. You just think of it as a means to an end . . . ending the pain.

I was totally, thoroughly devastated. I was ashamed of myself. I'd gone so long without drinking. I lived in a dark, stormy cloud.

Not long after I broke my sobriety, I attended a luncheon and sat beside my friend Kathleen and her husband, Carl. My subconscious was at work. I said hello and pretended that I hadn't been drinking and that no one would notice. But as soon as I opened my mouth, and maybe as soon as he saw my eyes, Carl turned to his wife and said, "She's been drinking."

Before leaving, I pulled Kathleen aside and in confidence told her that I'd been drinking.

"I know," she said without judgment, though her clear blue eyes were judgment itself.

"But I have it under control," I lied. "It's all fine."

"Really?"

"I'm happy, yes. I'm handling it."

I really honestly believed that. And that's the tragic part of this illness. Two weeks later when I was passing out, I could still convince myself that I was happy and not in any danger of drinking myself to an early grave.

Yet, while I was telling myself everything was under control, I couldn't stop my mind from worrying. I fixated on having turned thirty-nine, the age I always thought my career would end. I figured it was over for me. I worried about what I would do. I worried about my disappointments in childbearing. And I worried about Roger.

About the same time, Roger's bouts of exhaustion and weakness came more frequently. He couldn't get to meetings. Household chores became a struggle. Sometimes he literally had to will himself to stand, dress, and walk out of the bedroom, otherwise he wouldn't have gotten up. Roger was so weary, so de-energized, that he didn't seem as concerned about my drinking as he should have been, and that might have worried me even more. But I was too deep into my alcoholic haze.

Neither of us knew what was the matter. He promised to make a doctor's appointment. He never did.

It was inevitable that something had to give. One morning I woke up from a stupor at four a.m. and said to myself, "No more!" I wanted to call Kathleen, as I'd done on several occasions in the past when I had been tempted to drink, with good results. This time, though, since I'd already broken my sobriety, I decided to be polite and not wake her up.

About fifteen minutes later, Roger wandered into the kitchen looking tired but concerned. My place in our water bed was vacant, and he'd wondered where I'd disappeared to at such an unusual hour for me and expected to find the worst. Instead, I was as awake as a prowler, sitting at the kitchen table and pleased to see another human being.

"I'm going to call Kathleen," I announced, "but it's still too early. I don't want to wake her up."

"Wake her up," Roger said.

Everyone needs an angel. Kathleen was mine.

She had her regular weekly doubles-match with three ladies who were also in the organization and invited me over to watch. I arrived dressed in a black cashmere, black stretch pants, a wool scarf, a hat, and dark sunglasses—my version of incognito—and sat beside the tennis court as temperatures climbed toward one hundred while Kathleen and her pals played the best tennis of their lives.

They put on quite a show. They wanted me to see what they had in abundance—good health.

Afterward, we had tea. Four ladies beside the tennis court—three in tennis whites and one in black cashmere. We talked throughout the morning and afternoon about my frustrations over trying to get pregnant and the way I handled them. I recognized the soothing sense of relief that came over me as I unburdened myself. I knew that I didn't want to go on that way anymore, and I didn't. That evening Roger and I went to dinner and a recovery meeting, my first in months, with several of my supportive friends.

That was June 20, 1980. I haven't had a drink since.

38

WITH MY HEAD CLEAR AGAIN, I FIGURED TO HECK
with retiring. As long as my fans were still interested, I'd
grow old with them. It was Roger who I worried about.

His mind was busy, shuffling dates and scripts as if they
were a deck of cards. But while Roger plotted a world tour,
picture deals, and even the prospect of us finally working
together in a limited-run play, Gretchen Cryer's *I'm Getting
My Act Together and Taking It on the Road,* his body
would not oblige. Listless and depleted of energy, Roger
couldn't even get out of bed at Caesars Palace in Vegas to
go home.

A Lear jet waited at the airport and a car idled downstairs
in front of the hotel, but I doubted whether we'd actually
make it that far. Roger, struggling to just sit up in bed, had
absolutely no strength. I told him the car was in front; he
didn't have to walk any further than that. But he couldn't
move. Trying to revive him, I soaked towels in cold water
and wet his face, but he didn't budge.

Finally, I asked our friend Neal Peters and a few other
guys to help me lift Roger and assist him downstairs. I was
determined to get home and get him to a doctor. We'd
already inquired about specialists and had an appointment
with Dr. Gregory Walsh at St. John's Hospital in Santa
Monica.

When Roger woke up the next morning, he was too weak
to make a fist. Somehow, he dragged himself to the car and
sat next to me, in deep silence, as I drove him to the hospital.

After taking down Roger's medical history and exam-
ining him, Dr. Walsh felt fairly certain about what was

going on, but, he explained, before he could be positive, he needed to conduct a particular test—an anticholinesterase test. We had no idea what that meant. Dr. Walsh, explaining that the test measured the response at the nerve-muscle juncture, performed it right away.

Alas, the test confirmed the diagnosis of myasthenia gravis. At least we finally had a name to attach to this dreadful sickness that was crippling Roger.

We immediately acquired all the literature we could find in libraries, and the news wasn't good. Myasthenia gravis was a rare, chronic disease affecting the transmission of nerve impulses to the muscles they control.

Furthermore, the disease was unpredictable, and sometimes fatal. As we lay next to each other in bed, I read down the list of obvious symptoms.

"Weakness?"

"Check," Roger said.

"Double vision?"

"No."

"Thank God," I said. "Droopy eyelids?"

"No."

"Difficulty in carrying out simple tasks?"

"Yes."

"Swallowing?"

"I've had trouble with that, too."

The literature painted a disturbing portrait, and Roger fit it to a tee. Both of us were devastated. Inwardly, I cried, but I might've pulled off the best performance of my acting career by keeping a tough, positive exterior. Roger's only comment was true to his character. He wanted a second opinion.

Neither of us accepted bad news without a good fight.

Suddenly, our priorities changed. My career was put on hold, nightclub dates were canceled, movie scripts sent back, TV specials postponed, and everything on the drawing board was erased. The only thing that mattered was Roger's health.

Over the next few months the disease followed its own erratic blueprint. His neck weakened. He had trouble holding his head straight. He struggled to swallow. It became hard for him to eat. Often he needed liquid to force food down his throat and occasionally that didn't work and he'd choke. One morning he woke up gagging. Roger couldn't draw the air into his lungs and then exhale without really concentrating on making each fiber in each muscle do its job. Simply breathing required all his thoughts and energy and consumed an entire day at a time.

Though Roger's condition seemed grim, I never thought that he might not pull out of this horrible condition.

The rest of the world wasn't as kind. One day I picked up the phone, something I did routinely now that Roger wasn't able to speak easily, and a woman identified herself as a reporter from one of the better known tabloids.

"How long do you think your husband has?" she asked.

"I beg your pardon?" I responded incredulously.

"Your husband is dying," she said. "How much longer do the doctors expect him to live?"

I didn't know how this reporter got our unlisted number. Nor did I know how she could ask such a question. I slammed the phone down.

Roger started taking the drug Mestinon, but that caused too many side effects and he had to quit. There were days when everything seemed hopeless. But we both knew Roger had to continue to think positively and to fight. Hence, we got the names of two specialists in myasthenia gravis at UCLA—Drs. John Keesey and Christian Hermann. They informed us of a test, which would give us a more sophisticated analysis of Roger's condition. Although they warned us the test was painful, we just wanted to be as well-informed as possible and told them to go ahead. They stuck needles into Roger's arms, then stimulated his muscles with an electrical charge while the doctors measured the strength of the muscle.

"There's no doubt," we were told. "Roger has an acute case of MG."

Still, there was a bright side. Muscle weakness was measured by specific values. The higher the number, the more severe the case of MG. They figured that at his worst Roger had probably been at the high end, but now the numbers were low. We asked what that meant.

"It could mean nothing," we were told. "However, it could also indicate that he's begun a period of remission."

From the way he looked and felt, that was hard to believe. But we clung to even that thread of hope.

As the months went by, Roger did as much as he could. He took a drug called Prednisone, and started a macrobiotic diet. We were reeducated about eating by nutritionist Hermien Lee. On good days, he attempted to move around, even exercise a bit, doing anything he could to give his body a chance to fight back.

When he felt up to it, Roger read medical books, journals, and phoned experts and hospitals across the country and basically learned that there were two possible treatments—not cures—for people in his situation. One was a blood-cleansing procedure called a plasmapheresis, in which blood was filtered and then returned to the body. It proved beneficial, we were told, about forty percent of the time. But the downside was that this cleansing also removed a lifetime of immunities. The second option involved the surgical removal of the thymus gland, which is supposed to go dormant after puberty, but, we were told, often reactivates in MG patients. By removing the gland, doctors hoped to put him into remission.

We leaned toward surgery—a thymectomy—but first Roger and I read all the literature on the procedure. Because of the location of the thymus below the neck, the operation could be done two different ways. Either the chest could be split open as in heart surgery; or doctors had the option of positioning the patient so his head hung off the edge of the table and then performing the surgery through the throat.

In typically stubborn fashion, Roger couldn't decide which method was best—or best suited for him. Lying in bed, weak, tired, and hard of breath, he occupied his time with endless research, talking to doctors as well as to people who'd actually gone through the operation. I pressed him to decide, hoping for a miracle cure. Even our doctors pushed him to reach some conclusion. Roger might've been sick, but he didn't change as a person, and thus methodically took his time.

I also stood at a crossroads of sort, a point in my life where I had to make a decision vital to our existence. Could I step into his shoes and take over running the business, house, everything that he did with such ease? Was I strong enough to do that? Or was I, as many people suspected, too fragile and frightened to emerge from the protective cocoon? I simply did what I had to do, and as the months went by, I assumed the bulk of Roger's responsibilities, leaving him free to rest and pursue his medical research. I tried to shield the kids, too, helping them with their problems and trying to be cheerful on the outside so they wouldn't know how terrified I was within. Understandably, they were frightened, even panicked to see their once powerful father so incapacitated. They were scared. We all were.

Slowly, I became a different woman inside. The dependent, shy Ann-Margret slipped away by necessity, and a confident and competent woman came in her place. I could not only sing, act, and dance, but buy stocks and bonds, hire a plumber, and make business decisions about my career.

For many women, all this is a given, but for me it was a quiet triumph, an unexpected good that emerged from a state of crisis. Now, if only Roger would get better. Miraculously, he did. As the months passed, both of us noticed a strange and unexpected occurrence. Gradually and almost imperceptibly, Roger's health improved. He continued to debate the different thymectomy procedures, and we made arrangements to visit the Mayo Clinic in Minnesota. However, his breathing got easier. The muscles in his neck had less difficulty supporting his head. His legs felt as if they'd like to walk around the house, and soon they did.

In early 1982 we met with doctors at the Mayo Clinic, who put Roger through more of the same tests and answered his questions about the operation. Yet they told us that he probably shouldn't have the operation, and then offered even more heartening news. New tests suggested he was definitely in remission—the reason he had been feeling better.

As to why this had happened, the doctors were stymied. Roger believed that maybe his diet or vitamins played a part. I attributed it to all of the above as well as rest, no stress, the body's amazing power to rejuvenate, and prayer. But I'll never forget the morning Roger, beginning to look like his old self, asked over breakfast, "You know what?"

"What?" I replied.

"I feel kinda good."

There was such celebrating at the house. Nothing equaled that moment. Doctors confirmed the improvement. They said that it appeared that the disease, true to its unpredictable nature, had reversed itself. Roger had gone into remission.

"Why?" we asked.

"We don't know," they answered.

"Will it come back?"

"Again, we don't know. It could start up again tomorrow. Or it might never reappear."

"But he's better?" I asked, wanting reconfirmation.

"Look at him," they said. "He looks like he could do a couple of laps around the UCLA track."

It was as if the sun began to shine again after a lengthy dark spell.

If there was a lesson to be learned, it was to never surrender—no matter what the experts tell you. The human spirit is indomitable. The gift of life is too precious.

When Roger's strength appeared to be on its way back, we sat down and made a conscious decision to squeeze every drop of happiness from our lives. There would no longer be wasting of any time or postponing travel or adventure. We would live for the moment, the day, and not the future. Once Roger was his old self, we began skiing the gorgeous mountains in Aspen, and we scuba dived in Maui. I traipsed through the Egyptian desert in high heels that had sharper points than the great Pyramids. Roger strode happily by my side.

Doctors would not speculate on Roger's condition. The file Roger had started the day we went to the library to find out about this strange-sounding disease had grown into a whole drawer. He networked with others who had the disease, such as Bob Chernove, who produced a number of MG fundraising dinners, including one that honored us. We also spoke to people who've been in remission for thirty years and longer.

There was hope, not just for us, but for everyone suffering from myasthenia gravis as well as the twenty-six neuromuscular diseases related to it. Every year researchers learn more about it and believe one day there will be a cure. If a cure is found for just one of the diseases, then all the others will fall into place like a game of dominoes.

We hope and pray.

39

THE SOUND WAS LIKE NOTHING I'D EVER HEARD. Standing several feet behind the curtain at the China Theater, Stockholm's resplendent old showcase, I looked askance at Roger, who stood in the wings. As the curtain rose, the noise grew louder, frightening, like the low rumble of the ground during an earthquake. I turned to the front and through the lights discovered what was causing that sound. The audience wasn't just clapping, they were stomping their feet.

Instead of starting the first song as planned, I said a heartfelt thank-you. In the middle of my speech, though, I found myself struggling with my native language to find the words that would describe how I felt. Turning to the trombone player, a native Swede, I asked the correct way to say "goose bumps"—one euphemism I didn't know. The audience hung with me.

"You are so kind and wonderful, so very warm. I can't get over this reception. See, I have goose bumps," I said, showing them my arms. "Gås Hud."

The audience reacted with a chorus of loud guffaws. It was as if they'd never heard that phrase before. Then I laughed with them. It was a great way to start my first ever performance in the country where I was born.

In the fall of 1982 we *needed* a good laugh. Although Roger's health was nearly back to normal, we were wary of returning to work too quickly. We'd just come from London, where I tested my English accent opposite a great English cast—Alan Bates, Julie Christie, and Glenda Jackson—in the movie *The Return of the Soldier,* which didn't reach the U.S. until 1985. The movie, which had a relatively relaxed filming schedule, had given us a chance to start slow. And our mini-tour of Sweden was a triumphant finale.

Then, Roger and I debated long about what we should do next—what we should do and *how much* we should do. In fact, we had just returned from Europe and were resting in New York when the script for *Who Will Love My Children?* arrived. I said no without even reading it. I didn't want to overdo it. Tracey had recently made us grandparents for the first time, and that called for a certain amount of attention. But most importantly, I'd watched Roger closely and although he bore no resemblance to the man who'd spent the previous year in bed, he would never be his old self totally.

If it meant Roger's health, I didn't care if I ever set foot on stage or in front of a camera again. I was Mrs. Smith first. Then I was Ann-Margret. Some women may find this outdated and silly, but it was the way I had lived my life. Yes, I was newly competent, newly assertive, but still old-fashioned.

The *Who Will Love My Children?* script wouldn't go away. I received a call from Dr. Lu, who was also acquainted with the movie's director, John Erman. I'd actually met John at a party at her house.

"You know, he would really love for you to read it," she said. "He says it's exceptional."

Two more copies of the script arrived at the house. That night, Roger and I sat up in bed and read the true story of Lucile Fray, a terminally ill Iowa farm wife, whose final mission in life was finding a home for each of her ten children before she passed away. Three-quarters of the way through the script, I turned to Roger. I had tears streaming down my face. He did, too.

"I've got to do this," I said.

"You really do," he agreed.

The next day I called John Erman.

"John, I've never given birth to a child," I said. "I have three stepchildren whom I love like my own. But how can you consider me for this?"

"You're perfect," he replied.

"Really. I want to know how you thought of me for this. We met at Lu's party for what, five minutes?"

"And in those five minutes I saw the strength in you that made me believe you could play Lucile."

That's all I needed to hear. As strongly as John believed in me, I believed with all my might that Lucile Fray's story absolutely had to be shown to people as a testimony to strength and courage and character and tremendous dignity.

She was the first real person I'd ever played, and I vowed to try to do justice to this real-life heroine. It was so important. Her children would watch; this would be part of the legacy they'd have of their mother. It was a heavy responsibility.

I researched her valiant struggle to live long enough to place each of her children in a good home. I learned that she never shed a single tear in front of her children or her friends. Only her husband, who battled alcoholism, saw her cry. Despite severe pain, she refused strong drugs to ensure she did not get fuzzy-headed as she raced against time to find a home for the last child.

As the director, John had deep feeling for the story. He also had the kind of insight and understanding that inspired confidence and made it easy for me to take risks, to open myself up for the camera. Yet John was also stern. The day before the first scene, he reminded me that Lucile was a dying farm woman—not a city woman.

"In other words, no makeup," he said. "Nothing that hints you are Ann-Margret."

I understood. John was just reiterating the emotional depths I must reach for. The makeup was symbolic of something much greater. But actors, like anyone else, don't always want to let go completely.

"Can I curl my eyelashes?" I asked.

He smiled, and that is when I took the final leap.

"You'll have to trust me," he said.

When the movie aired on Valentine's Day 1983, I was in the middle of a short engagement at Caesars in Las Vegas. That evening I did my two regularly scheduled performances and then a special "gypsy show"—a free act at three a.m. for all the people who worked on the Strip. It used to be a tradition among performers. Between shows, we arranged for a small screening of *Who Will Love My Children?* in our suite. While everyone watched in the living room, I stayed in the bedroom.

But the reaction was the same: Everyone sobbed through the entire movie.

Who Will Love My Children? received a handful of Emmy nominations—and I was nominated Outstanding Actress in a Limited Series or Special for my portrayal of Lucile. I didn't expect to get it, and indeed, Barbara Stanwyck won for *The Thorn Birds* miniseries. Yet as she stood at the podium, she made me also feel like a winner.

"Now I would like to pay a personal tribute at this time," the legendary actress said, "to a lady who is a wonderful entertainer. She gave us a film last season in which I think she gave one of the finest, most beautiful performances I've ever seen. Ann-Margret, you were superb." Then she blew me a kiss.

I buried my head in Roger's jacket so no one could see the tears. I couldn't believe Miss Stanwyck's incredibly generous, touching mention of me in the midst of her acceptance speech. Nor could I get over another tribute. Over Christmas, I'd received a card from Lucile Fray's surviving children, who'd addressed it "To our other Mom" and signed off, "Love, the children."

Not long after the Emmys, Roger suffered a temporary relapse. For no apparent reason, his strength suddenly vanished. It happened as he supervised some changes in my nightclub act. Both of us were consumed by fears as Roger returned to bed. Privately, I shuddered at the thought of the disease returning to wreck its strange, unforgiving damage on Roger's body. Although I put on a brave face to Roger, I knew there was no predicting its course. I also knew there was no predicting Roger's ability to fight it. After several days, he remained too weak to attend an MG fundraiser that was, ironically, held in our honor in Beverly Hills. It was one of the few times in our married life that I went to an event without Roger. But I couldn't cancel. I'd promised to sing.

Over several weeks, Roger did rebound, but I didn't want to take any chances or tempt fate. We decided not to add any more nightclub dates other than those already scheduled, and instead to concentrate on films, which didn't put nearly as much stress on Roger. At the same time, an old idea resurfaced—a TV remake of Tennessee Williams's classic *A Streetcar Named Desire.* I'd discussed starring in a TV version almost a decade earlier. I even learned Tennessee himself had asked that I play Blanche DuBois.

So when the opportunity arose again in 1983, I realized it was for a reason. My first inclination was to seek out Tennessee and ask what it was about me that made him see Blanche. What were the similarities? What were the characteristics of mine that reminded him of this tragic Southern belle?

Tragically, he died three days after I signed the contract, and I never got a chance to meet or talk with him. Yet, instinctively, I sensed why the great playwright had seen me as Blanche. That led to my only request, which was really an outright demand. I wanted John Erman to direct. I knew the depth I would have to go to in order to become Blanche. It was similar to reaching inside Bobbie Templeton in *Carnal Knowledge,* and I wanted John there to make sure I did not fail.

In order to get Blanche's Southern mannerisms, I spent several weeks in Alabama visiting with a friend of John's who lived on a wonderful plantation. For several days, I lunched and had tea with different groups of ladies, asking them questions and tape-recording their answers so I could continue to study their accents back in L.A. I also met one of Tennessee Williams's good friends in a bar, and as soon as he heard me talk in my Southern drawl, he said, "Indeed, you're what he imagined."

After three weeks of rehearsals with cast members Treat Williams, Beverly D'Angelo, and Randy Quaid, we shot the picture in chronological order, leaving out the scenes John saved for location in New Orleans. By the time the production arrived in Bayou country, I was a quivering wreck. Down ten pounds (which was not unpleasant in that, like most women, I always want to be thinner). I felt dazed and psychologically beaten. Just as I had in *Carnal Knowledge,* I retreated inside the character, which was frightening for the others in the cast. During the scene where Treat Williams as Stanley Kowalski rapes Blanche, an ugly, brutal display, I insisted he really grab and physically pummel me. As black-and-blue marks surfaced on my skin, Treat apologized profusely and backed off the hard stuff.

"Don't," I pressed. "We've got to do it this way. Otherwise it won't look real."

"But look what it's doing to you," he said.

"Don't worry," I said.

Sydney Guilaroff, who had styled Vivien Leigh's hair when she filmed *Streetcar* in 1951, and had allowed me to persuade him out of retirement, asked every morning if I was okay. I said I was—at that moment.

On the second to last day of shooting, I froze. I wouldn't leave my dressing room. John was quickly summoned, and found me in a chair, twisted and shaking, confused, agitated, and staring ahead in a daze. I'd lost my grasp on reality. Quickly, John ordered the room cleared and took hold of my hands.

"Ann-Margret!" he said.

"Yes?"

"Listen to me!"

"What?"

"This is just a movie! You have to realize that this is just a movie!"

As Roger had feared, Blanche didn't disappear after the film had ended—a repeat of Bobbie's refusal to leave after *Carnal Knowledge.* After the last scene of *Streetcar,* which had started at midnight and gone till seven a.m., I flew to L.A. and began rehearsals for a show to be staged in San Francisco. Four days later, I had just stepped on stage at the Golden Gate Theater in San Francisco when Blanche decided to make a public appearance.

It was a matinee, the first of two shows that day, and I was midway through the opening, an old-fashioned strut, a big production number, when suddenly everything blurred in front of my eyes. I forgot the steps. I couldn't hear the music. With a frightening abruptness, I just stopped and stood in the center of the stage with a glazed look on my face, trembling.

"Ladies and gentlemen," I said, bewildered, "I think I'm going to have to leave the stage. I think I have to lie down for a moment."

Instantly, my dancers huddled around me and helped me off the stage. As I neared the side curtain, Roger took hold of me and sat me on a chair, where I shook uncontrollably. Roger and others tried to calm me.

Someone threw a blanket around me, and one of my backup singers gave me an energy drink, which I gulped down. Roger guided me through deep-breathing exercises. Slowly, I returned to reality. After ten minutes of relaxation, I limbered up again.

"Okay, we're gonna do it," I said.

"Are you sure?" Roger asked.

I could hear the audience chatter nervously and shuffle their feet—even over the band, which improvised without pause. Even my musicians were clueless as to the drama taking place beyond the curtains at the side of the stage. No one had made an announcement of any kind yet.

"I'm going to do it," I said, standing up and shaking off the hands that wanted either to steady me or pull me back.

Oblivious to the applause that greeted me on returning to the stage, I took the precaution of sitting down on the bench beside Donn Trenner, my pianist and conductor. He looked at me reassuringly and went to the next number on the set list as if this had been rehearsed while I held onto him and began to sing. Gradually my head cleared and senses returned, and I heard the music clearly. By the end of the song, I stood at the edge of the stage, gazing out at the audience with a broad smile on my face. I reached out to those seated in the front row, shaking hands as the applause buoyed my weak legs.

"I was wondering if you'd still be out here," I said.

The applause increased. Somebody from the dark middle of the theater, the part I could not see, yelled, "We're always here for you. We love you."

"And I love you, too," I said.

Then I looked toward Roger, watching from the same spot behind the curtain, where he'd stood since my first performance at the Riviera in 1967, and sang the stirring ballad "Wind Beneath My Wings." Afterward, I blew him a kiss and saw the same glint in his eyes that was there when we met. For old time's sake, we made a pilgrimage to the lobby of the Fairmont Hotel, where we'd begun our love affair twenty years earlier.

Famed San Francisco columnist Herb Caen once described Roger's and my relationship. "They met in that revolving door at the Fairmont," he wrote, "and they've been going round together ever since."

40

TOWARD THE CLOSE OF 1983, I STOOD ON STAGE OF Stockholm's China Theater, where I had made my Swedish debut not long before. This time, I announced my retirement from live performing.

Roger and I had talked about it for some time. Very simply, I was exhausted and mostly, I feared that my performance schedule would further damage Roger's health. After the music had faded into the background, we only had each other and our family, and there wasn't any reason to jeopardize that. Between movies and nightclub performances, we had little time to walk the trails that ran across our property at home. I wanted more time to cuddle.

Before we left Sweden, I decided I had to take everyone in the company who wanted to go to Valsjobyn. As long as they were witnessing the end, they might as well see the beginning, too. Because of foul weather, we canceled the helicopter scheduled to take us there, and faced a seven-hour drive. I promised everybody it would be worth it. There was no question, after a feast of reindeer, herring, moose meatballs, and potatoes—all topped off by Swedish pancakes and cloudberries for dessert.

In the midst of the dinner, I stole away to the little white church in nearby Hotagen, where my mother had been baptized, confirmed, and married. Outside, in the small, carefully tended graveyard, her parents—Mooma and Moofa—were buried. In that emotional setting, I knelt beside Mooma's grave and whispered, "Thank you for my mother."

Knowing what a vital role my mother had served in helping me get through the rough patches of the past, I returned home determined to make one final effort to beat the biological clock. I wasn't desperate, but I did have to come to terms with the longstanding desire. If it happened, my dream would be fulfilled. If not, it wasn't meant to be.

In April 1984, I turned forty-three and doctors pronounced me in perfect working order. Roger and I tried natural methods throughout filming of *Twice in a Lifetime*. As soon as the movie wrapped, I agreed to try an experimental fertility pump, a device that looked like two plastic cups. A needle was inserted beneath the skin around my waist and the cuplike pump attached. The pump released hormones every two hours, every day, over a thirty-three-day period.

I tried it three separate times—none successful—and then I gave up for good on trying to get pregnant. I had been trying for more than a decade. Clearly, I told myself, it wasn't meant to happen. I'd tried everything; I resolved not to suffer any regrets. I had three wonderful stepchildren whom I loved and helped to raise as if they were my own. I reasoned God had other plans for me.

I explained to Roger that I'd made my peace and then reminded him of a prayer I'd learned more than ten years earlier, a prayer that gave me the courage and conviction to accede to the uncertainty of fate. "God, grant me the serenity to accept the things I cannot change, the courage to change the things I can and the wisdom to know the difference."

About that time, we downshifted to a slower speed. As Roger sifted through scripts, we planned on making maybe one movie a year instead of two or three and several months of nightclub gigs. We had no plans to rest on our laurels, merely to enjoy them with family and friends. It took a lot to entice us out of the comfort of our hilltop refuge. But in early 1986, director John Frankenheimer talked me into working on *52 Pick-Up,* an adaptation of an Elmore Leonard novel about blackmail and murder that starred Roy Scheider.

As soon as it finished, I found myself confronted by a higher authority. Ever since he heard that I'd ended my nightclub performances, George Burns had been on my back to reconsider. He had pushed me when I'd guested on a TV special celebrating his eightieth year in show business in 1983, and he continued to do so when I appeared on a 1986 special honoring his ninetieth birthday. After *52 Pick-Up,* he called.

"Annie, do all the dramatic stuff you want," he said. "Movies are great. I remember when they were invented. But you're a performer. You gotta get back on stage."

"But Roger's health," I said. "We're being careful."

"He looks wonderful," Mr. Burns retorted. "At my age if you can walk without help, you're healthy. Know what I mean?"

I did. As we began to consider his point, John Erman phoned with an offer—costarring in the TV adaptation of Dominick Dunne's novel, *The Two Mrs. Grenvilles.* The part of Ann Grenville, a woman whose marriage to a young socialite pits her against his controlling mother, was irresistible. The other Mrs. Grenville was played by Claudette Colbert. I treasured the opportunity to work opposite one of the really great women of movies.

Once the picture finished, I took on *A Tiger's Tale,* a sweet coming-of-age story. We hadn't planned on starting another project so quickly, but we realized that the performer's habit of always looking ahead to the next job was as strong now as it had been when I was starting out.

For both of us, it was hard to stay at home. We loved to work, loved being part of an exciting, stimulating, challenging business. Many of our closest friends were people we'd met during projects. Burt Reynolds is a good example.

We became acquainted with Burt in Toronto when I was making *A New Life.* Burt wasn't even in the picture, but he was in the same hotel, directly across the hall from our room.

Roger and I knew Burt only in passing. We'd met several years earlier at a Dinah Shore show, and then said hello at various events. But I'd always heard about Burt's wonderful sense of humor; he was among the most entertaining storytellers in Hollywood. One night we noticed the light on in his room, and Roger walked across the hall and invited him to dinner.

We got together a few evenings later and discovered a mutual love of sports. Actually, it was more of an obsession, particularly with me. Burt, who'd played running back at Florida State—number 22—was amazed at how much I knew about football, especially the L.A. Raiders.

"How do you know so much?" he asked.

"Once a cheerleader, always a cheerleader," I smiled.

A man of great passion, Burt chartered a jet the next weekend and flew all of us to Florida State University to watch his beloved alma mater in action. Before the game, he and Roger even went onto the field and joined the motivational pregame huddle. It was a great day. Florida State won by some incredible margin. Back in L.A., we started a tradition of spending weekends at each other's house, watching the different games. One week at our house, one week at Burt and Loni's. Just joking around.

In fact, Burt changed our viewing habits. After we watched on his satellite dish and a ten-foot-screen TV, we also got one.

But there was a serious side to our friendship. Burt had been going through an extremely difficult period since he was accidentally hit on the side of his face with an iron chair in 1984, while making the movie *City Heat*. I knew all about mishaps; however he wasn't as lucky as I was. The blow crushed his temporomandibular joint, harmed his inner ear, and—until he had reconstructive surgery on his jaw—resulted in almost two years of constant, debilitating pain.

When we met, Burt was trying to climb out of this nightmarish existence. By his own admission, Burt's injury transformed him from a fitness buff to someone who'd lost nearly seventy pounds and who daily took sleeping pills as an antidepressant. He simply wanted to dull the pain, which was something I understood.

As soon as I learned the extent of his dependency, I stepped in and tried to help Burt kick the habit. I told him about my problems with alcohol.

"Call me every time you want to take a pill," I said.

"I'm going to be calling you a lot," he replied.

"Good. Call me."

Burt is a real guy, one hundred percent macho on the outside, but a pussycat with a big heart on the inside. I saw that closely guarded sensitive side surface.

"You know, I slipped," he confessed.

"So did I," I responded.

I saw in Burt's eyes the same look of reassurance and relief that I once felt. He told me that he'd always expected his rescuer to be someone like Clint Eastwood.

"Not a little Swedish girl," he said. "But you're a helluva lot stronger than anyone knows."

You have to be. I felt that Burt could clean up and step back into the spotlight he deserved, and I wasn't going to stand aside. I was willing to risk our friendship to make sure he knew that he had the choice. I pushed him to take control of his life, to seek professional help, and I'm glad I did.

41

SLIGHTLY MORE THAN EIGHT YEARS HAD PASSED now since Roger first got sick. We had weathered the intensity of the illness, and the recurrence, and once again Roger seemed to be in a state of remission. We had reordered our priorities and tried to cut back, but total retirement, we now knew, was not the answer. Roger needed the diversion of managing a busy career, and I thrived on activity. The decision was clear: I would return to the stage.

When the time came to get back in shape, I thought I had a choice. Either I could do it the easy way, or I could do it the hard way. But at forty-seven, who did I think I was fooling? There *was* no easy way.

About six years had passed since I'd retired my nightclub act, and both Roger and I were happy to be back. There was no use fooling ourselves. We were gypsies at heart. He enjoyed the creative part of shaping a show, from organizing the songs to writing my dialogue, while I knew no substitute for the energy and enthusiasm of a live audience.

Five months before my scheduled return at Caesars, I went into training. I climbed the one hundred eighty-seven stairs Roger constructed down a hill in our backyard. I swam sixty laps in the pool. I did two and a half hours of aerobics, lifted weights, jogged the canyon, and cut out all the fatty foods I loved but that my costumes didn't.

After opening at Caesars, I realized how right Mr. Burns had been in urging me back on stage. As always, the nerves I felt beforehand disappeared as soon as I heard, "Good evening, ladies and gentlemen, and welcome to Caesars Palace. Tonight Roger Smith is proud to present Ann-Margret." It seemed as if I'd just danced across the stage months earlier instead of years.

Following that engagement was a command performance for the King and Queen of Sweden, who were touring the U.S. in celebration of Sweden's three-hundred-fifty-year relationship with America. I'd also spent much of 1988 traveling through America as Sweden's official goodwill ambassador. At the King and Queen's request, we brought the whole show to Minneapolis during a snowstorm that reminded me of Sweden itself.

While we toured the act during most of 1989 and 1990, Roger relieved himself of a lot of stress by letting our longtime friend Alan Margulies, who'd worked for two of our favorite hotels, the Fontainebleau and Caesars Palace, co-manage my career. Alan also talked about playing Radio City Music Hall, an idea that first occurred in 1973 when our friend, Neal Peters, sent me a petition signed by several thousand people requesting that I play New York City.

I rejected it then. I rejected the same offer when I did the *Rockette* television special. And I didn't feel any different about it now. New York was my Mount Everest. I wasn't frightened as much as I was wary. I worried that my style of performing, which was very Las Vegas, wouldn't go over, a block from Broadway.

"This is one of the best shows we've ever done," Roger said in an attempt to convince me.

"You've got to play Radio City once," Alan chimed in.

Once again, director John Erman rescued me from having to make a decision by asking me to star in the TV movie *Our Sons*, about the plight of two gay lovers, one of whom was dying of AIDS, and their mothers' opposite reactions. Julie Andrews portrayed Audrey Grant, a wealthy woman who had accepted her son's homosexuality, while my character, Luanne Barnes, a cocktail waitress, had disowned her son upon learning he was gay.

I marveled at Julie. Prior to a scene, she could carry on as Julie Andrews the wife, mother, and businesswoman, while I disappeared in my dressing room and talked to myself in my Arkansas accent to stay in character.

We were such opposites. Julie had everything under control. She was always cheerful, prepared, well-organized, and perfectly dressed, Mary Poppins–like. She never forgot anyone's name. Her dressing room was always tidy whereas five minutes after I arrived, my dressing room was a disaster—shoes, clothes, bags, makeup, scripts everywhere.

My hope was that at least one person in a similar situation as these women would understand the story, and say I love you to a loved one dying of AIDS.

Afterward, I got scores of letters from women recounting exactly those experiences, and I cried over each one.

I had no idea what road my career might take me when I left Northwestern on a gamble for a singing job in Las Vegas. For a brief spell, it looked like that road might be a dead end. Then, even after I made a name for myself, my career seemed to be over more than once. Yet, I seemed to have a remarkable ability to resurrect myself. I was philosophical about it all by this point, especially after Roger's illness. Finally, I felt I had my life in perspective.

A month after *Our Sons* aired, I turned fifty. There was no reason to carp or complain, to mourn or feel distress. Instead, I felt adventurous and liberated. It was time for a new challenge.

"Let's do Radio City," I told Roger.

"I can't believe it," he said. "What happened to change your mind? Why?"

There had not been a lot of soul-searching. After all, it was just a stage show I was talking about. A show that worked, that proved itself over and over. Obviously people made much more important decisions every day.

"I want to do it while I still can," I answered. "While I can still kick."

The six-night, eight-show engagement, launched in mid-October 1991, confirmed the best things in life are worth waiting for. Throughout rehearsals, I repeated to my friend Neal Peters that I did not believe I would ever really end up on that fabled stage. However, at eight-thirty on October 22—my daddy's birthday—the lights dimmed, my stomach twisted in knots, the announcer said how pleased Radio City Music Hall was to present this special event, lights flashed, the curtain rose, and suddenly, Ann-Margret Olsson, the little girl out in the audience, jumped back into her fairy tale.

I slowly descended a staircase, trailing a seemingly endless yellow feather boa. For the next hour, I glided through a show that opened with "Stepping Out" and then touched on the past with *Birdie*'s "A Lot of Living to Do." After intermission, twelve leather-jacketed dancers on motorcycles purred "Black Cat" while I writhed out front on my own twenty-one-year-old Harley 1000 Sportster.

I described to the audience the lifelong impression left by my very first visit to Radio City, then fronted a leggy chorus line of Rockettes doing "How Do You Get to Be a Rockette." As we kicked, I glanced at Roger, who was clapping in his usual spot beside the curtain. Then I saw my mom out in front, grinning proudly. I hoped that somewhere in the audience, maybe somewhere way in the back, there might be a little girl, perhaps a little girl from a foreign country, who was getting her first taste of show business.

And I hoped it was magic for her, too.

EPILOGUE

"CONGRATULATIONS, YOU DID IT," ROGER SAID AS I came off stage.

"I did?" I smiled. "I don't believe it."

But then, despite everything I've done over the years, I still have never taken anything for granted. As soon as John Erman asked me to play Sally Jackson in *Queen,* the miniseries based on Alex Haley's book of the same title, I accepted. Three days later, Alex passed away. But John told me he'd lunched with him the afternoon of the day he died, mentioned that I was going to play Sally, and the author had been pleased.

During filming, I was made up to look like a humpbacked eighty-five-year-old woman. With my face and hands altered, carbuncles and broken blood vessels painted on, and my teeth browned for the occasion, I avoided mirrors as if they were the plague. Decked out in this geriatric getup, I celebrated twenty-five years of marriage to Roger.

"At least you know what's in store for you," I teased him.

Soon after, while filming Warner Brothers' *Grumpy Old Men,* with Walter Matthau and Jack Lemmon, in Minneapolis, I had another accident. As I drove Jack on the back of my snowmobile, I took an icy turn very fast and careened into a steel Dumpster. Worried about losing Jack, I clung to the bike as if my life depended on it.

I desperately looked around for Jack. Then someone told me that he'd bailed out far back and was fine. I nursed a broken wrist for a while. But no big deal. Life goes on.

* * *

It's ironic to think that some people thought I was a flash in the pan. I always wanted to be in this business for the long haul, and I guess I've been fortunate enough to have it work out. Stars often talk about their need to reinvent themselves. I think I've stayed the same. I'm finishing this book while on a film location in Romania and Roger and Alan are considering a television series. Some things never change. My idealism has survived along with me. Also my sense of fun. I enjoy myself immensely. I hope that it's still apparent in my work.

The past year has been very turbulent, full of highs and lows. I've lost two of my dearest friends—songwriter Peter Allen to AIDS and choreographer Lester Wilson, who died of a massive heart attack four days after helping stage a memorial benefit for Peter. Both were great men, true inspirations who contributed so much joy to the world. I miss them greatly.

Writing this book has certainly given me a diversion. But I've benefited, I'm sure, from doing some emotional house cleaning in preparing my story. The pain caused by reliving some of these memories was often too much. Other times I wished I could've remembered more. Overall, I'd say I've been fortunate to have such a full, rich, and exciting life.

Some of the rewards are easily displayed, some aren't, like our children. They're our proudest accomplishment. Tracey is a graphic artist and the mother of three. Jordan, a video recordist, is also married and a parent. And Dallas is an emergency-room doctor.

Of course, the tale would have been completely different were it not for Roger. People have often asked what has kept us together for almost three decades, not only still married but still really liking each other. I've finally figured it out. He concentrates on me, while I concentrate on him. And neither of us is a saint. Yes, we still fight and have our differences, but we also laugh a lot, fortunately at the same things. We've learned to joke about things that go wrong at home or on stage, instead of agonizing as we once did, and laughter can get you through anything.

Many years ago Peter Allen and Dean Pitchford mentioned that they wanted to write a song for me and asked if I had any suggestions. Just make it dramatic, sensitive, emotional, and personal, I said. They came up with ''Once Before I Go,'' which says in just a few lines the way I feel about a lifetime:

> *Once before I go,*
> *I want you to know*
> *That I would do it all again.*
> *I'm sure I'd make the same mistakes*
> *I'd even suffer through the pains*
> *and joys and aches*
> *I suffered then,*
> *But I'd do it all*
> *Oh yes, I'd do it all again.*